# VOTING THE AGENDA

# VOTING THE AGENDA

## CANDIDATES, ELECTIONS, AND BALLOT PROPOSITIONS

*STEPHEN P. NICHOLSON*

PRINCETON UNIVERSITY PRESS

PRINCETON AND OXFORD

Library of Congress Cataloging-in-Publication Data

Nicholson, Stephen P., 1966–
Voting the agenda : candidates, elections, and ballot
propositions / Stephen P. Nicholson
p. cm.
Includes bibliographical references and index.
ISBN: 0-691-11684-9 (cloth : alk. paper)
1. Elections—United States. 2. Voting—United States. 3. Direct
democracy—United States. 4. Political psychology. I. Title.
JK1976.N47 2005
324.973—dc22       2004042189

British Library Cataloging-in-Publication Data is available

This book has been composed in Sabon

Printed on acid-free paper. ∞

pup.princeton.edu

Printed in the United States of America

10  9  8  7  6  5  4  3  2  1

*To Jennifer and Kylie*

# CONTENTS

# FIGURES

# TABLES

# PREFACE

As a graduate student living in California, I found a marked disjuncture between what I was learning about congressional and gubernatorial elections in the scholarly literature and what I learned about them from watching television, reading the newspaper, and talking to people in and outside of academia. I found that scholarly accounts of voting and elections focused on particular types of electoral contests (e.g., House elections) and factors exclusive to them such as the candidates' party affiliations, campaigns, and issues. With the exception of national issues such as the economy or approval of the president, the larger political environment of issues seemed to be shortchanged. National issues are important, of course. Nonetheless, they only partly define the bustling marketplace of elections. In many states, to anticipate the argument of this book, ballot measures play an important role. Nowhere is this more conspicuous than in California, where ballot propositions regularly define the electoral agenda. Is this a unique feature of California politics, or do initiatives and referenda play an important role in other states' elections? If they do, what does that mean for traditional approaches to the study of voting for congressional and state offices? Are scholars missing an important piece of the electoral puzzle?

Although salient ballot measures certainly do not play an important role in each election cycle of every state, they do appear regularly in many of them. In addition, ballot propositions could well be the proverbial tip of the iceberg. States have an electoral environment all their own, driven by high-profile candidate contests and news media. Surely, the issues from these sources define agendas. But the difficult case is ballot measures, which are by definition restricted to state policy. Students of congressional elections, for example, do not consider ballot measures because, the logic goes, voters do not connect state issues to federal races. Besides, congressional candidates probably ignore these issues, further dampening the prospects for a relationship between the two.

Yet a major theme of most scholarly work on voting and elections is that the typical voter lacks a sophisticated understanding of politics. If so, we would hardly expect most voters to fine-tune their voting decisions to match the job responsibilities of particular offices. Nor would we expect them to match issues judiciously to the contests from which they came. Instead, we would anticipate that most voters draw heavily from the information environment in the form of the electoral agenda to which they are exposed.

Voters absorb the agenda. Should the issues on it have a partisan bent, it seems reasonable that they would apply the same issue understanding of the election across a variety of offices. Thus, we expect that voters go to the polls with a Democratic or Republican Party "mindset," primed to evaluate candidates with issues favorable to a party. Incumbency, name recognition, party identification, and other factors strongly associated with voting surely continue to figure prominently, but something "big" is missing from many accounts of nonpresidential elections. My purpose in this book is to direct attention to this missing element in standard accounts by focusing on the essential features of the larger political environment within which elections take place and voters make decisions.

I have many people to thank for helping me with this book. To begin with those closest to the project, I thank Bob Jackman and Gary Segura. Bob and Gary provided valuable comments and suggestions from which this project greatly benefited both as a dissertation and as the book before you. My debts to Gary and Bob extend beyond helping me with this project, however. Both were especially important in helping me develop as a scholar. I have learned a great deal from them, and I am in their debt. Their enthusiasm for the study of elections and voting behavior is contagious.

Gary gave a first-year graduate student without any direction other than, "I want to study American politics," much-needed guidance. After speaking with him at a department barbeque before my first year of graduate work, I worked for him as a research assistant. Although he called me about research projects long before I would have ordinarily gotten up in the morning, I am grateful to him for giving me direction and impressing on me the value of conducting strong theoretical and empirical research (and getting it done!). Although Gary left UC–Davis before I was very far along on my dissertation research (he stayed just long enough to tell me that my first idea was too small), he continued to give me significant feedback. I am grateful to him for these things as well as continuing to be a valued friend and coauthor.

Bob probably read more chapters of this manuscript than anyone else (and more than he cares to think about, I'm sure). He read, reread, and reread yet again many drafts. Many of these early drafts came back in a sea of red ink, something that he may not know he is (in)famous for among UC–Davis graduate students. But my recidivism was driven by the care he took in responding to my ideas and helping me strengthen their exposition. I am grateful for his continued support and friendship.

Gary Jacobson and Scott James also helped shape this project, and I am indebted to them as well. Although at UCSD, Gary was kind enough to serve as a member of my dissertation committee. He offered valuable comments on theory and empirical models, especially the need to focus the project. His deep understanding of congressional elections was also valuable. Before he left UC–Davis, Scott and I had marathon-long conversations about my ideas that were critical to moving me in the direction of studying ballot initiatives and congressional elections. But more than that, he suggested that I get outside the literature now and again because he saw it hindering my theory building—his nudging encouraged me to do just that, and the book is much better for it. Scott also slugged through multiple drafts of chapter 1, both during the writing of the dissertation and long afterward, when I was revising it for publication.

I also extend a hearty thanks to the following people for providing comments on one or more chapters: Monica Barczack, Shaun Bowler, Dave Damore, Jamie Druckman, Stacy Gordon, Jennifer Jerit, Peter Lindsay, Jennifer Nicholson, Dave Nixon, Dave Redlawsk, and Roger Rose. I am also grateful to the anonymous reviewers at Princeton University Press who provided feedback that led to important changes in clarifying my argument and improving the presentation of results. In addition, conversations with Jo Andrews, Scott Gartner, Elisabeth Gerber, Scott Graves, Tom Hansford, Stuart Hill, Brian Lawson, Ross Miller, Randolph Siverson, Jim Spriggs, and Nayda Terkildsen were helpful in many different ways. Edmond Costantini also helped write the questions we submitted to the Field Poll and acted as the faculty sponsor. All of these people provided valuable comments that helped strengthen the project, sometimes considerably so.

Without data, this project would not have been possible. Both the Institute of Governmental Affairs (IGA) and the Social Science Data Service (SSDS) at UC–Davis were very helpful in providing me with some of the data used in this book. I also thank Jean Stratford of IGA, Henry Brady of UC Data, and Mark DiCamillo and Merv Field of the Field Institute in helping Ed Costantini and me get our questions on the California Field Poll.

Chuck Myers has been a wonderful editor, and I am grateful for all his work on behalf of the manuscript. He was enthusiastic about the project early on and did a wonderful job guiding an assistant professor through the review and publication processes. Jennifer Nippins and Mark Bellis have also been helpful in ushering this book through the publication process.

I also thank Glenn Abney, the chair of the Department of Political Science at Georgia State University, for clearing away many of the distractions that come with faculty life. Joel Turner, Carrie Myers, and Eric Hurst, my graduate research assistants at Georgia State, also helped with various tasks and I thank them as well.

To my parents, brother, and grandparents, I thank you for all the love and support you have shown me over the years. My parents, in particular, are my biggest fans, and I am grateful for their encouragement. A few friends who helped, directly and indirectly, also deserve thanks. The Hollywood flavor found in chapters 1 and 6 belongs to my friend Richard Gale, a writer and director of movies. Rick deserves thanks for reading those chapters and the many conversations we had about the creative process of writing. Chris Andre and I also discussed this project because of his interest in initiative politics, something he had long before I did. I would also like to thank my Tuesday night running friends at Fleet Feet Duluth for asking about the project and giving me an opportunity to get away from work for a while.

My biggest debt of gratitude, however, is to Jennifer and Kylie Nicholson. I thank Jennifer, my wife, for all the love and encouragement she has given me over the years, and I thank my eighteen-month-old daughter, Kylie, for enriching my life and for reminding me of the wonder and humor in everyday things. I am also grateful to Jennifer for being supportive of this project even though it meant time away from her and Kylie— Daddy can go to the pool this summer. To them, I dedicate this book.

Despite all of this help, I alone am responsible for any errors and shortcomings.

# VOTING THE AGENDA

*Chapter 1*

## KINDRED VOTES: AN INTRODUCTION

Pete Wilson was in trouble. With California smarting from an economic recession, the Republican governor's reelection prospects looked dim. More than a year before his 1994 reelection bid, Wilson had the lowest approval rating of any California governor in the history of the California Field Poll and trailed his likely Democratic opponent, Kathleen Brown, by more than twenty percentage points. Although a relative newcomer to California politics, Brown had some impressive qualities. She was the state's treasurer, an adroit fund-raiser, and well-known among voters. In short, many believed Wilson's defeat a foregone conclusion.

Wilson wasn't the only one in trouble. Michael Huffington, the Republican nominee for U.S. Senate, was also a long-shot candidate that year but for different reasons. In contrast to Wilson, Huffington was unknown to most California voters. He had thin political credentials limited to a single term in the House and few legislative accomplishments. On the other hand, Huffington's opponent, Diane Feinstein, was a popular, well-recognized figure in California politics. Few pundits thought Feinstein would have any trouble defeating Huffington for the seat that she had easily won just two years prior (in a special election). Indeed, a little more than a year before the election, the California Field Poll showed Huffington trailing Feinstein by twenty-seven percentage points.

In an ending that few anticipated, both Republican candidates surpassed expectations. Wilson defeated Brown by a fourteen-point margin and Huffington, although falling short of defeating Feinstein, lost by a two-point margin. What helped these long-shot Republicans? In a word, the "agenda." In California's 1994 elections, the agenda included hot-button ballot initiatives, most notably Proposition 187, an initiative that sought to deny illegal immigrants public benefits. The initiative was the topic of extensive political debate in the media as well as in the candidate races, resulting in a majority of voters naming it the most important political event of the elections, including the Senate and governor's contests (Lubenow 1995, 124). Support for Proposition 187 was also high; roughly three out of five voters favored it throughout the campaign season. Since the parties had taken clear positions on the initiative—Republicans were for it and Democrats against it—Proposition 187 cast the election in terms favorable to Republican candidates. Thus, illegal immigration helped define the meaning of the election, boosting the electoral fortunes of Republican candidates, especially Wilson, who had made it the cornerstone of his campaign.

The story of Pete Wilson, Michael Huffington, and Proposition 187 is dramatic but not unique insofar as it illustrates how direct legislation may define the agenda. Although the frequency of direct legislation use varies across the states, in the 2002 elections, voters in forty states cast their ballots on 202 statewide ballot measures (Waters 2003, 8).[1] The last twenty years have seen the heaviest use of initiatives (Waters 2003, 8), the types of direct legislation most often associated with politically charged issues. In the last few election cycles, for example, controversial issues such as affirmative action, animal rights, abortion, medicinal marijuana, school choice, gun control, same-sex marriage, physician-assisted suicide, taxes, health care reform, environmental reform, and bilingual education were the topics of ballot initiatives. Issues of this kind, the focus of my research, play an important role in shaping the agenda and thus the types of considerations voters make in judging candidates.

Despite the fact that ballot measures take place alongside candidate races, scholars seldom consider them together. The omission is curious given the aforementioned increase in the frequency of initiative and referendum use over the last twenty years, especially in light of how many ballot measures contain controversial issues, strong ideological overtones, and/or expensive campaigns. Of course, I do not expect all ballot measures to play an important role in candidate races since not all of them have strong partisan or ideological overtones. Nevertheless, a good number do fit this description; many interest groups involved in the initiative process turn to ballot measures precisely because legislators are unwilling to handle many controversial issues.

The study of agendas, of course, is broader than the role of direct legislation in candidate races. Although I focus on a single phenomenon, my goal is to illuminate the role of agendas in elections. The conclusions of this book, therefore, should be applicable to not only how ballot measures affect voting in candidate races but also how issues from one candidate race spill over into another. They should also speak to how issue ad campaigns waged by interest groups and political parties affect voting behavior (Magleby 2002).

I define agenda as the one or more policy issues that matter to voters in a given electoral environment. While actors raise multiple issues within a given electoral environment, typically only a few achieve agenda status. Thus, even though a good number of issues might be well-known, the agenda consists of the most salient issues. My principal argument is that agendas play a profound role in U.S. elections by establishing the criteria voters use in making candidate judgments. Agendas introduce common elements into voters' candidate judgments, and not just for a single office.

Thus, agendas structure voting decisions along a common evaluative dimension and do so for offices that are as seemingly different from each other as U.S. Senate, House, and governor. By highlighting decision making at the constituency level, agendas also emphasize the diversity of issues that structure voting decisions across the United States. Taken together, I hope to elucidate how agendas unify voting decisions *within* a constituency and alter the foundations of candidate evaluation *across* constituencies.

It is curious that political scientists seldom consider voting for candidates in nonpresidential contests from the perspective of agendas. Instead, voting behavior research typically stresses the uniqueness of voting decisions by distinguishing voting decisions by office or issue on the ballot. The underdog candidates from the beginning of the chapter illustrate the shortcomings of isolating voting decisions. Not recognizing how voting decisions belong to the same family, conventional approaches would consider these contests apart, grouping the Wilson versus Brown race with other gubernatorial contests and the Huffington versus Feinstein race with other Senate contests. In so doing, analysts would likely stress the role of state issues, especially the state economy, in the gubernatorial races (e.g., Chubb 1988; Stein 1990) and national issues in the senatorial contests (e.g., Abramowitz and Segal 1992; Hibbing and Alford 1982). To be sure, these issues play an important role in voting for both types of offices and may even have the greatest overall effect. However, Wilson likely owed much of his reelection to the illegal immigration issue, and although Huffington lost by a slim margin, had illegal immigration not been on the ballot he probably would have lost by a larger margin.

Traditional approaches, therefore, exaggerate the individuality and disconnectedness of voting decisions across issues and candidates on the ballot. Consequently, scholars seldom consider whether direct legislation affects voting in candidate races or the broader question of spillover effects in which "outside" issues influence the criteria voters use to judge candidates. Although political scientists have learned much about elections and voting behavior from the methodological choice of studying elections in isolation from each other, it has privileged some explanatory variables at the expense of others. By using analytical frameworks that stress the distinctiveness of electoral choices, scholars lose sight of how voting decisions—up and down the ballot—belong to a single family by sharing a common understanding of politics centered on the information environment. To be clear, I am not arguing that scholars abandon the study of elections by office type. Rather, I am arguing that voting decisions across offices are not as unique as traditional approaches suggest. In the remainder of this chapter, I critically evaluate conventional approaches and how they elevate considerations that differentiate types of elections while obscuring the electoral information environment, especially the vital role of agendas.

## THE CONSEQUENCES OF METHODOLOGICAL CHOICE

Why study elections apart from each other? Why look at certain types of electoral information and disregard others? More specifically, why ignore issues that share space with candidates on the same ballot? To answer these questions, I begin with the simple insight that elections are busy and confusing marketplaces. In each election, candidates running for different offices try to flood the electorate with campaign messages. Candidates running for president, governor, Congress, and state assembly, to name a few, compete for scarce voter attention not only with their opponents in a given race but also with candidates running for different offices and not all that infrequently the campaigns for and against ballot measures. The electoral process thus generates a cacophony of messages sent by many actors—candidates, mass media, political parties, and interest groups—with the intention of reaching and persuading voters.

To make sense of voting decisions for candidates amid this chaos, analysts isolate different types of elections by office. Studies of electoral behavior treat each office, often implicitly, as self-contained and exempt from external influences.[2] In much political science research, critics often direct their energies toward models that leave political processes "inside" the box unexamined, labeling such neglect as "black box" approaches. I take the opposite tack by arguing that students of elections often neglect to look "outside" the box at the broader information environment.

Studying elections and voting decisions by office type is typically done for the sake of unit homogeneity, which requires that cases be identical, or nearly so, for the sake of making causal inferences. The unstated assumption is that the act of voting is largely not comparable across different types of offices, so that organizing the study of voting behavior by office is necessary for comparability. But observe the implication of this assumption: the act of voting varies *considerably* across elected offices.[3] From this vantage point, it is not surprising that voting behavior research orbits around difference rather than similarity.

The notion of unit homogeneity does not require units to be identical, however, but simply that they be comparable. As King, Keohane, and Verba (1994) note, it is never possible to achieve strict unit comparability because units of analysis always differ in some respect. Instead, "two units are homogenous when the expected values of the dependent variables from each unit are the same when our explanatory variable takes on a particular value" (91). Thus, the comparison of voting decisions across different elected offices simply requires that independent variables have a comparable effect on the dependent variable.

Studies of voting behavior provide considerable evidence that independent variables *do* have common effects across different offices. Few students of voting behavior, for example, dispute that partisan identification is the most important explanatory variable when looking at individual voting behavior across a variety of offices, especially low-information elections. Furthermore, few would disagree that variations in the effects of partisan identification are likely specific to the vagaries of electoral contests rather than the process of voting. Voters in low-information contests rely heavily on partisan cues (Schaffner and Streb 2002) while voters in information-rich contests will be somewhat less reliant on partisan cues given the abundance of other data. The insight here is that the mix of ingredients is the same; what differs is the amount. Gronke (2000) makes much the same point with reference to House and Senate elections when he argues that the "inputs" of voting for these offices are the same—the difference lies in the amount of a given input.

Nevertheless, many studies of voting behavior emphasize how *institutional responsibilities* (the job requirements of an elected office) and *campaign-specific issues* (information from a particular race) vary the foundations of candidate evaluation for different offices. If voters draw on institutional responsibilities, they compare the candidates' records against a set of criteria based on the responsibilities associated with a particular office. For example, the local orientation of the House of Representatives directs voters to evaluate House candidates by their ability to handle casework and bring federal projects to the district. The implication of this tendency is that voters use different criteria for evaluating candidates running for different offices.

On the other hand, if voters use campaign-specific issues as evaluative criteria, they focus on policy issues from a given contest.[4] According to this approach, voters evaluate candidates in a given race based on the issues the candidates discuss in their campaigns or the issues most prevalent in media coverage of their contests. The implication of this approach is that voters only consider campaign issues (policy issues) relevant to a particular contest and screen out campaign messages from other contests. The picture that emerges from these approaches is one of voters pondering very different criteria as they move down the ballot, considering candidates for governor, senator, or representative. Although many scholars would balk at the notion that voters use subtle distinctions in making candidate judgments, the methodological choice of studying electoral behavior from the vantage point of the office or the flow of campaign information about a particular race nevertheless imposes this type of fine-tuning into the study of the voting decision.

Below, I address a seldom recognized but nonetheless real puzzle in voting research: If most voters pay little or no attention to politics, why do we assume that they correctly link numerous campaign messages with the appropriate candidates or assign certain institutional responsibilities to particular offices and vote accordingly? I argue that, in large part, voters do not make these distinctions and instead rely on the most salient morsels of information available. Often this information takes the form of partisan or incumbency cues, but it might also include prominent policy issues located within electoral environments such as states.

## The Methodological Choice of Institutional Responsibilities

As mentioned, the institutional responsibilities approach implies that each office has its duties and requirements, and voters fine-tune their vote choices based on the particular demands of various political offices. Given this logic, the national orientation of the Senate requires voters to evaluate Senate candidates based on national issues such as the economy or presidential approval. Similarly, the Senate's reputation for handling international affairs requires voters to evaluate Senate candidates based on foreign policy. In contrast, because House members have a local orientation, pork barrel politics and constituency service play a large role in voters' decisions. Finally, because voters presumably understand the fine distinctions between federal and state offices, gubernatorial elections should turn on statewide considerations rather than national influences. These perceptions largely guide analysts in deciding what information matters in these races.

But scholars have found little evidence that citizens make meaningful institutional distinctions between voting for House and Senate candidates (Gronke 2000; Krasno 1994). Gronke (2000, chap. 6) found that voter evaluations of the job requirements of House members and senators do not turn on institutional distinctions. Instead of differentiating House members from senators by job requirements, voters ascribe the same duties to both offices, thus debunking the notion that national issues play a greater role in evaluations of senators and local issues play a greater role in evaluations of House members. Similarly, Stein and Bickers (1994) debunk the notion that House incumbents' reelection prospects are intimately tied to their ability to bring home pork barrel projects, a responsibility political scientists strongly associate with House members' institutional roles. Although this may be true for a small segment of voters, the authors find that "[m]ost members of the general public remain indifferent to alterations in the flow of new [pork barrel] rewards" (394). Thus, in many studies, the traditional wisdom that the institutional roles and responsibilities of elected officials shape mass political behavior often is not supported empirically.

Further, citizens' disregard of institutional distinctions between House and Senate extends beyond the electoral arena. For some time, scholars generally believed that House and Senate members have different representational roles because of the institutional differences between the two chambers, and that citizens appreciated the distinction.[5] Scholars typically assumed that House members, given their role as the institution "where the people speak," have closer representational relationships with their constituents than do senators. Questioning this wisdom, Oppenheimer (1996) found that the distinction between House and Senate (the institutional setting) is much less important to constituent-representative relationships than state population size. Indeed, he found that senators from small population states have closer relationships with constituents than do House members.

Some scholars explicitly argue that voters use institutional criteria by differently evaluating senatorial and gubernatorial candidates according to federal-state responsibilities (Atkeson and Partin 1995, 1998; Stein 1990). According to Atkeson and Partin (1995, 1998), voters evaluate candidates running for Senate on national political concerns such as the economy and presidential approval while they evaluate candidates running for governor on matters such as the state economy.

On its face, the case for voters making state versus federal distinctions appears stronger than that for distinctions between the House and Senate. Indeed, the institutional distinction between the House and Senate, both federal offices, appears smaller as compared to that separating the federal and state governments. Yet even here the evidence is mixed. For example, although Stein (1990) and Carsey and Wright (1998) find that state economic conditions affect gubernatorial voting, they also find that national conditions play an important role. Moreover, some scholars have found that national conditions are the primary force behind gubernatorial elections and that state-specific factors play a secondary role (Chubb 1988; Kenney 1983; Peltzman 1987).

The case for voters making institutional distinctions is especially unconvincing examined in light of citizens' lack of political knowledge. The amount of political knowledge, not to mention willingness, required for voters to use institutional distinctions as criteria in voting decisions is contrary to research documenting citizens' minimal knowledge about American politics (e.g., Converse 1964; Delli Carpini and Keeter 1996).[6] Delli Carpini and Keeter (1996) show that citizens lack knowledge about basic institutional features of the American political system, many seemingly easier than reasoning about institutional responsibilities for different elected offices. Many citizens, for example, show great ignorance of the president's institutional powers, believing he "has the power to adjourn Congress at his will (29 percent), to suspend the Constitution (49 percent), and to appoint judges to the federal court without the approval of the Senate (60 percent)" (99). Similarly, despite arguments to the contrary, citizens do not have any better grasp of federal versus state powers. The enterprise of distinguishing between federal and state responsibilities, of course, is inherently problematic given the extensive mixing of policy responsibilities. Given the ambiguity of federal-state relations, citizens do not fare well in assigning responsibilities on this basis (Delli Carpini and Keeter 1996, 99). While there is a tendency to assign some policy areas to the states or the national government, partisanship and ideology, explicitly political factors, largely account for these attributions (Schneider and Jacoby 2003). But even if citizens do know a lot about federal and state policy responsibilities, it is unlikely that they would apply this knowledge in evaluating candidates. Put differently, it is doubtful that institutional distinctions are chronically accessible considerations that guide voters' evaluations of candidates (see Arceneaux 2003).

Although the lack of importance citizens and voters ascribe to institutional distinctions are likely surprising to some scholars, they probably would not be surprising to most citizens. Few voters have the knowledge, or desire, to adjust their voting decisions in keeping with institutional responsibilities. When voters do appreciate institutional distinctions, it is likely more the product of the electoral information environment than their knowledge of American political institutions. Therefore, if institutional distinctions matter, they are likely dependent on candidates in high-intensity races, running campaigns that stress the job requirements of their offices. For example, if senatorial and gubernatorial candidates in hotly contested races have stressed issues consistent with institutional responsibilities, voters may draw on such distinctions. The "institution" effect, if it exists, is indirect rather than direct—information environments structure evaluative criteria; institutionally savvy voters do not impose different criteria for different offices. Rudolph (2003) reached the same conclusion in his study of citizen responsibility attributions and institutional context. Although Rudolph found that state institutional context (e.g., the amount of budgetary power given governors) had a significant effect on evaluations of governors, he did not attribute the effect to well-informed, institutionally savvy citizens. Rather, he believes this process likely operates through the flow of information about budgetary politics in states, thus making citizens act as though they were knowledgeable about state institutional structures (210).

## The Methodological Choice of Campaign-Specific Issues

A second implication of studying elections by office type is that voters use a narrow range of campaign-specific issues sent by or communicated about the candidates. To test for campaign effects, analysts match a vote choice for a given election to the relevant issues discussed by a candidate or the media about that election. For example, if candidates discussed taxes and crime in their campaigns, scholars examine whether these issues influenced the voting decisions for those candidates. To be sure, campaigns do influence voting decisions. Under a variety of circumstances, scholars have found that Senate (Druckman 2004; Franklin 1991; Kahn and Kenney 1999; Goldstein and Freedman 2000), gubernatorial (Carsey 2000), and House campaign issues (Abbe et al. 2003) affect voter decision making.

However, for campaigns to "matter," voters must receive and accurately link campaign messages to the appropriate candidates. Thus, the less recognized but equally important key to understanding campaign effects from the vantage point of traditional approaches concerns whether voters *correctly* match issues to candidates. In presidential elections, where information about campaigns is relatively plentiful, fewer voters encounter difficulty recalling important issues and associating them with the presidential contest. Consequently, many scholars have found that presidential campaigns "matter" (Alvarez 1997; Finkel 1993; Holbrook 1996). Nevertheless, elections are bustling affairs involving many different issues floating around with most voters receiving and processing electoral information in a haphazard manner.

Given research on voter sophistication, including revisionist accounts that depict voters as making informed decisions with low-cost sources of information, it is unrealistic to expect voters to be able to make all, or even most, of the linkages between candidates and the issues found in their campaigns. Sometimes issues from the candidates' campaigns stick, but quite often they do not (Dalager 1996; Kahn and Kenney 1999). Kahn and Kenney (1999), for example, found that only 19 percent of voters asked to identify an issue from the Senate contest in their state could do so correctly. Although the authors found that the ability of voters to correctly identify an issue increases with the intensity of Senate campaigns, the fact that so many voters could not strongly suggests that scholars need to look elsewhere for the origins of voter information in low-information contests. When voters make little effort to become informed about elections, as do most voters, it is unlikely that they keep the issues and candidates carefully associated with each other.[7]

The ability of voters to correctly match issues and candidates depends on the volume (and perhaps clarity) of information available about a contest. For instance, voters choosing Senate candidates are more likely to be knowledgeable of them and use ideological and issue-based criteria in high-intensity campaigns (Kahn and Kenney 1999; Wright and Berkman 1986). Under certain conditions, especially high-spending campaigns,

House candidates may influence voting decisions (Herrnson and Patterson 1998). Moreover, voters are most likely to use the campaign messages supplied by presidential candidates because these contests provide abundant information. As a rule of thumb, the more information available about a given contest, the greater the likelihood voters will use criteria from that contest to evaluate candidates.

Despite the fact that some Senate and gubernatorial races are information rich, few of these candidates dictate the terms of debate. Information about issues from these contests is simply less plentiful, and although the candidates from these races do their best to set the agenda, they may often fail in defining the "big" issues. Indeed, for this reason, I refer to all nonpresidential elections as low-information (while recognizing variation within this category). For down-ballot candidates running for House of Representatives or the state legislature the problem is much worse. Their voices are seldom heard among the louder, better-financed, and higher-profile contests that take place within a state (see Wolak 2004). Thus, without the ability to shape the agenda, candidates in low-information elections regularly contend with issues not of their making.

As mentioned, I am *not* suggesting that students of elections ignore offices. Organizing elections by office type lends analytic tractability to a cluttered electoral marketplace. It makes studying voting behavior a manageable task. Rather, my argument concerns misplaced emphasis. Elections supply an abundance of electoral information, and the content of this information has important implications for voting, and not just for one office type. By emphasizing institutional differences among offices or candidate campaign issues from a specific contest—a by-product of studying elections by office type—researchers often overlook information germane to voters, namely the broader information environment of which agendas play a leading role.

## ISSUE VOTING AND AGENDAS

The influence of agendas on voting is unmistakable. As democratic and social choice theorists alike have emphasized, it is difficult to overstate the importance of agendas. Barber asserts, "He who controls the agenda—if only its wording—controls the outcome" (1984, 181). Similarly, Riker posits, "Agendas foreshadow outcomes: the shape of an agenda influences the choices made from it" (1993, 1). In discussing his theory of conflict displacement, an agenda-based approach to studying democratic processes, Schattschneider declares, "*[T]he definition of the alternatives is the supreme instrument of power*; the antagonists can rarely agree on what the issues are because power is involved in the definition" (1960, 68; emphasis original).

In contrast, some of the earliest quantitative research on voting behavior found little support for issue voting among the mass public, a necessary requisite of agenda voting. Campbell et al.'s *The American Voter* (1960) cast doubt on the ability of voters to make issue-based voting decisions. In their classic study, partisan identification and candidate characteristics exceeded the effects of issues. According to Campbell and colleagues, voters lacked the necessary information to vote for presidential candidates on policy issues. Converse's (1964) research on belief systems in the electorate advanced this line of research when he found that voters did not demonstrate a sophisticated enough understanding of politics to link candidates and issues.

Yet scholars have found evidence of issue voting, mostly in presidential contests. Predating *The American Voter*, Berelson, Lazarsfeld, and McPhee's (1954) research on the 1948 presidential election demonstrated how changes in the weight voters assigned to issues affected standards of candidate evaluation. Specifically, the authors found that the shift in voter support toward Truman followed changes on the weight voters assigned to issues on which they agreed with him. The research following Campbell and colleagues focused on the electoral information environment and how it may help or hinder the ability of voters to make issue-based voting decisions. Key (1966) was among the first to point out that the capability of voters to make informed decisions (e.g., policy based) is contingent on the information available to them. Subsequent research found that voters were more likely to choose candidates based on issues because the information environment had changed (Nie and Anderson 1974; Nie, Verba, and Petrocik 1976; Pomper 1972). Nie, Verba, and Petrocik (1976) showed that changes in the national agenda during the 1960s were responsible for making voters more politically aware and likely to engage in issue voting than were voters during the 1950s. Vietnam and the civil rights movement shaped the politics of the day in a way that differed greatly from the restrained politics of the Eisenhower era.[8] In contrast to the 1950s when Campbell and colleagues did their research, Nie, Verba, and Petrocik argued that later decades provided greater opportunities for voters to make issue-based voting decisions. Thus, the change in political climate hastened a greater awareness of and reliance on policy issues in making voting decisions. Despite methodological problems in the revisionist accounts (e.g., see E. Smith 1989; Sullivan, Piereson, and Marcus 1978 for a discussion), contemporary scholarship on voting and elections finds that the electoral information environment, especially campaigns, shapes voter attitudes in presidential elections (Alvarez 1997; Bartels 1988; Gelman and King 1993; Popkin 1991; Repass 1971).

Even though scholars of presidential elections have been comfortable with the notion that policy issues matter, their counterparts who study low-information elections have been less so. The scholarly consensus had been that policy issues are relatively unimportant in these types of contests. Stokes and Miller (1962) found that issue voting was absent in House elections: "[T]he increment of strength that some candidates, especially incumbents, acquire by being known to their constituents is almost entirely free of policy content" (543). Despite research at the aggregate level of analysis demonstrating the effect of national issues on congressional elections (e.g., Tufte 1975), much of the evidence on congressional elections largely supports Stokes and Miller's finding that many voters in congressional elections do not use policy-based considerations. In contrast to studies of presidential elections, many studies of congressional elections demonstrate that "local forces," as defined by the incumbency advantage (e.g., Cain, Ferejohn, and Fiorina 1987; Mayhew 1974), campaign expenditures (e.g., Jacobson 1980), and candidate quality (e.g., Jacobson and Kernell 1983) make up the major ingredients of voting in congressional elections. Taken together, the dominance of "local forces" in congressional voting left little room for policy-based issue voting. No doubt "local forces" explain most of what happens in House elections, especially those races with an incumbent and an unknown challenger. Yet, studies of issue voting in congressional elections have largely neglected salient issues, the type most likely to be on voters' minds.

Studies of gubernatorial elections also neglect salient issues if they are not economic considerations. The major research question for studies of gubernatorial elections is whether these contests turn on national or state economic variables and to a lesser extent presidential approval (Chubb 1988; Holbrook-Provow 1987; Howell and Vanderleeuw 1990; Leyden and Borrelli 1995; Partin 1995; D. Simon 1989; Stein 1990). Thus, although the scholarly debates that characterize studies of congressional and gubernatorial elections help define the relative effect of subnational versus national influences, these debates have largely obscured how policy-based voting follows the rhythms of issue agendas in the states.

Evaluating the effects of the electoral information environment, of which agendas play a central role, is a crucial step toward understanding how voters make decisions in low-information contests. Indeed, if some information environments educate citizens on matters of public policy better than others (Kuklinski et al. 2001; Jerit and Barabas 2003), it is not far-fetched to expect related effects for the less Herculean task of evaluating candidates in nonpresidential elections. Studies of issue voting in these types of contests suggest that salient issues have a significant effect on voting for candidates in gubernatorial (e.g., Carsey 2000; Cook, Jelen, and Wilcox 1994; Hutchings 2003), Senate (e.g., Jacobson and Wolfinger

1989; Hutchings 2003; Kahn and Kenney 1999), and House (e.g., Iyengar and Kinder 1987, chap. 11; Zaller 1992, chap. 10) elections. Few analysts, however, take the crucial step of looking outside a particular contest to examine the broader information environment and how it might prime voters to assign greater weight to some issues. And while the candidates' campaigns may play a major role, especially if an electoral contest is highly visible, I contend that agendas, whether discussed by a pair of candidates in a given race or not, may play an equally important or perhaps even greater role.

## A Preview of Coming Chapters

I offer a theory of agenda voting in chapter 2. Here, I bring together well-known analytical tools in the study of political behavior and opinion—agenda-setting, priming, spillover effects, and partisan stereotypes. Together, these concepts provide the theoretical framework for how agendas infuse voting decisions with common meaning. Although these concepts are not new to political science, my use of them is somewhat novel for political science. For example, most applications of priming in political science examine how a prime shapes evaluative criteria for a single politician. In contrast, I recognize how priming effects influence multiple voting decisions. Priming effects, therefore, ignore institutional boundaries, showing little regard for institutional arrangements or the content of candidate campaigns. Thus, priming effects travel much further than previously recognized.

In chapter 3, I address questions of research design. Central to my research strategy is the use of direct legislation or ballot measures as a means of assessing the influence of agendas. Using direct legislation has several advantages. With the exception of a few states, most have some kind of process where voters decide matters of public policy at the polls. Institutionally defined as a state-level concern, ballot measures are often well-known and are often the focus of their own campaigns. Furthermore, they are often distinct from candidate campaigns and thus offer an opportunity to examine how "exogenous" issues affect voting decisions.

In contrast to the conventional approaches that characterize policy issues in congressional elections as exclusively national, chapter 4 examines the agenda-setting effects of statewide ballot measures in House and Senate elections. Here, I show that direct legislation has a substantial agenda-setting effect in these contests, controlling for rival explanations such as candidates' campaign messages. Using data from the National Election Study/Senate Election Study, I find evidence that statewide ballot measures on the environment, taxes, and abortion influence the agenda in congressional elections.

In chapter 5, I examine how agendas—via priming—affect voters' choice of candidates running for a variety of offices. Taking advantage of a natural experiment from the 1982 elections wherein some voters were exposed to freeze campaigns through initiatives and referenda and others were not, I examine whether nuclear freeze ballot measures affect the standards of candidate evaluation in congressional and gubernatorial elections. Comparing voters in states with and without freeze ballot measures, I find evidence of substantial priming effects. Voters in states with freeze measures were primed to evaluate candidates using this issue regardless of whether the freeze was a part of the campaign or relevant to a particular office.

Chapter 6 examines the interplay of candidates and ballot measures. The focus of this chapter is the use of ballot propositions as agenda-setting tools of candidates and political parties. Although direct legislation issues are mostly exogenous to candidate races, on occasion, and with increasing frequency, candidates and political parties make them endogenous to their campaigns. In the cases examined in this chapter, I look at how California's Republican Party used the issues of illegal immigration and affirmative action in 1994 and 1996, respectively, to infuse the "wedge issue" of race into elections.

Finally, in chapter 7, I discuss the democratic implications of agendas in light of my research findings and conclude with some thoughts on future research.

*Chapter 2*

# A THEORY OF AGENDA VOTING

How do agendas affect voting behavior? In this chapter, I propose a theory of agenda voting built on concepts from the study of public opinion and mass political behavior: *agenda-setting*, *priming*, *spillover effects*, and *partisan stereotypes*. Although these concepts are not new to political science, I bring them together into a cohesive framework of political judgment and voting. By integrating them, I offer a new perspective on voting behavior in which the major issues of the day affect myriad voting decisions. After briefly outlining the theory, I discuss each part in detail and how they interrelate to bring about agenda voting.

Agenda voting happens because voters do not pay all that much attention to politics and elections. While voters are not empty receptacles for issues since issues must resonate with them, voters choose among elite supplied agendas in deciding which issues matter. As relatively undiscriminating consumers of politics, voters use information that is available at the lowest cost. Voters do not seek out election issues; election issues find them. The major issues of an election—the agenda—emanate from what voters have seen, read, or heard. If abortion is a widely discussed issue, abortion *becomes* an important issue.

Highly accessible, agendas prime voters to evaluate candidates, often implicitly, alongside prominent issues. The process is likely automatic, taking place outside conscious awareness, affecting evaluations of candidates in the contest where an issue is discussed as well as spilling over into contests in which the issue is absent or voters have little or no information. Spillover effects occur because priming influences political judgments indiscriminately, regardless of whether a prime (the issue) is explicitly related to a target of evaluation (candidate). Consequently, priming shapes candidate judgments across multiple offices. If an issue is on the agenda, even if only discussed in one type of race, its effects will be widespread, shaping voters' candidate judgments up and down the ballot. To be sure, not all voters will be equally susceptible given differences in political sophistication and attachment to parties, but agenda issues will likely influence most voters to some degree.

How do agendas shape judgments of candidates if candidates do not discuss agenda issues or if voters never receive information about the candidates' positions? Partisan stereotypes do the heavy lifting of linking agenda issues to candidate evaluations. Voters ascribe issue positions to candidates because the Democratic and Republican Parties have reputations for handling issues (e.g., the notion that parties "own" issues). Given these strongly embedded stereotypes, agendas shape voting decisions along partisan lines. This process is likely automatic, requiring little thought on the part of voters since people frequently use stereotypes, partisan or otherwise, in judging others without recognizing it. Indeed, partisan stereotypes are so powerful that voters nevertheless assign certain issue positions to candidates based on stereotypes, even when a candidate holds an issue position contrary to that of the party (Rahn 1993). Thus, an election that is about taxes and crime—Republican-owned issues—will benefit Republican candidates and an election about education and the environment—Democratic-owned issues—will benefit Democratic candidates (Petrocik 1996), even if candidates do not discuss the issue or take opposite positions from their party on the issue.

In the remainder of the chapter, I discuss the building blocks of agenda voting: agenda-setting, priming, spillover effects, and partisan stereotypes.

## AGENDA-SETTING AND PRIMING

Agenda voting rests on the shoulders of rationally ignorant voters—voters with minimal interest in and knowledge of politics. In contrast to the many hours people spend researching an automobile or home purchase, voters typically do not investigate candidates and issues (see Popkin 1991). The basis of this inattention is the low incentive associated with acquiring political information (Downs 1957, chaps. 11–12; Popkin 1991). Coupled with research on social cognition that shows individuals do not attend to the full range of considerations when making decisions (see H. Simon 1957), it is not surprising that few individuals acquire much information about politics. Consequently, voters rely on information thrown at them from newspaper headlines, direct mail, television commercials, and social contexts. Because the costs of acquiring political information are high while the potential benefits to individuals of a vote this way or the other are low, most voters, most of the time, rely on these relatively inexpensive sources of information (Downs 1957; Popkin 1991). In short, citizens do not find politics important enough to expend the effort to stay informed and if they did, they would only attend to a few matters.

Since politics is seldom more than a passing concern for most voters, the policy issues that receive the most attention define agendas. Since elections are supposed to be about issues, it is not surprising that in the course of any campaign, candidates and political parties engage in a seemingly continuous effort to develop and float issues they hope will connect with the voters. What *is* surprising is how few of the issues discussed actually connect with voters and thus become part of an agenda. Thus, while issues are central to agendas, the latter typically involve only a small subset of the former. Further, while some components of electoral agendas stem from the efforts of candidates for office, a good part of the agenda in a given election has other origins, reflecting the activities of political parties, interest groups, and other actors.

As discussed in chapter 1, democratic and social choice theorists have stressed the importance of agendas (Barber 1984; Dahl 1989; Riker 1982, 1986, 1993; B.D. Jones 1994; Schattschneider 1960), and empirical research shows how agendas shape public opinion and voting behavior (Abbe et al. 2003; Berelson, Lazarsfeld, and McPhee 1954; Iyengar and Kinder 1987; MacKuen 1984; McCombs and Shaw 1972; Petrocik 1996). Foremost among empirical studies on agenda-setting is work on the mass media and how it plays a potent role in shaping the public's issue priorities.[1] Working from this tradition, Ansolabehere, Behr, and Iyengar define agenda-setting as "[t]he idea . . . that the public's social or political priorities and concerns—their beliefs about what is a significant issue or event—are determined by the amount of news coverage accorded an issue or event" (1993, 142). Lippmann (1922) was among the first to note that the media were largely responsible for "the pictures in our heads." Although he did not use the language of agenda-setting, Lippmann laid the groundwork for this research by revealing how the media's priorities strongly influence the public's agenda.

McCombs and Shaw (1972) were the first to empirically examine the agenda-setting effect of media on public opinion. Using the 1968 presidential campaign as their setting, the authors found that the mass media, as measured by content analysis of media coverage, had a substantial impact on the public's agenda. Weaver et al.'s (1981) year-long, nine-wave panel study found similar agenda-setting effects in the 1976 presidential election. Iyengar and Kinder (1987), drawing on both experimental and quasi-experimental designs, also found that media coverage of issues had a significant agenda-setting effect. In one of their experiments, subjects exposed to particular news stories were more likely to mention those stories when asked about what issues were the most important problems facing the nation. Likewise, at the aggregate level they found that changing patterns of television news coverage affected public opinion as to what was the nation's most important problem. In elections, of course, the source of information may vary substantially given that candidates, parties, interest groups, and other actors join the familiar chorus of journalists in setting the public's political priorities. West (1997), for example, shows that candidate advertisements in presidential elections have a substantial agenda-setting effect in shaping citizens' perceptions of the most important problem facing the nation.[2]

The "priming effect" is the means by which agendas shape political judgments. Priming is based on the notion that not all considerations are attended to in the decision-making process. Instead of considering the full range of alternatives, then, individuals call on earlier considerations that have been *recently* or *frequently* activated in memory (Fiske and Taylor 1991; Higgins 1996; Taylor and Fiske 1978). The assumption behind many priming models is that memory is organized according to an associative network of linkages between nodes that represent concepts or knowledge constructs. Within this associative network, the activation of a knowledge construct will spread to related constructs (Collins and Loftus 1975; Fiske and Taylor 1991). Given this *spreading activation*, "priming describes the effects of prior context on the interpretation of new information" (Fiske and Taylor 1991).[3] Although accessibility is the working assumption behind most priming research, some scholars find that the perceived importance of issues plays a larger role (Miller and Krosnick 2000).[4] Although such debates fall outside the scope of this book, I assume that accessibility plays a larger role by priming issue considerations automatically and indiscriminately (see below).

Regardless of the psychological mechanism at work, priming approaches provide a powerful tool for looking at information exposure and political judgment. Iyengar and Kinder (1987) found substantial priming effects in Connecticut's 1982 Third Congressional District race. Participants exposed to different considerations (e.g., issues, candidate information) assigned greater weight to these matters when evaluating candidates. For example, participants shown stories about the national economy were more likely to mention it as a basis for choosing candidates. Further evidence of priming effects in experimental settings are found in studies of the 1988 (Mendelberg 1997; Schleuder, McCombs, and Wanta 1991), 1992 (Ansolabehere and Iyengar 1995), and 1996 (Valentino 1999) presidential contests.

Evidence of priming effects, however, is not restricted to experimental research. Krosnick and Brannon (1993) and Iyengar and Simon (1993) found that media coverage of a "real world" event, the Gulf War, significantly increased President Bush's public approval standings. Krosnick and Kinder (1990) found that the Iran-Contra affair also had a significant impact on evaluations of President Reagan's job performance. Jerit (2004) found that priming had a significant effect on shaping public support of the Clinton healthcare reform plan. Survey-based research has also provided evidence of priming effects in elections. Druckman (2004) found that the 2000 Minnesota Senate campaign primed voters to evaluate the candidates in terms of issues and candidate images. Mendelberg (2001) found that in the 1988 presidential election, the Bush campaign's use of implicitly racial messages (e.g., Willie Horton ads) primed voters' evaluations of the candidates. Using a rolling cross-section survey, Johnston et al. (1992) showed that the Canada-U.S. Free Trade Agreement primed voters in Canada's 1988 elections. In particular, the party campaigns that revolved around this issue through debates and political advertising influenced citizens' judgments of the candidates. Looking at the same elections, Mendelsohn (1996) found that media priming of candidate attributes played an increasingly important role over the course of the campaign. Early in the campaign voters were inclined to vote on the basis of partisan leanings, but later in the campaign this tendency gave way to candidate-specific considerations as a result of news coverage that focused on candidate attributes.

In summary, agendas prime voters to consider particular issues, while neglecting others, in making candidate judgments. In so doing, they do not bring about attitude change (e.g., persuasion) but rather alter the weight voters assign to issues through varying the salience of considerations. But this is not the whole story. My theory advances the theory of agendas and priming by arguing that they shape the criteria voters use to evaluate candidates in *myriad* contests. How can agendas and priming have such an effect, especially in contests where candidates and the ensuing news media coverage do not mention agenda issues?

## INDISCRIMINATE PRIMING

Agendas have far-reaching effects, up and down the ballot, because priming works bluntly or indiscriminately. By way of introduction, priming research suggests that information exposure, at least where there is sufficient categorical match, indiscriminately affects subsequent evaluations (Higgins 1996). In making social judgments, for instance, a person exposed to a news story about society's declining manners may interpret the behavior of individuals he or she encounters with this construct in mind. This type of priming effect is ubiquitous in studies of social cognition (e.g., Higgins 1996). Priming in elections likely works in a similar fashion. If voters are heavily exposed to an issue, regardless of its source, voters will view candidates in a variety of contests with the issue in mind. Ceteris paribus, issues absent from a given contest, but salient otherwise, may nonetheless have a profound effect on voting decisions for that contest. In some low-information elections, such as House races, this might even be the norm.

In contrast to research in social cognition, many studies of priming effects in political science typically examine *explicit* or unambiguous linkages between the prime and the target of evaluation. For instance, Krosnick and Kinder's (1990) study of the Iran-Contra scandal demonstrates that the scandal—clearly associated with President Reagan—influenced evaluations of Reagan's job performance. Likewise, the customary approach to studying issue voting is to match campaign messages from a specific contest to voters' decisions in that contest. Many studies implicitly take this approach because researchers are simply looking to see whether "campaigns matter." However, as mentioned, priming effects may shape judgments regardless of whether a target and prime are explicitly connected (Fiske and Taylor 1991; Bargh 1989; Bargh and Pietromonaco 1982; Wyer and Srull 1989). Kunda remarks that "social psychologists have demonstrated repeatedly that a concept that has been recently primed is especially likely to be applied to the interpretation of novel information, *even in unrelated contexts*" (1999, 22; emphasis mine).

The question of the applicability of a knowledge construct to a stimulus, according to Higgins (1996, 154), is contingent on whether there is a sufficient *categorical* match. Higgins states that stimulus information is "unambiguous" when only one construct is applicable, such as the case with the Iran-Contra scandal and President Reagan. On the other hand, stimulus information is "ambiguous" when at least two constructs are equally applicable, such as the issue of gay marriage and House and Senate candidates. Whereas the Iran-Contra scandal is strongly related to Reagan, the issue of gay marriage, generally speaking, is not specific to any one candidate or contest. Thus, most policy issues, regardless of their origin, provide a sufficient match with candidates. Consequently, a salient policy issue not explicitly connected to a particular contest will nevertheless be accessible to voters—at the top of their heads—when evaluating the candidates in that contest.

The voter also need not consciously make the linkages between issues and candidates because priming effects can be automatic (Bargh and Pietromonaco 1982; Bargh 1989; Higgins and King 1981; Higgins 1996; Mendelberg 2001; Moskowitz and Roman 1992; Sherman, Mackie, and Driscoll 1990; Terkildsen 1993). Although there are certainly limitations to "automatic" priming models (Martin and Achee 1992; Stapel, Koomen, and Zeelenberg 1998),[5] this type of phenomenon appears commonplace in making political judgments. For example, Iyengar and Kinder (1987) found an implicit relationship between evaluations of President Carter and news stories on inflation that did not mention the president or his administration. Similarly, Valentino (1999) shows that racially stereotypic crime stories that made no explicit mention of Clinton and Dole nevertheless primed evaluations of the candidates during the 1996 elections. Implicit primes may even be more powerful than explicit primes since priming effects are more potent when individuals are unaware of them (Bargh and Pietromonaco 1982; Lombardi, Higgins, and Bargh 1987; Moskowitz and Roman 1992; Strack et al. 1993). Indeed, if voters are aware that they are being primed, as when they view a blatantly racist campaign advertisement, they are likely to scrutinize the information to a greater degree than if the information has no apparent intent (Mendelberg 2001).

Thus, when looking exclusively at campaign messages and the intended recipient's vote choice, scholars may ignore important, seemingly unrelated primes. The significance of agendas, therefore, is that they may prime voters similarly across multiple voting decisions. This effect happens because elections are noisy affairs with multiple information sources (e.g., campaigns, the media, political discussants) that overwhelm voters with a large amount of electoral information. The most salient issues take hold and the least salient are left aside. Information gets lost in the process and slippage between issues and candidates is common. In sum, by looking exclusively at candidates' campaign issues we are likely ignoring important primes.[6]

## SPILLOVER EFFECTS

Priming effects have far-reaching consequences for voting and elections. Candidates able to saturate voters with campaign issues—either through deep financial pockets or media coverage—prime voters to evaluate them based on standards of their own choosing. By working indiscriminately, however, priming effects have much greater breadth—they can affect the standards of evaluation for multiple candidates. Spillover effects address this crucial point. Spillover effects occur when one or more issues from a contest (or contests) influence the criteria voters use to judge candidates in another, separate contest.[7] For example, a spillover effect happens if voters evaluate House candidates based on an issue featured in a gubernatorial contest. By this definition, spillover effects may also happen if voters choose candidates running for lower offices based on issues from a presidential contest, a circumstance that heightens coattail voting (Mondak 1990). In addition, as I demonstrate throughout this book, issues on the ballot can shape the criteria voters use to evaluate candidates. Spillover effects differ from traditional campaign effects in that spillover effects require an issue be absent or nearly so from the contest in question or voters must have had little or no awareness whether the issue was featured in that contest. On the other hand, traditional campaign effects require voters to evaluate candidates based on issues from the candidates' campaigns.

Spillover effects presume that voters disregard the source of an issue. On this point, Dalager's (1996) research on U.S. Senate elections examines whether voters correctly identify campaign issues found in the candidates' campaigns. Using the 1988 NES Senate Election Study, Dalager reports that "almost three fourths of the electorate cannot recall even one of a number of issues raised in the campaign"(509).[8] Investigating the voters that mentioned an issue, Dalager found that 42 percent of them, nearly half, incorrectly identified an issue. Interestingly, these "misinformed" voters were nearly as politically sophisticated as respondents who were able to correctly identify an issue from a Senate contest. Dalager surmises that voters were getting these issues from outside campaigns and suggests that presidential campaign issues were one source. Not surprisingly, given the low visibility of House elections, Abbe et al. (2003) found that 76 percent of voters did not agree with the candidates about the most important issue in House campaigns. To the extent that campaign issues matter, then, many voters make judgments about candidates based on issues from outside sources. In sum, there is little evidence, at least in congressional elections, that voters properly link issues and candidates. With a substantial number of voters not "getting it right," research on U.S. elections should begin to consider where voters get their information and how that information affects voting decisions.[9]

Ansolabehere and Iyengar (1995) take an important step in this direction by looking at how information from distinct contests spills over into each other. Using an experimental design, the authors found that the likelihood that subjects would mention issues in their evaluations of candidates (likes and dislikes) in one race increased when exposed to information from another. Focusing on the 1992 presidential election and both of California's U.S. Senate contests that year, the authors found that the mention of issues not only crossed over between the two Senate races, but also between the Senate and presidential elections.

> Exposure to an advertisement from the presidential campaign, for instance, boosted (by a significant margin) the likelihood that voters would cite issues when asked about their impressions of the candidates in either Senate race. In reciprocal fashion, exposure to advertising from either of the Senate races more than doubled the frequency of issue-oriented comments aimed at Bush and Clinton. (Ansolabehere and Iyengar 1995, 46–47)

Although Ansolabehere and Iyengar did not find evidence of spillover learning effects for candidates' issue positions (as mentioned, this process may take place outside conscious awareness), their findings suggest that voting for a particular office does not take place in isolation and that information from one race may affect others.

If spillover effects take place among elections for federal offices, do they happen between levels of government? This question is critical given that few scholars entertain the idea that issues from state politics affect federal elections. A handful of studies on Senate and gubernatorial elections, however, suggest that voters do not discriminate against issues that appear to fall outside the responsibility of a particular office. National economic conditions and political issues affect voting in gubernatorial elections (Chubb 1988; Simon, Ostrom, and Marra 1991; Stein 1990), and state factors affect voting in U.S. Senate elections (Jacobson and Wolfinger 1989; Westlye 1991). These studies emphasize that elections are not neat and tidy affairs. Consequently, agenda issues may—and most likely do— spill over into a variety of contests where they, to a greater or lesser degree, shape voters' candidate judgments.

## PARTISAN STEREOTYPES

Once an issue has made its way to the top of the voter's head, that is to say it has become accessible, how does the voter know the candidates' positions? After all, if voters have little knowledge of the candidates or their campaigns they certainly do not know the candidates' issue positions. Yet even in the United States where political parties do not have elaborate control mechanisms over candidates, voters nonetheless strongly identify candidates with particular issue positions based on the candidate's party affiliation (Cain 1995; Conover and Feldman 1989; Koch 2001; Petrocik 1991, 1996; Rahn 1993). Furthermore, the homogenization of the two parties in the 1990s (Republicans becoming more conservative and Democrats becoming more liberal) has solidified such understandings among the electorate (Jacobson 2000).

Partisan stereotypes underlie the idea that voters ascribe certain issue positions to candidates based on party affiliation. Petrocik's (1991, 1996) theory of issue ownership addresses the origins and effects of these stereotypes. Issue ownership is the idea that some issues belong to or are owned by political parties (Klingemann, Hofferbert, and Budge 1994; Petrocik 1991, 1996). The theory of issue ownership assumes that the issues that receive "attention from a party are those associated with the groups that are a part of the party's normal constituency" (Petrocik 1991, 18). What follows, according to Petrocik, is that parties establish reputations for particular issues. A party's reputation, in turn, affects the issues the party discusses (the agenda element), what it has to say about issues (solution element), and whether voters perceive it as able to handle an issue successfully (credibility element). In an election, then, each party seeks to set the agenda with issues it owns for which a majority of the electorate shares the party's position. For example, Republicans are perceived as the party most capable of delivering tax cuts—a position popular with many voters. Hence, Republicans "own" the issue of taxes and will discuss taxes and other issues in which they have an electoral advantage and ignore issues that Democrats own. Not surprisingly, Democrats will do the opposite. In effect, Democratic and Republican campaigns seldom converge on the same issues (Damore, 2004; Klingemann, Hofferbert, and Budge 1994; A. Simon 2002; Spiliotes and Vavreck 2002). Given that parties cannot credibly take any position on an issue, agenda formation is the key to influencing voting. Thus, "Both parties/candidates are trying to establish an advantageous interpretation of the issue 'meaning' of the election and, implicitly, the criteria by which voters should make their decision" (Petrocik 1991, 22). In the end, whichever party succeeds in setting the agenda defines what the campaign is about (Petrocik 1991; Riker 1993).[10]

What evidence is there for issue ownership? Petrocik (1996) found that voters in the 1980 election strongly associated parties with solving certain problems or issues. Not surprisingly, voters perceived Democrats as more capable of protecting social security and Republicans as better suited to handling tax policy. These distinctions matter in important ways for voting behavior. Holding ideology and partisan identification constant, Petrocik found that respondents more attentive to a party's issue agenda were significantly more likely to vote for that party's presidential candidate. In an experimental setting, Iyengar and Valentino (2000) demonstrated that candidates who run on issues "owned" by their party have greater success attracting voter support than those who run on the other party's issue strengths. Using survey data of voters and candidates from the 1998 elections, Abbe et al. (2003) found that the amount of agreement between House candidates and voters about the most important issues in a campaign affects voting decisions if the candidate's party "owns the issue."

A wealth of research supports the notion that voters draw on partisan stereotypes or schemas in ascribing issue positions to candidates. Scholars using both experimental and survey research have found that partisan stereotypes or schemas affect perceptions of candidates' issue positions (Conover and Feldman 1989; Koch 2001; Lodge and Hamill 1986; Norpoth and Buchanan 1992; Rahn 1993; Riggle et al. 1992). These perceptions are so strongly ingrained that individuals may incorrectly ascribe the party position on an issue to candidates who have taken contrary positions (Koch 2001; Rahn 1993). This effect appears especially powerful in the context of low-information elections. Koch (2001), for example, demonstrates that many voters are unlikely to know when House candidates "issue trespass" on abortion because they ascribe pro-choice positions to pro-life Democrats and pro-life positions to pro-choice Republicans. In sum, voters' partisan stereotypes, their understandings about which party owns issues, bridges the gap between agendas and candidates.

The link between agenda issue and party is also apparent in voting on ballot propositions. For a long time, it was conventional wisdom among scholars that voting on ballot propositions was devoid of partisan cues. For example, in Magleby's (1984) study of voting on ballot propositions in California between 1972 and 1980 he concludes that although party cues appear to matter in voting on a few measures, party is rarely important. Recently, however, scholars have found a strong partisan basis to voting on ballot propositions. Smith and Tolbert (2001) found that partisanship was the strongest predictor of voting on California ballot propositions between 1994 and 1998. Similarly, Branton (2003) found that from 1992 to 1996 party identification was the most consistent predictor of vote choice on ballot propositions, especially on social/moral ballot initiatives. Thus, at least in recent years, party labels constitute important cues for voting on ballot measures and likely help strengthen the partisan link between ballot proposition issues and candidates.

## Explaining Agenda Effects

The most blunt and powerful agenda effects include the capacity of agendas to infuse contests for different offices with common criteria and to differentiate the criteria voters use to evaluate candidates in different electoral environments. These characteristics of agendas are nothing new. In presidential contests, the national agenda affects voting for presidential candidates as well as the vote for candidates running for lower offices (coattails). Mondak (1990), for example, shows that coattail voting—voting for House candidates based on presidential candidate preference—happens most often when voters exhibit a high degree of issue agreement with their preferred presidential candidate. Thus, scholars have known for some time that agenda issues infuse disparate voting decisions with common meaning. Similarly, the content of the national agenda changes across election years. Thus, scholars have also known for some time that agendas alter the foundations of candidate evaluations.

However, looking at agendas from a subnational point of view, (e.g., ballot propositions) reveals a different perspective on nonpresidential elections that is lost when focusing exclusively on national agenda issues. Agendas homogenize the criteria voters use to evaluate candidates within a state or constituency. In so doing, voters evaluate candidates in myriad contests along similar issue dimensions, riding roughshod over distinctions that turn on candidates' campaigns or institutional requirements of an office (see chapter 1). Highly visible issues place candidates from the same party along a common issue continuum. If Republican candidates running for governor, senator, and representative are on the winning side of an issue, Democratic candidates for these offices would be on the losing side. The implication is that elections that are seemingly unrelated because they involve different offices (such as House and gubernatorial contests) may share more of a common evaluative basis than elections for the same type of office in different states. Agendas, in short, unify voting decisions within a constituency.

Agendas also differentiate political discourse across constituencies. In contrast to holding constant the electoral environment, agendas, examined at the constituency level (e.g., states), produce substantial information differences. Were all agendas national, we would see few differences in the issues voters consider important across states or regions. Although some elections have more national content than others, a substantial amount of campaign and issue information varies across electoral environments. As put by Huckfeldt and Sprague, "When television newscasters MacNeil and Lehrer interview the editors of newspapers across the country, they recognize the disjunctures in information flow that can only be observed from a local perspective" (1995, 5).

The variance in flows of information provides voters with distinct evaluative criteria across constituencies. Ballot proposition campaigns, the empirical focus of this book, constitute a major source of agenda issues across the United States. Consider the role of nuclear freeze ballot propositions in the 1982 midterm elections (see chapter 5). The unemployment rate was nearly 10 percent, and Reaganomics was at the forefront of many election campaigns. Despite the importance of economics in 1982, the freeze was an important issue for voters in states with referenda on the issue. It influenced voting for House, Senate, and gubernatorial candidates in states with freeze ballot measures regardless of whether the candidates discussed the freeze or not. But the freeze did not play a similar role in states without ballot measures. Voters' attitudes about the freeze played an insignificant or small role in states without freeze ballot measures. In sum, agendas differentiate the content of electoral discourse across the United States.

## THE CONDITIONAL EFFECTS OF AGENDAS

Agendas, of course, are not all-powerful. In some elections, such as contests between a well-funded, popular incumbent and a poorly funded, unknown challenger, agendas will seldom be decisive. Issues, even important ones, are but one ingredient in deciding electoral outcomes and the fact that many voters split their tickets attests to the variety of influences that account for the vote. Yet, as discussed, agendas play a significant role in many contests by influencing the criteria underlying candidate judgment. Nevertheless, agenda effects are not uniform, and I expect their effects to wax and wane depending on informational conditions. The visibility of an agenda issue, candidate visibility, and the interplay among them constitute the major determinants of how prominently an agenda issue will figure in the voting decision.

Agendas matter to voters. They establish what the election is about and thus the standards voters use to evaluate candidates. Although I make blunt distinctions among agenda issues, some are more salient than others, and differences in voter awareness likely affect how importantly issues figure in the voter's decision-making process. In chapter 3, I elaborate the factors that account for the visibility of direct legislation issues, the empirical focus of this book. For now, suffice it to say, the more prominent an issue on the agenda, all else equal, the greater weight voters assign it in making candidate evaluations.

Agenda effects also vary according to how much information is available from and about a given candidate race. Since candidates in low-information elections have relatively little control over the information voters use to evaluate them, these races are best characterized as understructured, and the porosity of these contests enables agendas to spill over into them. The influence of presidential campaigns on voting behavior in lower offices underscores the ability of information from "outside" a specific contest to affect voting decisions for candidates within that contest. Thus, issues on the agenda, regardless of their origins, may routinely spill over into multiple contests, even in contests where candidates do not discuss them. A Senate race in which crime is central might affect the criteria voters use to evaluate candidates running for governor, U.S. House, and state legislative races. In other instances, as explored in this book, direct legislation may shape agendas.

Although I categorize all nonpresidential contests as low-information, there is, of course, substantial variation among what voters know about candidates and issues in these elections. Compared to Senate elections, the visibility of challengers in House elections is relatively low (Abramowitz 1980; Krasno 1994). Yet I do not expect candidates running for higher-profile offices to be immune from agendas. To the contrary, I expect candidates running for these offices (e.g., governor, senator) to be more susceptible to agenda influences. Initially, such an expectation appears counter to the theory of campaign effects. By effectively communicating their messages, candidates in highly visible races should be in a better position to shape the criteria voters use to evaluate them, thereby inoculating themselves from "outside" issues. Nevertheless, visibility is precisely why agenda issues spill over into these contests.

Why do visible candidates heighten agenda effects? Recall that memory is organized in an associative network of linkages between knowledge constructs. In an election, candidates, parties, and issues constitute the primary knowledge constructs. Frequent activation of certain knowledge constructs builds an association between them. Thus, heavy exposure to an issue and candidate, regardless of whether an explicit connection exists, helps establish an association between them. Candidates running for more highly visible offices, then, will likely have greater visibility by virtue of the amount of attention given these contests by the media, higher levels of campaign spending, and greater competition. On the other hand, since voters receive so little information from or about the typical House candidate, the opportunity for a link to form, not to mention a strong link, between a House candidate and an agenda issue diminishes. As a result, the cues of incumbency and party identification dominate voting for House candidates and the effect of agendas may only be realized in competitive down-ballot races where candidates are sufficiently visible to voters.

Although the variance in informational environments is most pronounced between the average House contest and the average Senate or gubernatorial contest, information differences also exist among races for the same office. Indeed, the distinction between high- and low-intensity Senate contests is an organizing principle behind research on Senate elections (Kahn and Kenney 1999; Westlye 1991). Candidates running high-intensity elections are more capable of controlling the criteria that voters use to evaluate them (Kahn and Kenney 1999). Nevertheless, voters choosing candidates in high-intensity races are also more susceptible to agenda effects. Again, for agendas to matter, the candidate and issue must be sufficiently visible for an association between them to form, especially a strong association. None of this is to say that agendas do not matter in House contests or low-intensity Senate or gubernatorial races but rather that the agenda effect is somewhat muted in these races because of the lack of candidate visibility.

By way of comparison, presidential elections most likely do not follow the same patterns of agenda influence outlined for other candidate elections. In voting for presidential candidates, at least compared to voting for candidates running for lower offices, voters have a substantial amount of individuating information. Even the most inattentive voter generally knows something about a presidential candidate's appearance, personality, character, and the issues he or she is talking about. In contrast, voters have less individuating information in low-information elections such as those for governor, Senate, and House. With lower visibility and fewer resources to shape campaign discourse, candidates in low-information contests cannot do much to stay the tide of agenda issues. Despite their best efforts, prominent issues may play a major role in these contests. Agendas are thus inescapable for most candidates in low-information environments. No matter what many of these candidates do or say, their electoral fortunes are inextricably tied to the basket of issues voters deem important. Consequently, agendas impose themselves on most candidates running in low-information contests. Thus, agendas matter for most, if not all, nonpresidential or low-information contests, but the above-mentioned information differences among these contests increase or decrease how important a role they play.

In summary, all else equal, I expect to find the largest agenda effects where issues are highly prominent and so are candidates. Because I look primarily at nonpresidential elections, I expect highly salient issues to play an important role in shaping gubernatorial or senatorial voting decisions and a lesser role for races such as those for the House or state legislature. Again, the higher visibility of candidates and issues is the key to potent agenda effects since less opportunity exists for the political environment to link lower-visibility candidates to prominent issues. The variability of information about agenda issues also makes a difference in how prominently the agenda issue will matter. Less visible agenda issues will have less potent effects on shaping the standards of candidate evaluation, but this, too, varies by candidate visibility. While the effect of a lower-visibility agenda issue on highly visible contests will be less than that of a highly visible agenda issue, the effect of a lower-visibility agenda issue on low-visibility candidates will produce the weakest agenda effects.

Even though my discussion largely characterizes candidates as agenda benefactors or victims of issues that they did not include in their own campaigns, candidates may also help shape the agenda and/or speak to those issues already on the agenda. By campaigning on agenda issues, the nexus between candidate and agenda is strengthened. The connection will be further bolstered by high-intensity campaigns where the candidates' campaign messages are reaching voters. In chapter 6, for example, I examine the California Senate and gubernatorial races mentioned in chapter 1. Governor Pete Wilson campaigned on an illegal immigration initiative, thus making the choice of Wilson and anti–illegal immigration policy nearly inseparable. Wilson's counterpart running for U.S. Senate, Michael Huffington, also campaigned on the initiative, but he did so late in the campaign and amid allegations that he had employed an illegal immigrant (making him appear hypocritical). Given the vast amounts of money spent in both the gubernatorial and Senate contests, each was a high-intensity campaign, but the significance of the agenda issue—illegal immigration—varied according to the rhythms of the candidates' campaigns and news coverage.

Despite the prominence of the anti–illegal immigration initiative, most candidates did not attach themselves to it. Indeed, even where I found extensive political party involvement in initiative politics, few candidates addressed initiative issues. At first blush, this neglect is curious. Assuming that candidates want to win elections (a safe assumption), the question becomes, why would candidates neglect popular issues that might help them win? Neglecting popular agenda issues appears peculiar if you are a candidate whose party is on the winning side, but it is consistent with an institutional mindset that many candidates exhibit in their reelection campaigns. Although I argue that the institutional lines delimiting offices are unimportant to voters, I believe they are important to politicians, especially incumbents. Members of Congress largely talk about issues that they are responsible for handling, as do governors. Atkeson and Partin (2001), for example, show that governors and senators talk about different kinds of issues that fall along state-federal functional responsibility lines.[11] Thus, political candidates craft campaign messages relevant to their offices. Yet, as discussed, voters do not take the same care in linking these issues to offices. Thus, despite the fact that some issues may rise to prominence on the state's agenda through direct legislation, this does not mean members of Congress will say much about these issues because they view them as outside their control or area of responsibility.

More important, initiative issues differ from typical campaign issues in a significant way. In contrast to candidate races where candidates largely control the presentation of campaign issues, the meaning of ballot issues is contested given that they are sometimes the subjects of their own campaigns (Bowler and Donovan 1994; Joslyn and Haider-Markel 2000). Once an issue is on the agenda, its meaning is defined through the campaign. Riker (1986) discusses how the very definition of an issue affects how individuals decide to vote on an issue. One example he provides is how Senator Warren Magnuson (D-Washington) redefined a bill concerning the shipment of toxic chemicals to his state to be considered as a bill that would, if passed, impend on the prerogatives of the U. S. Senate (106–13). In so doing, a critical number of senators reconsidered their initial opposition to the issue, thus providing the margin of votes necessary for Magnuson's alternative to prevail.

Although Riker is discussing agendas in legislatures, his point is germane to mass voting behavior; support for an issue can be volatile depending on how the issue is defined.[12] For candidates, aligning themselves with a popular ballot issue early in the campaign season may cause problems if voter support for it declines. Indeed, support for many ballot propositions changes over the course of an election, usually downward (Bowler and Donovan 1994; Joslyn and Haider-Markel 2000). For example, the Democratic Party in California made a strategic miscalculation in the 1990 midterm elections by aligning with an environmental initiative, Big Green, which had early voter support but was defeated on election day. Additionally, ballot measures can be divisive (e.g., abortion, affirmative action), and candidates try to avoid such issues because they may lose votes. Thus politicians may avoid these issues because of uncertainty about the popularity of ballot proposition issues as opposed to abstract campaign talk about issues.

## Conclusion

Agendas, through priming, work indiscriminately in shaping the electoral landscape. Agendas capture the attention of voters, thus priming voters to assign greater relevance or weight to some issues than others when making candidate evaluations. In contrast to traditional approaches that separate elections from each other, agenda voters use the same criteria to evaluate candidates for each office. When making candidate evaluations in low-information contests the issues at the top of the voter's head, in many cases, will not change across voting decisions for different offices. Thus issues may spill over from one contest into another.

Working from the premise that interrelated cognitive structures organize memory, partisan stereotypes link agenda issues to candidates. Agendas consisting of "party-owned" issues will benefit, or disadvantage, a political party depending on which party's issues are most prevalent. Consequently, voting for House, Senate, and gubernatorial candidates may share a common evaluative basis if issues strongly attached to partisan divisions, such as abortion or taxes, define the agenda.

Agendas include not only unifying voting decisions within a constituency but also differentiating the criteria voters use to evaluate candidates across constituencies. As the basket of issues varies across different states, so do the standards of candidate judgment. Taking a closer look, the effects of agendas will wax and wane according to the electoral information environment. The more prominent an agenda issue, all else equal, the greater role it will play in shaping candidate evaluations. Agenda effects will also vary according to candidate visibility. Highly competitive races such as those found in open-seat contests or contests featuring high-quality, well-financed challengers increase the visibility of candidates and thus links with salient issues. Candidates in lackluster races will likely be "out of sight" and thus "out of mind," hindering an association between them and salient issues.

*Chapter 3*

# STUDYING AGENDAS AND DIRECT

# LEGISLATION IN U.S. ELECTIONS

Direct legislation issues may provide voters with a common basis of candidate evaluation and at the same time diversify the criteria voters use to make candidate judgments across constituencies. Yet, despite the importance of ballot propositions and other statewide issues on the agenda, they are seldom considered as determinants of the vote in candidate elections. Implicit in many studies is the assumption that citizens are not exposed to, knowledgeable about, or concerned with issues found in their home states. With such little recognition of local information environments, it is not surprising that analysts ignore state agendas. In this chapter, I discuss the agenda-setting properties of direct legislation and sketch my research strategy for studying them.

## DIRECT LEGISLATION AND AGENDA-SETTING

The dramatic increase in the number of well-known ballot propositions, especially the initiative, has led many scholars and observers to note their importance in setting the agenda (Berg and Holman 1989; Ellis 2002, chap. 4; Garrett 1999; Magleby 1984, 1995; Thomas 1990; D. Schmidt 1989, 30). Since voters must either abstain or vote to accept or reject a ballot proposition, a choice is institutionally presented. In presenting this choice, the initiative is an agenda-setting institution that focuses attention and informs citizens about what is important. To borrow from Rourke, Hiskes, and Zirakzadeh, "[R]eferendums institutionalize political talking—they make political discussions more than mere grumbling or cocktail party small talk" (1992, 166).

The myriad effects of ballot measures on political behavior, especially the quality of civic life, suggest that it is not a stretch to argue that direct legislation has potent agenda-setting effects. Scholars have found that direct legislation promotes political efficacy (Bowler and Donovan 2002; Gilens, Glaser, and Mendelberg 2001; Mendelsohn and Cutler 2000), knowledge (M. Smith 2002; Smith and Tolbert 2004; Tolbert, McNeal, and Smith 2003), and voter participation (M. Smith 2001; Tolbert, Grummel, and Smith 2001; Magleby 1984). States with initiatives also have larger and more diverse interest group populations (Boehmke 2002), including a citizenry more likely to contribute financially to groups (Tolbert, McNeal, and

Smith 2003). Finally, direct legislation enhances representative democracy by promoting legislative responsiveness to median voter preferences (Gerber 1996, 1999). The cumulative picture that emerges is that direct legislation shapes the political life of citizens in meaningful ways.

Despite these broad effects, only a handful of studies have examined direct legislation's role in candidate races (Jacobson and Woflinger 1989; Westlye 1991). Since voting on direct legislation can be demanding, scholars of voting in these elections are keenly sensitive to the makeup of the electoral information environment, especially the presence of cues (Bowler and Donovan 1994, 1998; Gerber and Lupia 1995, 1999; Karp 1998; Lupia 1994; Magleby 1984). And while research on direct legislation voting typically looks at politicians and candidates as cheap sources of information, students of candidate voting seldom acknowledge ballot measures. The omission is unfortunate given that the use of initiatives and referenda has increased dramatically over the last twenty years (Donovan and Bowler 1998; Waters 2003). For example, the 1998 elections saw 235 ballot measures in 44 states, of which 61 qualified as either popular initiatives or referenda (Initiative and Referendum Institute 1998). In the 2000 elections, voters cast their ballots on 204 statewide measures including 71 popular initiatives and referenda (Initiative and Referendum Institute 2000). Recently, the 2002 elections witnessed 202 statewide ballot measures in 40 states, 53 of which were placed on the ballot by popular initiative or referendum (Waters 2003).

So how does direct legislation set the agenda? Although there is more to the story, as I will discuss shortly, social choice theory helps illustrate the agenda-setting capabilities of direct legislation. In social choice theory, there is no guarantee that equilibrium exists when three or more voters with dissimilar ranked preferences choose among three or more issues (Arrow 1963). Consider the classic example: voter one prefers a > b > c, voter two prefers b > c > a, and voter three prefers c > a > b. If the voters are asked to choose between issues a and b, a is the majority choice. A glance at the three preference orderings shows that although only voter one ranks alternative a first, voter three also prefers a to b. Only voter two prefers b to a. If the voters are given a choice between a and c, c is the majority choice. If voters are asked to choose between b and c, b wins. And so on. Thus, the winner depends on which pair of alternatives is offered and there is no equilibrium majority choice. In theory, the process may continue indefinitely.

However, the outcome of a vote is not simply the aggregation of preferences (Riker 1982). The outcome of a vote may depend on the agenda (Riker 1982, 1986, 1993). In states with initiatives, actors may define the important issues by placing an issue on the ballot. Since voters are confronted with a "take it or leave it" choice (Romer and Rosenthal 1978), they must accept the agenda-setter's proposal, reject it (status quo), or abstain. Typically, we characterize a, b, and c from the example above as alternatives *on an agenda* since they constitute the choice set from which voters must choose (we did not get to choose from x, y, and z after all). To illustrate agenda-setting effects for voters in a typical U.S. election, however, I redefine a, b, and c as potential agenda issues (rather than as alternatives on an agenda). In other words, the agenda is endogenous—voters are choosing the important issues. Voters cannot manipulate the agenda (by proposing different issue pairings) but only accept or reject an issue from a given pairing. Candidates and parties attempt to manipulate the choice set so that their preferred issue finds its way onto the agenda. If they succeed, the agenda changes.

Assuming all candidates have an equal ability to propose alternative issue pairings (which is not typically the case), no equilibrium exists because the candidates will indefinitely propose different issue pairings so that their preferred issue is on the agenda. However, in an election voters may have the same preference rankings or opinions about which issues matter. In other words, voters typically find some issues more compelling than others. Thus, suppose voters one and two have identical preferences, say a > b > c. The equilibrium, issue a on the agenda, is preference induced. However, if issue c is placed on the ballot, an institutional move, it is fixed onto the agenda. This equilibrium is rule imposed.[1] Direct legislation, therefore, may focus attention on an issue in which the underlying distribution of voter preferences (e.g., what is an important issue) would not support.

Of course, not all ballot measures make it onto the agenda. Despite the attention that accompanies the institutional "push" given to an issue on the ballot, it is not a necessary or sufficient condition for inclusion on the agenda. Many ballot measures reside in obscurity with few voters knowing anything about them. Furthermore, among the ballot measures that do rise to prominence, not all have the same visibility. What factors account for these differences? Elsewhere, I have shown that the visibility of California ballot propositions, a plausible proxy for agenda status, varies according to the political environment (Nicholson 2003). For example, initiatives involving civil liberties, civil rights, and morality issues heighten awareness of ballot propositions. In the 1998 through 2002 election cycles, direct legislation covered such controversial topics as affirmative action, abortion, medicinal marijuana, gun control, same-sex marriage, physician-assisted suicide, and the death penalty (Initiative and Referendum Institute 1998, 2000; Waters 2003). Not surprisingly, these types of issues have a greater chance of capturing media and public attention than do obscure bond measures.

High levels of campaign spending and media coverage also boost awareness of ballot propositions. Campaign spending, especially by opponents, increases awareness of ballot propositions (Bowler and Donovan 1998; Nicholson 2003). Recent spending on some initiative campaigns suggests that awareness of ballot measures can be high. In 2002, for example, groups spent an estimated $173 million on ballot measure campaigns. Surprisingly, this amount was down from 1998, the prior off-year election, where it was estimated that $400 million was spent.[2] In many instances, direct legislation campaigns can involve greater spending than that in statewide races for governor or U.S. senator (e.g., the 1988 California auto insurance initiatives). Although many ingredients go into explaining the awareness of ballot propositions, these factors likely play an especially significant role in explaining which ballot measure issues make it onto the agenda.

Further meshing the worlds of direct legislation and candidate races is the cultivating of initiatives by candidates and political parties (See Ellis 2002, chap. 4; Smith and Tolbert 2001). As discussed in chapters 2 and 6, this strategy is risky, but it does happen. Several California gubernatorial candidates, for example, have taken this approach to setting the agenda. Hoping to bolster his credentials as a political reformer, Democrat Jerry Brown's successful campaign for governor in 1974 centered on Proposition 9 (it won), an initiative to bring about campaign finance reform. Republican Pete Wilson also succeeded with this strategy by running on Proposition 187 (it won), an initiative to deny public benefits to illegal immigrants. Many candidates using this strategy, however, do not fare well. In his unsuccessful bid for governor, Republican State Senator John Briggs sponsored initiatives proposing to deny civil rights to homosexuals (it failed) and buttress California's death penalty (it won). Democrat Tom Bradley's failed bid for governor in 1986 was tightly linked to Proposition 65 (it won), an initiative that sought to regulate toxics and ensure clean water. While the success or failure of candidates running on ballot propositions is another question, the mixed results underscore how shaping the agenda may not be sufficient to influence election outcomes where other factors such as incumbency play an important role.

In sum, the vast sums of money and media attention surrounding direct legislation issues, especially those that invoke controversy, help them make their way into the minds of voters. The link between direct legislation issues and candidates may be further reinforced as political parties and candidates tie these issues to their campaigns.

## STUDYING THE AGENDA-SETTING EFFECTS OF DIRECT LEGISLATION

### Laboratories of Democracy

In 1932, Justice Louis Brandeis wrote, "It is one of the happy incidents of the federal system that a single courageous State may, if its citizens choose, serve as a laboratory; and try novel social and economic experiments without risk to the rest of the country" (quoted in Osborne 1990). Although Brandeis's comment concerned public policy experiments, his insight is no less valuable for students of U.S. elections. Research on U.S. elections, especially congressional elections, has not taken full advantage of states as natural experiments to investigate the environmental consequences of information. In large part, this neglect is a by-product of surveys conducted to assess the behavior of a national electorate. Since our research tools are national in scope, so are the questions we ask and, consequently, the answers we get (see Huckfeldt and Sprague 1995). Further, many national surveys do not allow us to make valid inferences about state-level phenomena such as direct legislation because of the over-representation of large states.

Yet electoral politics play out, in many ways, state by state. Presidential elections take place with an eye toward winning the electoral college, a state-based strategy. Candidates running for the U.S. Senate and governor are involved in statewide races that involve an even more explicit recognition of statewide concerns. Even candidates running for the House must occasionally adopt strategies that focus on statewide issues given that the interests of their constituents are inextricably tied to state politics. Brace and Jewett (1995) agree: "While it is widely acknowledged that members of Congress think about what is going on back home, and typically allocate large portions of their time and resources to strengthening their state base, many congressional studies pay remarkably little attention to state-level factors" (645). Further emphasizing statewide concerns and issues are the many media markets that coincide with state boundaries.

U.S. citizens are also Californians, Minnesotans, New Yorkers, and Georgians, who share a common pool of electoral information with their fellow state citizens. Voters within a state have a shared evaluative basis for politics based on this commonality. The corollary, of course, is that states break the national electorate into many subelectorates. Each state electorate may use different criteria, more or less, to judge candidates. But how important are state electoral environments? For some scholars, they are very important. Erikson, Wright, and McIver (1993) note that relatively stable factors such as party identification and ideology, what Campbell et al. (1966) refer to as long-term forces, leave much of the variance in state-level voting unexplained. Erikson and colleagues conclude that short-term forces (factors that change from election to election) dominate statewide elections, especially those for governor and U.S. senator: "Although important, state partisanship leaves vast amounts of the unexplained variance in state outcomes, particularly in elections below the presidential level. State elections for senator and governor are largely the result of short-term forces independent of state partisanship." If these authors are correct, especially in light of the emphasis placed on local forces in studies of congressional elections, the neglect of issue agendas in the states is a major lacuna.

A modest step toward filling this lacuna is to examine direct legislation. It is important to underscore the fact, however, that all states have issue agendas, not just those with direct legislation. Elections and campaigns within a state can introduce new issues or reintroduce longstanding ones that shape electoral behavior. In this respect, then, direct legislation is only one means, although perhaps a preeminent one, of identifying salient statewide issues.

Studying direct legislation is an effective strategy for identifying distinct electoral environments. All fifty states allow the legislative referendum, the process whereby state legislatures may place ballot measures before voters. Yet the most controversial issues, those likely to achieve high agenda status, typically make it to the ballot through the popular (citizen-initiated) initiative. By collecting a required number of signatures, initiatives permit citizens to place a statute or constitutional amendment on the ballot for voters to accept or reject. As seen in figure 3.1, twenty-four states allow initiatives.[3] The popular referendum also permits citizens to participate directly in the law-making process by collecting signatures.[4] In contrast to initiatives, however, referenda involve voters approving or rejecting laws enacted by state legislatures. As shown in figure 3.1, twenty-four states also permit this method of direct legislation. Taken together, twenty-seven states have adopted the initiative, referenda, or both. While most states allow both types, three states that allow the initiative do not allow the referendum and vice-versa (Waters 2003).

The variation among issues on the ballot across states takes advantage of strengths inherent in both surveys and controlled experiments. The tradeoff between surveys and controlled experiments is that surveys have high external validity and controlled experiments have high internal validity. In the laboratory, the experimenter can, for the most part, hold constant the environment. The weakness of controlled experiments, however, is that external validity is limited. When survey data are used, we can be reasonably assured that our findings are generalizable to the population we wish to make inferences from. However, what is gained in external validity is lost in internal validity. That is, we do not have the same confidence regarding causal inference as we do in laboratory experiments.

Mondak (1995, chap. 2) speaks to this concern. Specifically, he discusses how naturally occurring political situations can be used as experiments to increase the internal validity of survey data. The quasi-social experiment he used involved two cities during the 1992 elections. A sample of residents from Pittsburgh, or the treatment group, had no local newspaper during the election because of a newspaper strike. The control group, a sample of residents from Cleveland, had uninterrupted newspaper service. The natu-

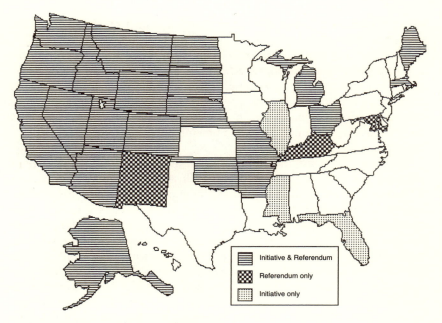

Fig. 3.1.  Direct Legislation in the States
   Source: Waters, 2003.

ral absence of a newspaper in Pittsburgh, holding constant other factors, varied the two groups according to the presence or absence of a local newspaper. Mondak reasons that within the survey research tradition, this setting not only has external validity but also takes the best from controlled laboratory experiments—high internal validity. Since the treatment (information variance) occurs naturally in the research design, we have greater confidence in our ability to make causal inferences.[5]

In contrast to Mondak's study where the population characteristics of Pittsburgh and Cleveland were similar, the characteristics of state populations can vary a great deal and the greater heterogeneity of state populations introduces internal validity problems. However, these problems may be addressed, in part, through individual-level control variables. These variables may account for many of the factors that determine candidate judgments and voting decisions so that the effects of varying flows of electoral information can be isolated adequately.

Studying the effects of ballot measures has additional methodological advantages. Since I am concerned with agendas spilling over into candidate races, direct legislation provides an ideal setting for looking at whether "outside" issues shape the standards of evaluation for judging candidates down the ballot. One of the most obvious benefits is that direct legislation diminishes the ambiguity associated with what issues are important to voters *within a state*. By definition and constitutional design, ballot measures address only policy matters under state control. Finally, besides having a campaign life of their own, initiatives and referenda are the statewide issues about which survey researchers ask the most questions. Hence, state ballot measures constitute the best means we have for examining statewide issues.

## An Alternative Explanation of the Agenda-Setting Effects of Direct Legislation

My argument depends on the ability of direct legislation to set the agenda. But it is possible that issues on the ballot reflect what voters in a state consider important. Put differently, one might reasonably ask whether direct legislation increases information flow about an issue or whether an issue on the ballot simply means that the issue has already reached a certain level of importance for a state's voters. Although I believe that direct legislation triggers popular interest (its effects are exogenous) rather than reflects it (its effects are endogenous), it is important to address this potential limitation. Here, I take up this potential criticism on substantive grounds. In later chapters, where possible, I address it empirically.

The major argument on behalf of the view that initiatives reflect an issue's importance is that citizens share common concerns that run deeper than the issues prominent in a given election. For example, some states such as Oregon and Washington, big initiative users, have reputations for placing a high priority on environmental issues. Issues that resonate with a state's voters may very well "play big" there. However, with the exception of issue publics, issue concerns are more likely to be latent than chronically accessible. In other words, certain issues might resonate with voters in a state, but if the information flow about these issues is scarce, few voters are thinking about them. Indeed, most scholars of public opinion and voting behavior believe that issues make it into the public mind from the top down, a process whereby elites structure the information environment (e.g., Carmines and Stimson 1980; Iyengar and Kinder 1987; Kuklinski and Segura 1995; Kuklinski et al. 2001; Zaller 1992). Students of initiatives also subscribe to a top-down view of how the process works. Whereas Populist reformers designed the initiative process as a tool for citizens to engage in grassroots organizing, interest groups and policy entrepreneurs dominate the process today (Broder 2000; Ellis 2002; Gerber 1999; Magleby 1984; McCuan et al. 1998; D. Smith 1998).

But what about the fact that some ballot measures, the popular initiative and referendum, must meet a signature requirement to qualify for the ballot? Obtaining a substantial number of signatures suggests that an issue has, at minimum, a modest level of popular interest in the state. But most scholars believe that initiatives get on the ballot independent of the depth of popular sentiment (and therefore less open to endogeneity issues). While a good number of issues on the ballot may appear to be important to voters, we can point to many that do not appeal to most of the electorate. In 1998, for instance, California had a ballot proposition (6) on banning the killing of horses to curb consumption of horse meat—an initiative that was likely not all that important to voters.

Studies of direct legislation do not support the notion that meeting a signature requirement signifies that lots of people think that the issue is important. Although it is true that quite a few signatures are required to qualify a ballot proposition, the percentage is not substantial. For instance, Tolbert, Lowenstein, and Donovan (1998, 28) report that signature requirements range "from a low of 2% in North Dakota to a high of 15% in Wyoming." In California, signature gatherers need 5 percent of the vote from the last gubernatorial election. To be certain, these requirements are financially burdensome for those trying to qualify initiatives. However, as Donovan and Bowler conclude, signature requirements are "modest" obstacles for qualifying an initiative (1998, 9).

The signature-gathering process for qualifying a ballot proposition demonstrates that the public's perception of the importance of an issue has little, if any, relationship to whether it will qualify. Qualifying an initiative or referendum is seldom, if ever, done without the strong involvement of interest groups and money to "buy" signatures. Gerber (1999) maintains that the impetus behind qualifying initiatives and referenda rests squarely with interest groups and, to a lesser extent, politicians and political parties. She does not consider popular sentiment as an obstacle to qualification. In her research, *money* and *time* are the primary barriers interest groups face in trying to qualify an initiative or referendum (also see Ellis 2002; D. Smith 1998; Tolbert, Lowenstein, and Donovan 1998).

To overcome these barriers, interest groups use the "initiative industry" to qualify an issue for the ballot. Tolbert, Lowenstein, and Donovan note, "In the past two decades, virtually all successful drives [to qualify an initiative] have relied, at least predominately, on professional circulation firms" (1998, 35). To support these claims, the authors cite a major study on this question conducted by the California Commission on Campaign Financing: "Professional signature-gathering firms now boast that they can qualify *any* measure for the ballot (one 'guarantees' qualification) if paid enough money for the cadres of individual signature gatherers, and their statement is probably true. Any individual with approximately $1 million to spend can now place any issue on the ballot" [emphasis original] (1992, 265). In sum, the reality of the "initiative industry" means that the electorate's opinion of an issue's importance is of little significance in qualifying it for the ballot. As discussed, money, organization, and time are the crucial ingredients necessary for qualifying an issue on the ballot—not citizens' belief that it is an important issue. By addressing this concern on both empirical and theoretical grounds we can be satisfied that endogeneity is not a problem.

## Conclusion

This chapter argues that agendas vary the flow of political information across electoral contexts and to propose a research strategy for investigating such effects. By neglecting agendas, analysts hold constant the electoral information environments that vary the issues important to voters. The states are the unit of analysis best suited to evaluating environmental effects as embodied in agendas. U.S. states constitute the primary constituency grouping for elections, and a wide variety of studies suggest that information differences among the states should influence electoral attitudes and behavior. Using direct legislation, I take advantage of a naturally occurring experimental manipulation that enables me to investigate how differences in issue saliency across states shape candidate judgments.

*Chapter 4*

# BALLOT MEASURES AND CONGRESSIONAL ELECTION AGENDAS

The purpose of this chapter is to test an implicit but widely held assumption among scholars that state issues—ballot measures—do not play a role in shaping evaluations of congressional candidates. As mentioned in previous chapters, issues on state agendas are conspicuously absent from studies of House and Senate elections. By isolating federal races—House and Senate contests—from the electoral environment of states, scholars may be missing a significant piece of the puzzle of congressional elections. Former Speaker of the House of Representatives Tip O'Neill famously remarked that all politics are local. If all politics are local, shouldn't we at least look to see if he was right?

In this chapter, I examine whether issues on a state's agenda, as measured by state ballot measures, shape the agenda in congressional elections. In so doing, I compare the criteria voters use to evaluate congressional candidates across states with (and without) direct legislation on abortion, taxes, and the environment. Using a merged data set of ballot measures and the NES Senate Election Study, I find that direct legislation affects the issues that voters attach to congressional candidates. The ability of ballot measures to set the agenda in congressional races demonstrates that federal versus state distinctions do not figure prominently in how voters assemble candidate evaluations and that (local) agendas differentiate the standards of candidate evaluation for federal candidates across states. The results also demonstrate that spillover effects happen more often than students of elections typically recognize.

## DATA AND METHODS

To evaluate the effects of ballot measures, I need to make inferences about state electoral environments. Unfortunately, many surveys are inadequate for studying state-level phenomena because they rely on national samples. This is a problem since most national surveys overrepresent large states, making inferences about state-level phenomena less reliable. Westlye (1991) found this problem in studies of Senate elections where previous researchers had erroneously concluded that these races, as a category, were highly competitive because national surveys disproportionately selected respondents from large states (also see Lee and Oppenheimer 1999, chap. 4).

To remedy these problems, the Survey Research Center at the University of Michigan conducted the 1988, 1990, and 1992 NES Senate Studies. The sample is drawn by state with roughly equal numbers of respondents. Since the sample design enables researchers to make state-to-state comparisons, it is a valuable resource for looking at electoral phenomena at the state level. Although the Senate study is ideally suited for state research, it does not contain questions about state ballot measures. To overcome this limitation, I merged these data with data on ballot measures. The merged data set includes all fifty states and three election years—1988, 1990, and 1992.

The political landscape of each election showed considerable variation in the national electoral environment despite the marginal gains and losses of congressional seats. One obvious difference, of course, is that 1990 was a midterm election. Without the centralizing force of a presidential contest, midterm elections typically turn on local politics. In contrast to the 1988 and 1992 elections, national politics was noticeably absent from the 1990 elections. Struck by this localism, *Congressional Quarterly* wrote that the 1990 congressional elections "looked like a series of hard-fought city council contests, shaped largely by personalities, local issues and a pronounced absence of clear-cut national themes" (*CQ Almanac* 1990, 901). The lack of "clear-cut national themes" in 1990 likely created an information environment hospitable to ballot measures. Indeed, voters demonstrate a greater awareness of ballot measures at the midterm (Nicholson 2003).

The amount of information devoted to national politics, on the other hand, swells during presidential election years. However, the amount of information devoted to policy issues appeared to differ across the two presidential election years. In the 1988 presidential contest between Republican George Bush and Democrat Michael Dukakis, voters witnessed a race in which policy issues were noticeably absent (Hershey 1989; Patterson 1989; Quirk 1989). Indeed, the candidates were reluctant to discuss programmatic concerns. Dukakis campaigned on technical competence for most of the campaign while Bush engaged in negative campaigning, referring to his opponent as a liberal who, unlike himself, would not "stay the course" navigated by outgoing President Ronald Reagan.

In contrast, the 1992 elections emphasized policy issues (Quirk and Dalager 1993). Above all others, the "It's the Economy Stupid" slogan from the Clinton-Gore campaign room summed up the dominant issue of the 1992 presidential election (Alvarez and Nagler 1995). The presidential contest was not the only source of political issues in 1992, however. Magleby, for example, reports that over $117.3 million was spent on ballot measures in 21 states during the 1992 election year, and this

TABLE 4.1
Ballot Measures, Initiatives, and Referenda, 1988–1992

| Year | Number of States with Ballot Measures | Number of Ballot Measures | Number of States with Initiatives and/or Referenda on Ballot | Number of Initiatives and Referenda |
|------|---------------------------------------|---------------------------|---------------------------------------------------------------|--------------------------------------|
| 1988 | 41 | 224 | 18 | 54 |
| 1990 | 44 | 225 | 17 | 72 |
| 1992 | 42 | 231 | 21 | 69 |

Note: Data for 1988 are from *Initiative and Referendum: The Power of the People!* fall 1988; data for 1990 and 1992 are from the Free Congress Foundation as listed in their reports, *1990 State Ballot Listing* and *1992 State Ballot Listing*, respectively.

figure understates spending because some states do not require expenditure disclosure (e.g., Arkansas, Nevada, and North Dakota) (Magleby 1994, 4, 2). By comparison, the major party presidential campaigns in 1992 officially spent $55.2 million each. Although Arterton (1993) reports that Clinton and Bush spent an additional combined estimated $75 million in "soft money," the millions spent on ballot measures in less than half of the states suggests that some ballot measures aggressively compete for voter attention with presidential candidates.

Although studies of congressional elections give scant attention to ballot measures, table 4.1 suggests that voters, at least during the 1988, 1990, and 1992 elections, could not hide from them. From the left side of the table, beginning with the number of states with ballot measures, it is evident that over four-fifths of states had some type of ballot measure (either through legislative or citizen impetus). In the fourth column, one can see that two-thirds of the states with the initiative and/or popular referendum had at least one ballot measure. Likewise, the total number of ballot measures for each year is surprisingly large. In column 3 the total number of ballot measures across all states in a given year is no less than 224. Among states with initiatives and referenda, column 5 shows that the lowest number is greater than 50.

The high volume of ballot measures found in table 4.1 suggests that voters are exposed to many more policy issues than commonly recognized. Of course, not all of these ballot measures achieve agenda status. As discussed in chapter 3, a good number of these ballot measures probably do not capture the public's attention. Nevertheless, many ballot measures contain one or more ingredients (e.g., a controversial issue, ample campaign spending) that make them likely agenda issues.

## THE POLITICS OF ABORTION, TAXES, AND THE ENVIRONMENT

I examine the agenda-setting capabilities of ballot measures on abortion, taxes, and the environment. As seen in table 4.2, a substantial number of U.S. voters considered ballot measures on these topics in the three election cycles under investigation. Note that table 4.2 includes ballot measures on these topics regardless of whether they were placed on the ballot through popular means (citizen initiated) or by state legislatures. I chose these issues because they represent longstanding concerns of varying significance to voters.

According to table 4.2, seven states had ballot measures on abortion across the 1988, 1990, and 1992 election cycles. (The appendix at the end of this chapter describes the coding for ballot measures and all other variables.) Among the three policy areas, I expect ballot questions on abortion to have the largest agenda-setting effects. Abortion is an issue that invokes great controversy and divisiveness (Craig and O'Brien 1993). Voters show greater awareness of ballot measures on moral issues (Nicholson 2003), making abortion a strong contender for inclusion on a state's agenda. Over the last thirty years, abortion has played an important role in U.S. elections by shaping partisan loyalties (Adams 1997) and voting decisions (Abramowitz 1995; Carsey 2000, chap. 7; Cook, Jelen, and Wilcox 1994).

Economics also play a prominent role in many elections (Fiorina 1981; Kiewiet 1983). Although the majority of scholarly attention has focused on economic performance, taxes are an important issue to the American voter. A potential problem in coding tax ballot measures, however, is that some are not just about tax cuts or hikes.[1] For example, Florida's Proposition 5 in the 1988 election proposed to extend the property tax exemption for widows. Not only did this proposition include only a small segment of Floridians, it involved a group that evoked deep sympathy. Other examples of ballot measures excluded from the analysis include California's 1988 initiative for a 25 cents per pack cigarette tax, Oregon's 1990 initiative to give a tax credit for school choice outside the public school system, and Massachusetts's 1992 ballot measure to require public reporting of corporate tax information. Because tax measures may involve multiple dimensions and target different groups, I only include ballot measures that involved a tax increase or reduction affecting most citizens.[2] Despite using a narrow criterion, a fair number of states, twenty-three in all, had ballot measures on tax policy across the 1988, 1990, and 1992 election cycles.

I expect tax ballot measures to have a substantial effect on the congressional agenda, but not uniformly. Some ballot measures that offer substantial tax cuts, for example, may play a larger role in the agenda politics of a state than others. In addition, even though I focus on ballot measures

TABLE 4.2
Abortion, Tax, and Environmental Ballot Measures, 1988–1992

| | Election Year | | |
|---|---|---|---|
| Issue/State | 1988 | 1990 | 1992 |
| **Abortion** | | | |
| Arizona | | | Prop. 110 |
| Arkansas | Amend. 3 | | |
| Colorado | Amend. 7 | | |
| Maryland | | | Question 6 |
| Michigan | Proposal A | | |
| Nevada | | Question 7 | |
| Oregon | | Measures 8, 10 | |
| **Taxes** | | | |
| Arizona | | | Prop. 108 |
| Arkansas | Amend. 4 | | |
| California | | Prop. 136 | Prop. 167 |
| Colorado | Amend. 6 | Amend. 1 | Amend. 1 |
| Florida | | | HJR 139, Measure 10 |
| Idaho | | | HJR 4, Measure 1 |
| Kansas | | | HCR 5007 |
| Massachusetts | | Question 2 | |
| Missouri | untitled | | |
| Montana | | Amend. 55 | |
| Nebraska | | Repeal LB 1059 | |
| Nevada | Question 9 | Initiatives 6, 9 | |
| New Mexico | Amend. 3 | | |
| Oklahoma | | Amend. 641 | Amend. 646 |
| Oregon | | Measure 5 | |
| S. Carolina | | county referenda | |
| S. Dakota | Amend. C | Amends. C, E | untitled |
| Utah | Initiatives A, B | Initiative A | |
| Virginia | | Amends. 1, 3, 4 | |
| Washington | | HJR 4231 | |
| W. Virginia | | | SJR 4 |
| Wisconsin | | | untitled |
| Wyoming | Amend. 1 | | |
| **Environment** | | | |
| Arizona | | Prop. 202 | |
| Arkansas | Act 636 | | |
| California | | Props. 130, 132, 135, 138 | |
| Colorado | | | Measure 8 |

TABLE 4.2 (cont'd)
Abortion, Tax, and Environmental Ballot Measures, 1988–1992

|  | Election Year | | |
|---|---|---|---|
| Issue/State | 1988 | 1990 | 1992 |
| Environment (cont'd) | | | |
| Maine | Bond 3 | Bonds 4, 7 | |
| Massachusetts | Question 4 | | Question 3 |
| Michigan | Proposal C | | |
| Minnesota | untitled | untitled | |
| Missouri | | Prop. A | |
| Montana | Initiative 113 | | |
| Nebraska | Measure 402 | | |
| New York | | Proposal 1 | |
| N. Dakota | | | Measure 7 |
| Oregon | Measure 7 | Measure 6 | Measure 6 |
| Rhode Island | Proposal 10 | | |
| S. Dakota | | Measure 2 | |
| Washington | Initiative 97 | Measure 547 | |

Sources: Inter-University Consortium for Political and Social Research Referenda and Primary Election Materials (ICPSR 0006) and Waters 2003.

that do not include specific groups (e.g., widows) or issues other than taxes (e.g., education), some ballot measures might be framed in these terms. For these reasons, the effects of tax ballot measures might be understated in the analysis.

While not typically as salient as abortion or taxes, environmental issues can also play an important role in electoral politics. Nevertheless, many studies of voting behavior neglect "green" issues. This disregard might be because the environment is seldom a momentous issue in presidential elections. However, the 1988, 1990, and 1992 election cycles registered numerous environmental issues, at least on the ballot. As seen in table 4.2, seventeen states had at least one environmental ballot measure across the three elections. I expect environmental ballot measures to have a considerable effect on setting the congressional agenda but less than that of abortion and tax ballot measures since morality and economic issues typically take center stage in electoral politics.

Identifying environmental ballot measures, like their tax counterparts, is a thorny task. Environmental ballot measures may consist of multiple dimensions (as found with tax measures), but more often the problem encountered in coding them is that they concern narrow proposals rather than broad environmental regulations. Although narrow and broad proposals both concern environmental factors, I exclude environmental ballot measures from the analysis that appear overly technical or narrowly focused. The idea is to include only ballot measures that capture a voter's unsubtle consideration of the environment. For example, South Dakota's ballot measure on surface mining reclamation (Measure 2 from 1990) is not included in the analysis whereas Washington State's initiative to establish a superfund for environmental cleanup (I-97 from 1988) is included. The former is a narrow policy question that may not tap environmental concerns while the latter is blatantly environmental.

## RIVAL EXPLANATIONS

Apart from the flow of information produced by ballot measures, voter attitudes, characteristics, and level of interest in elections help account for why voters use certain issue criteria in their evaluations of candidates. Although these variables constitute the control variables for the analysis, I briefly discuss their relevance to shaping voters' candidate evaluations.

Central to a voter's mentioning an issue, not surprisingly, is the degree of attitude strength or intensity associated with it. For example, research in social psychology finds that extreme attitudes exert a large effect on judgment (Judd and Johnson 1981), thus increasing the probability that a respondent will link an issue to a candidate. Fortunately, the NES Senate study asked questions about abortion, taxes, and the environment on one aspect of attitude strength: the degree to which an individual favors (disfavors) an issue.

Abortion attitudes likely play a significant role in explaining why a respondent would mention it when queried about a candidate. It is an issue with ardent supporters and opponents. Since two identifiable sides exist, respondents with strong attitudes on each side of the debate are examined separately. Few individuals, however, identify themselves as ardent tax increase supporters or anti-environmentalists. Therefore, I only look at respondents who are pro-environment and anti–tax increase.

Strong partisans are also likely to mention issues, especially when compared to weak partisans or Independents. Unlike the specific attitude measures for each issue, strength of partisanship taps a general proclivity toward issues. Since party identification may partially represent a long run tally of issues (Downs 1957; Fiorina 1981; Key 1966), strong Democrats and Republicans are more likely to have an opinion on these issues, and mention them, when asked about candidates.

Attention to political campaigns and education may also affect whether respondents mention an issue in conjunction with a candidate. Respondents with greater interest in campaigns are more likely to pay attention to issues and mention them when asked about candidates. Education, unlike most other demographic characteristics, is a mainstay in predicting electoral behavior. According to Price and Zaller (1993), educational attainment is positively correlated with the ability to recall news stories, holding other factors constant. Although the precise effect that education has on electoral behavior is disputed, most would agree that it is either a direct or indirect measure of an individual's ability to process political information and use it in a meaningful way (but see Luskin 1990).

## AGENDA-SETTING IN CONGRESSIONAL ELECTIONS

Scholars typically define the agenda as the issues the public deems the most important problems facing the nation. Although this definition suits many agenda-setting studies, it is a blunt indicator of the issues that citizens deem important in an election. The research questions posed here demand a finer measure of agenda status because I am concerned with the issues that individuals deem important in voting for congressional candidates. Moving beyond measures that tap the general importance of issues, I look explicitly at the congressional election agenda by examining the issues citizens mentioned when queried about congressional candidates and campaigns.

To evaluate the agenda-setting effect of ballot measures on candidate evaluations, I used open-ended questions that asked citizens to mention which issues, if any, they deemed important to voting for House and Senate candidates. Unlike closed-ended or force-choice questions, open-ended questions do not direct respondents to think about any particular issue. I used two questions from the NES Senate study to code the dependent variables in the analysis. One question asked respondents to mention likes and dislikes about candidates, and the other asked respondents to mention the issue most talked about in the campaign.[3] As mentioned, the issues I examined include abortion, taxes, and the environment, and for each model—one for each of the three issue areas—the dependent variable is coded one (1) if the respondent mentioned the issue and zero (0) otherwise. Included in the dependent variable are mentions of these issues for either the House or Senate since I am interested in picking up the influence of ballot measures on federal offices.

The downside of using open-ended questions to measure the dependent variable is the high nonresponse rate. Broken down by election year, table 4.3 reports the number of respondents who mentioned an abortion, tax, or environmental issue. These data reveal that, in general, the distribution of the dependent variables is negatively skewed. In other words, there are many more nonresponses (zeros) than responses (ones). Given the low per-

TABLE 4.3
Percentage of Respondents Mentioning Abortion, Taxes, and the Environment in
Evaluations of Congressional Candidates, 1988–1992

| Variables | 1988 | 1990 | 1992 |
|---|---|---|---|
| Mentioned issue with regard to candidates | | | |
| Abortion | 4% | 12% | 9% |
| Environment | 8% | 12% | 6% |
| Taxes | 10% | 21% | 6% |

*Data Source*: NES Senate Election Study

centage of responses in the issue categories, the agenda-setting effect of state ballot measures in congressional elections is subject to a demanding test.

A few percentages from table 4.3 are noteworthy. Despite the attention abortion receives in the media, it is the issue with the lowest response rate in a given election year—only 4 percent of respondents mentioned abortion in 1988. Over the cycle, however, the number of responses on this issue increases to a high of 12 percent in 1990 and then falls to 9 percent in 1992. Also striking are the percentages of respondents who mentioned tax issues. Eclipsing the percentages in all other cells, over 20 percent of respondents associated taxes with congressional candidates in the 1990 elections. Furthermore, in 1988 taxes were the most frequently mentioned issue. Finally, the environment was neither the most nor the least mentioned issue. With the exception of 1992, environmental issues were the middle response category.

Overall, attention to congressional candidates increases during midterm elections. Looking at all three elections, voters devoted greater thought to congressional candidates at the midterm election. Without exception, respondents gave more answers in 1990 than in either presidential election year. These percentages suggest that the absence of a presidential election increases the amount of attention given to not only ballot measures, but also congressional candidates.

## ANALYSIS AND DISCUSSION

Recall that the dependent variables in these analyses are coded 1 if a respondent mentioned a given issue (e.g., taxes) and zero otherwise. Given the dichotomous nature of these variables, I estimated the models using probit analysis. Probit estimates for the agenda-setting effect of state ballot measures are reported in table 4.4. The goodness-of-fit measures, the percent predicted correctly, and the proportional-reduction-in-error indicate that each model is well specified. The percent predicted correctly for both the abortion and environment models are 91 percent while the taxes model successfully predicts 85 percent of cases. The proportional-reduction-in-error statistic indicates that the model on taxes saved .42 of the errors we would have expected to make and the models on abortion and the environment saved .45.[4] As expected, given the low percentage of issue mentions the models predict failure (0) much better than success (1).

The coefficient estimates in table 4.4 provide support for the hypothesis that ballot measures affect the agenda for congressional candidates. The coefficients for each ballot measure are statistically significant and in the predicted direction. Furthermore, they are considerably larger than the control variables. The comparisons are striking since ballot measures, and state issues more generally, are often neglected in research on congressional elections.

However, because probit coefficients are nonlinear, they are difficult to interpret. Figure 4.1 clarifies the effects of these variables by depicting changes in probabilities for each of the ballot measures (King, Tomz, and Wittenberg 2000; Tomz, Wittenberg, and King 2003). These quantities are calculated by looking at a discrete change in the independent variable (from 0 to 1) holding all other variables at their mean values. Across the three issue areas, abortion ballot measures have the greatest influence on voters who mention an issue on the congressional agenda. All else equal, voters in states without abortion ballot measures had a predicted probability of .07 of mentioning abortion when queried about congressional candidates whereas voters in states with them had a .20 predicted probability, a .13 change in probability of mentioning abortion across the two groups. This quantity is more than twice as large as comparable changes in probability—paying attention to politics (.05 change in probability) or strongly identifying as a partisan (.03 change in probability). Following abortion ballot measures, the next largest changes in probability are for pro-life identifiers and education. A minimum to maximum change in each of these variables increases the probability of mentioning abortion by .08.

Compared to abortion ballot measures, the changes in probability for environmental and tax ballot questions show less dramatic effects. All else equal, voters in states without environmental ballot measures have a probability of .08 of mentioning the environment whereas voters in states with environmental ballot measures have a probability of nearly .13, a change in probability of nearly .05. Contrary to my expectations, tax ballot measures had a smaller effect than environmental ballot measures in setting the congressional agenda. Voters in states without tax ballot measures, all else equal, had a probability of .14 of mentioning taxes on

TABLE 4.4

Probit Analysis of the Agenda-Setting Effect of Abortion, Environmental, and Tax Ballot
Measures on Evaluating Congressional Candidates, 1988–1992

| | Issue Mention | | |
|---|---|---|---|
| Variables | Abortion | Environment | Taxes |
| Ballot measure | .63*** | .27*** | .14** |
| | (.073) | (.049) | (.048) |
| Education | .10*** | .09*** | .06*** |
| | (.013) | (.013) | (.013) |
| Partisan | .06*** | −.005 | .02 |
| | (.022) | (.021) | (.022) |
| Attention | .17*** | .15*** | −.05* |
| | (.030) | (.029) | (.030) |
| Pro-choice | .06 | — | — |
| | (.045) | | |
| Pro-life | .44*** | — | — |
| | (.057) | | |
| Pro-environment | — | .24*** | — |
| | | (.040) | |
| Anti–tax increase | — | — | .11** |
| | | | (.042) |
| Constant | −2.14*** | −2.01*** | −1.32*** |
| | (.071) | (.070) | (.072) |
| N | 8,372 | 8,372 | 5,529 |
| Chi-square | 242.20*** | 186.32*** | 37.16*** |
| % Predicted correctly | 91 | 91 | 85 |
| Proportional reduction in error | .45 | .45 | .42 |

Note: Entries in parentheses are standard errors. Dependent variable = respondent mentioned policy
issue in answering likes or dislikes about candidates in a given race or mentioned issue most talked about
in the campaign.

     * significant at the .05 level (one-tailed test)
    ** significant at the .01 level (one-tailed test)
  *** significant at the .001 level (one-tailed test)

the congressional agenda whereas voters in states with tax ballot measures had a probability of .17—a probability change of .03.

    Although the probability changes for the environmental and tax models
are smaller than those for the abortion model, within-model comparisons
(looking at each model by itself) show that environmental and tax ballot
measures are relatively strong predictors. With the exception of educa-

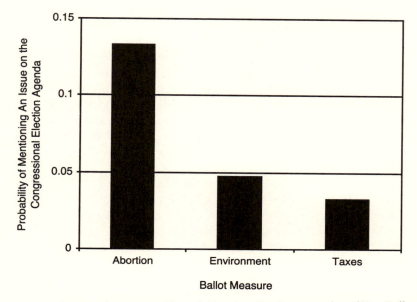

Fig. 4.1. The Agenda-Setting Effect of Abortion, Environmental, and Tax Ballot Measures on Evaluating Congressional Candidates, 1988–1992 (Change in Probabilities)

*Note*: Quantities represent changes in probabilities (based on Clarify simulations) calculated by examining the difference between states with and without ballot measures holding all other variables at their mean values.

tion, a variable that increases the probability of mentioning an issue by about .08 in both models, ballot measures on the environment and taxes make up the most potent variables of mentioning an issue. Thus, holding extreme issue positions appears less important to injecting issues on the congressional agenda than ballot measures.

Taken together, these analyses support the hypothesis that direct legislation shapes the agenda in congressional elections and thus the criteria by which voters evaluate congressional candidates. In contrast to the conventional wisdom, voters making decisions for these candidates do not distinguish among issues based on whether they are from state or national sources. Before rushing to judgment, however, I address a few methodological concerns.

## METHODOLOGICAL CONCERNS

Thus far, the results draw on the entire sample (all fifty states across three elections). However, it is possible that these findings are driven by factors other than ballot measures. Alternatively, as discussed in chapter 3, it might be that state demographics or long-term voter interest in an issue makes a state more apt to have a ballot proposition on a subject. Put differently, it could be argued that instead of ballot measures setting the agenda in congressional races, voters in these states are independently concerned with these issues. For example, the environment may be a common concern for citizens in Oregon, Washington, and Massachusetts, or abortion might be of longstanding interest to citizens in Arkansas, Maryland, and Michigan. If this were the case, then the results reported above would be spurious.

To evaluate this possibility, I reestimate the models including only respondents from the states that had a ballot measure on a given type of ballot proposition. For example, the abortion model includes the seven states listed in table 4.2 that had a ballot proposition on abortion: Arizona, Arkansas, Colorado, Maryland, Michigan, Nevada, and Oregon. Therefore, for each year, respondents in a state with an abortion ballot measure (e.g., Arizona in 1992) are pooled with respondents from that state from other election years (e.g., Arizona in 1988 and 1990) in addition to all the other states with abortion ballot measures in any given year. By reestimating the models, I hold constant the possibility that state characteristics are driving the importance of issues on the congressional agenda (e.g., abortion is always an important issue to Arizona citizens) rather than ballot measures.

Table 4.5 indicates that influences such as these are not causing states to have ballot measures on the issues of abortion, the environment, and taxes. The size and statistical significance of the probit coefficient suggest that the supply of direct legislation, not voter demand for them, is responsible for the salience of these issues. I also calculated the changes in probabilities and found few substantive changes. The most notable difference in the abortion results is that the change in probability for ballot measures shrinks by .01 while the same change for education increases by .05, making the effect of these two variables roughly comparable. The change in probability for environmental ballot measures also decreased by about .01 while the impact of education increased by roughly the same amount. Also notable from this analysis is the influence of paying attention to the campaigns. A minimum to maximum change for this variable—moving from not much interested to very much interested—increased the probability of mentioning an environmental issue by about .02, surpassing the effects of tax ballot measures. In contrast, the change in probability for tax ballot measures increased the probability of mentioning a tax issue on the congressional agenda by about .02, while the change in probabili-

TABLE 4.5
Probit Analysis of the Agenda-Setting Effect of Abortion, Environmental, and Tax Ballot Measures on Evaluating Congressional Candidates (Restricted Sample), 1988–1992

| Variables | Issue Mention | | |
| --- | --- | --- | --- |
| | Abortion | Environment | Taxes |
| Ballot measure | .57*** | .17** | .21*** |
| | (.096) | (.063) | (.065) |
| Education | .12*** | .09*** | .06*** |
| | (.032) | (.021) | (.021) |
| Partisan | .02 | −.00 | .03 |
| | (.052) | (.032) | (.034) |
| Attention | .25*** | .19*** | −.05 |
| | (.074) | (.049) | (.037) |
| Pro-choice | .17* | — | — |
| | (.103) | | |
| Pro-life | .40** | — | — |
| | (.153) | | |
| Pro-environment | — | .21*** | — |
| | | (.064) | |
| Anti–tax increase | — | — | .06 |
| | | | (.064) |
| Constant | −2.22*** | −1.93*** | −1.39*** |
| | (.179) | (.114) | (.117) |
| N | 1,186 | 2,802 | 2,350 |
| Chi-square | 76.12*** | 66.69*** | 21.40*** |
| % Predicted correctly | 86 | 89 | 85 |
| Proportional reduction in error | .43 | .44 | .41 |

*Note*: Entries in parentheses are standard errors. Dependent variable = respondent mentioned policy issue in answering likes or dislikes about candidates in a given race or mentioned issue most talked about in the campaign.
  * significant at the .05 level (one-tailed test)
  ** significant at the .01 level (one-tailed test)
  *** significant at the .001 level (one-tailed test)

ties for the control variables diminishes in size. Taken together, these results represent modest alterations in the quantities of greatest interest.

One last methodological concern involves the possibility that the agenda-setting effect is caused by candidate campaigns. To control for this effect, I look at a single year, 1988, where the NES Senate study included data on Senate campaign issues. Fortunately, 1988 is an off year for many states' gubernatorial elections, a rich source of campaign issues that varies substantially across states. It was, however, a presidential election year. Nevertheless, as mentioned, voters in 1988 received fewer policy issues from presidential candidates than in many other presidential election years. Moreover, presidential elections are less troublesome in this analysis, given that the national media help homogenize the content of presidential campaigns across states.

Until now, I have not discussed whether the agenda-setting effect of ballot measures is a spillover effect because I have not controlled for the possibility that candidate campaign messages are endogenous to ballot proposition elections. In other words, it could be that candidates' campaigns are where voters are receiving agenda information. Here, I am able to test the effect of campaign issues head to head with ballot measures to see whether the relationship between ballot measures and setting the agenda in congressional elections is driven by candidate campaign messages.

According to the NES Senate study, campaign content codes were culled from six secondary sources that covered Senate races in 1988.[5] From these sources, all campaign themes were coded. When more than seven themes were identified, the themes with the fewest occurrences across all sources were excluded. From these content codes, I constructed a variable to control for policy-relevant issues from Senate races.

The probit estimates in table 4.6 provide no support for the hypothesis that Senate campaign issues are driving the relationship between ballot measures and the congressional election agenda. Substantively, the results for ballot measures do not appear to change much. The size of the coefficients for the abortion and tax ballot measures increase, while the size of the coefficient for environmental ballot measures slightly decreases. Figure 4.2 depicts the changes in probabilities associated with ballot measures and Senate campaigns. Despite the presence of Senate races, the changes in probabilities for ballot measures are relatively stable across models. The abortion initiatives in Arkansas, Colorado, and Michigan appear to have a much larger effect on setting the congressional election agenda than Senate campaigns. Holding all other variables at their mean values, an abortion initiative increases the probability of mentioning abortion by a little more than .12 while a Senate campaign does so by only about .01. For the other two models, the changes in probabilities are similar to those reported in figure 4.1. However, we can see from table 4.6 that Senate campaigns that emphasized taxes did not appear to influence voters. The coefficient in this model is not statistically distinguishable from zero. In addition, the change in probability for Senate campaigns that emphasize taxes is less than .02, a modest influence compared to that of ballot measures.

TABLE 4.6
Probit Analysis of the Agenda-Setting Effect of Senate Campaigns and Ballot Measures on Evaluating Congressional Candidates in the 1988 Elections

| | Issue Mention | | |
| Variables | Abortion | Environment | Taxes |
|---|---|---|---|
| Ballot measure | .91*** | .23** | .21** |
| | (.131) | (.080) | (.086) |
| Senate campaign | .20* | .75*** | .10 |
| | (.122) | (.075) | (.076) |
| Education | .09** | .12*** | −.03 |
| | (.030) | (.024) | (.021) |
| Partisan | .19*** | .017 | .04 |
| | (.053) | (.040) | (.036) |
| Attention | .21** | .15** | .10* |
| | (.070) | (.056) | (.049) |
| Pro-choice | −.37** | — | — |
| | (.124) | | |
| Pro-life | .40*** | — | — |
| | (.114) | | |
| Pro-environment | — | .39*** | — |
| | | (.080) | |
| Constant | −2.81*** | −2.63*** | −1.48*** |
| | (.175) | (.139) | (.106) |
| N | 2,843 | 2,843 | 2,843 |
| Chi-square | 113.78*** | 219.11*** | 14.59** |
| % Predicted correctly | 95.8 | 92 | 90 |
| Proportional reduction in error | .49 | .45 | .44 |

Note: Entries in parentheses are standard errors. Dependent variable = respondent mentioned policy issue in answering likes or dislikes about candidates in a given race or mentioned issue most talked about in the campaign.
　* significant at the .05 level (one-tailed test)
　** significant at the .01 level (one-tailed test)
　*** significant at the .001 level (one-tailed test)

In the model on environmental issues, however, campaign themes from Senate elections have a larger effect than do environmental ballot measures. In table 4.6, the coefficient for an environmental Senate campaign issue is larger than environmental ballot measures. However, the changes in probabilities reveal a much smaller difference. A Senate contest that

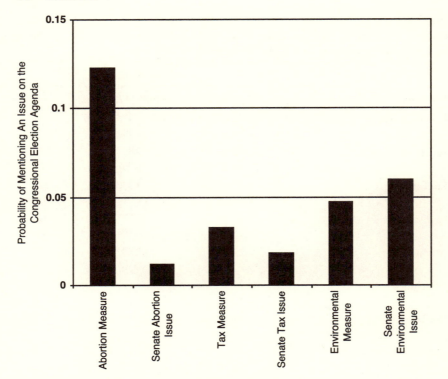

Fig. 4.2. The Agenda-Setting Effect of Ballot Measures and Senate Campaigns in the 1988 Congressional Elections (Change in Probabilities)

*Note*: Quantities represent changes in probabilities (based on Clarify simulations) calculated by looking at a minimum to maximum change in an independent variable holding all other variables at their mean values.

emphasized environmental issues increases the probability that a respondent will mention the environment by about .06 whereas environmental ballot measures increase the probability of mentioning the environment slightly less than .05. These results suggest that ballot measures have an effect on shaping the congressional election agenda independent of the most high-profile congressional campaigns.

CONCLUSION

In this chapter I show that ballot measures produce an agenda-setting effect in congressional elections. Given the small number of respondents who mentioned issues, this was a demanding test. Despite this limitation, the research in this chapter suggests that localized flows of information influence congressional races. As discussed in previous chapters, voters draw on information available at a low cost when making candidate evaluations and do so regardless of whether candidates or parties have explicitly linked an issue to a race. Therefore, at least in the cases of abortion, taxes, and the environment, issues from outside particular contests may define, in a rather blunt manner, what is important to electoral politics. State ballot measures shape voters' evaluations of congressional candidates, a finding that runs contrary to conventional thinking about congressional elections.

The results presented in this chapter also address potential problems of internal and external validity. The greatest threat—low internal validity—is addressed by including the effects of Senate campaigns and state characteristics. By controlling for these influences, as well as individual-level characteristics, we can be reasonably assured of the robustness of the results. Looking at external validity, the great strength of survey research, the analyses drew on three election cycles across all fifty states. The breadth of these results, then, should invite closer inspection of the ingredients of voter choice in congressional election studies.

The data analysis in this chapter, however, examines agenda status, not vote choice. The next question then, is how do agendas affect voting behavior? Although I would have liked to investigate whether the ballot measures in this study directly influenced voting for congressional candidates, it is difficult to evaluate them collectively given data limitations. For instance, to properly evaluate the effects of these ballot measures on voting decisions it would be necessary to identify their emphasis (e.g., was the measure pro-choice or pro-life?), campaign frames, and voter opinions, all factors that vary across each ballot measure. In the following chapters, I take such an approach.

## Appendix

| | |
|---|---|
| *Ballot measure* | Coded one (1) if a state had an abortion, environmental, or tax ballot measure in a given year and zero (0) otherwise; coded by issue area. |
| *Pro-life* | Coded one (1) if a respondent stated that abortion should never be legal under any circumstances and zero (0) otherwise. |
| *Pro-choice* | Coded one (1) if a respondent stated that abortion should be legal under all circumstances and zero (0) otherwise. |

| | |
|---|---|
| *Pro-environment* | Coded one (1) if a respondent wanted to increase federal spending on the environment and zero (0) otherwise. |
| *Anti–tax increase* | Coded one (1) if a respondent strongly opposed a tax increase and zero (0) otherwise. |
| *Partisan* | Coded one (1) if a respondent strongly identified as Democrat or Republican and zero (0) otherwise. |
| *Attention* | Coded two (2) if a respondent stated he or she was very much interested in political campaigns, one (1) if he or she was somewhat interested and zero (0) if he or she was not much interested. |
| *Education* | Coded zero (0) for respondents with less than an eighth-grade education to seven (7) for respondents with postgraduate degrees. |
| *Senate campaign* | Coded one (1) when a relevant issue was present in a Senate race and zero (0) otherwise. |

*Chapter 5*

PRIMING THE FREEZE: NUCLEAR FREEZE
BALLOT MEASURES AS A COMMON BASIS
OF CANDIDATE VOTING IN STATE
AND FEDERAL ELECTIONS

In this chapter, I examine whether agendas provide a common thread for evaluating candidates across different offices by spilling over into distinct electoral contests, even those where there is no obvious linkage. Building on the notion that political judgments are shaped by easily accessible, low-cost information, I examine whether agendas—via the priming effect—have far-ranging consequences that may affect voting decisions well beyond the confines of a particular contest. While the ability of agendas to indiscriminately prime voters choosing candidates in multiple contests is my central focus, this analysis will also explore how the electoral information environment, as embodied in agenda issues, varies the determinants of candidate choice across the United States.

To test these claims, I present a crucial case from the 1982 elections, which examines the effect of nuclear freeze ballot measures on voting decisions for congressional and gubernatorial candidates. According to David Schmidt, an expert on initiative politics, "[W]ith over 30 percent of the nation's voters casting ballots on the question [of a mutual, verifiable nuclear freeze], it was the closest equivalent of a national referendum ever to take place in the United States" (quoted in Cronin 1989). Although some claim that the freeze had a considerable effect on congressional races (Hunt 1983, 21–22; Mann and Ornstein 1983, 146), others neglect it (Abramowitz 1984; Jacobson and Kernell 1983; Petrocik and Steeper 1986). I argue that the freeze mattered, but it depends where you look. In an election year dominated by economic concerns and the Reagan presidency, the freeze was not likely a major issue nationwide, but I expect that it had a significant effect in those states with ballot measures on the matter.

Freeze ballot measures called for a mutual and verifiable freeze of nuclear weapons production with the Soviet Union. Comparing freeze ballot measure states with states that did not have them forms the basis of a naturally occurring experiment where the existence of a freeze campaign varies the amount of information available about the freeze issue. In sum, I explore the possibility that a salient issue on the ballot—even one not formally a part of the candidates' campaigns and/or relevant to a given office—may have a sweeping effect on the ingredients of candidate choice.

## THE NUCLEAR FREEZE AND THE 1982 ELECTIONS

The nuclear freeze issue appeared on the ballot in ten states during the 1982 elections. The California campaign served as the model for most of the freeze campaigns. Taking charge of California's freeze campaign, Harold Willens, a millionaire and Democratic Party insider, brought with him "an infusion of money, media attention, and mainstream legitimacy" (Meyer 1990, 111). As with the national discussion of the freeze, "Willens also successfully shaped the California freeze resolution in the image he thought most palatable to people like himself. He prevented the freeze from being linked to any other issues, defining it in as limited and moderate a way as possible" (112). Ultimately the Willens style came to dominate how the freeze issue was framed in statewide campaigns.[1]

Overall, as listed in table 5.1, ten states held initiatives and referenda on the freeze issue. Each state witnessed a campaign in favor of the freeze while only four had an opposition campaign. However, the opposition campaigns were not well funded. Although the spending figures varied across freeze states, the fact that campaigns existed gave the issue "legs." Further highlighting the freeze was the media coverage surrounding the ballot measures. According to Rourke, Hiskes, and Zirakzadeh, "The process—the freeze movement and referendums—was the story." Consequently, media coverage "would last only as long as the process itself persisted, that is, until the referendums were over in 1982" (1992, 164–65).

The two columns on the right-hand side of table 5.1 show that voters largely supported the freeze. With the exception of Arizona, every state passed it. The one-sided nature of the campaign spending suggests that lack of an effective opposition helps explain the outcomes of these elections. This is not to say that opponents were silent. Late in the 1982 elections, for example, the Reagan administration sent Secretary of Defense Caspar Weinberger to speak against the freeze in each of the states with a ballot measure (Zisk 1984, 219). However, this effort was largely ineffective. Without a well-organized opposition campaign, the debate over the freeze was one-sided and largely free of opposing considerations.

While President Reagan's bellicose rhetoric about the "evil empire" and his administration's efforts to defeat the freeze measures defined Republican opposition, Democrats staked out a strong position in favor of the

TABLE 5.1
Campaign Expenditures and Vote Returns for States with Nuclear Freeze
Ballot Measures

| | Campaign Expenditures | | | Vote Returns | |
|---|---|---|---|---|---|
| | For | Against | Total | For | Against |
| Arizona (Proposition 201) | $33,115 | $1,000 | $34,115 | 40.7% | 59.3% |
| California (Proposition 12) | $3,483,605 | $15,000 | $3,498,605 | 52.3% | 47.7% |
| Massachusetts* (Question 5) | $32,600 | $1,500 | $34,100 | 73.7% | 26.3% |
| Michigan (Proposal E) | $187,042 | none | $187,042 | 56.6% | 43.4% |
| Montana (Initiative 91) | $13,491 | none | $13,491 | 57.4% | 42.6% |
| New Jersey (Public Question 1) | $98,424 | none | $98,424 | 66% | 34% |
| North Dakota (Measure 7) | $6,000 | none | $6,000 | 58.4% | 41.6% |
| Oregon (Measure 5) | $55,571 | none | $55,571 | 61.6% | 38.4% |
| Rhode Island (Referendum 10) | $26,058 | none | $26,058 | 58.7% | 41.3% |
| Wisconsin** (untitled referendum) | $22,000 | $7,000 | $29,000 | 75.7% | 24.3% |

Note: Data for campaign spending and vote returns are from McGuigan 1985.
* These figures are from Zisk 1984.
** Wisconsin's referenda took place on September 14, 1982.

freeze. The beginning of the nuclear freeze's association with the Democrats began when Representative Edward Markey introduced a freeze resolution into Congress on February 10, 1982. However, it was not until Senator Edward Kennedy cosponsored a freeze resolution in the Senate that the issue became tightly linked to Democrats (McCrea and Markle 1989). Once the resolution built momentum, the freeze became a partisan issue. The link between Democrats and the freeze was formalized when "[t]he Democratic Party endorsed the freeze at their 1982 mid-term conference, believing that a large Freeze constituency could be mobilized to support Democratic candidates" (McCrea and Markle 1989, 136). This belief was realized through the freeze movement's role as "a junior partner in Democratic Party struggles" (Cockburn and Ridgeway 1983, cited in Hogan 1994).

## HYPOTHESES AND DATA

I test three hypotheses. First, I hypothesize that voters in states with freeze ballot measures were more likely to mention the freeze as important to their vote compared to voters in states without freeze ballot measures. As tested in chapter 4 for the issues of abortion, taxes, and the environment, this hypothesis examines the agenda-setting effect of ballot measures by looking at the criteria voters used to evaluate candidates. Given data limitations, this hypothesis is tested for House candidates only.

The second hypothesis is that the presence of freeze ballot measures affect voting decisions across numerous offices—Senate, House, and governor—by increasing the probability that citizens will vote for multiple Democratic candidates. If indiscriminate priming is common, the freeze will affect all types of contests. This hypothesis tests whether agendas provide a common evaluative basis to voting decisions and whether these standards of evaluation vary across states with and without freeze ballot measures.

The third hypothesis concerns the information environment of elected offices. As mentioned in chapter 2, the low visibility of House candidates diminishes the association between agenda issues and candidates. By contrast, the relative visibility of Senate and gubernatorial candidates provides opportunity for the establishment of a strong association between the freeze issue and the candidates running for these offices. Consequently, I hypothesize that freeze attitudes will have the least effect on voting for House candidates.

To test these hypotheses, I use the 1982 *ABC News/Washington Post* exit polls (ICPSR 8120). The full sample, conducted on election day with self-administered questionnaires, included 24,438 respondents across 40 states. The major drawback of using exit polls, of course, is that many fewer questions are included, making it difficult to measure important individual differences in exposure to political information. Although these data forgo a more nuanced analysis concerning which individuals (e.g., sophisticates versus nonsophisticates) are susceptible to political information (Bartels 1986; Zaller 1992), it is crucial for the purposes of this effort to have large sample sizes to assess the political behavior of voters residing in particular states (Wright 1990; Wright and Berkman 1986; see also Westlye 1991).

Of the ten states with freeze campaigns, seven are included in the sample for the analysis of voting for House candidates (N = 6,370). However, the pollsters did not ask questions about vote choice for senator and governor in all states, ostensibly because of small sample sizes. California (N = 1,677), Michigan (N = 1,160), and Wisconsin (N = 1,413) had adequately large samples, and voters in these states were queried about their vote choices for senator and governor. New Jersey (N = 1,394) did not have a gubernatorial contest, but its voters' choices for senator are included. Arizona (N = 166), Massachusetts (N = 390), and Montana (N = 68) had Senate and gubernatorial contests, but the pollsters did not ask voters in these states about how they voted for these offices. Oregon (N = 102) had a gubernatorial contest, but its voters were also not asked about vote choice for this contest. Voters in North Dakota and Rhode Island were not polled. Thus, the analysis concerning voting decisions for House candidates includes respondents from all states, regardless of sample size, and the analyses for senatorial and gubernatorial contests only include states with sufficiently large samples.

As mentioned in chapter 3, causality is a potential concern when examining the effects of ballot measures.[2] It could be argued that voters in states with freeze ballot measures were concerned about the freeze issue apart from the ballot measures. Indeed, one could argue that freeze initiatives and referenda appeared in the states they did because voter interest for the issue was greater in these states than elsewhere. But accounts of the freeze movement suggest otherwise. The movement had a strong organizational structure that used modern methods of political fund-raising and communication. The National Freeze Clearinghouse coordinated the activities of local chapters and centralized communications with the media. In addition, the movement was funded by large donations from wealthy patrons, foundations, and philanthropies (McCrea and Markle 1989, 117–22), a depiction consistent with top-down accounts of group mobilization (Walker 1991).

Another way to address the question of causality is to examine whether voters in states with ballot measures differ from voters in states without them in politically meaningful ways. As seen in table 5.2, voters in states with freeze ballot measures do not appear to be much different from voters without them. The demographic and political characteristics of voters are nearly the same. Taken together, the top-down nature of the freeze movement and the similarity of voters in states with and without ballot measures suggest freeze ballot measures caused, rather than mirrored attention to, the freeze issue.

TABLE 5.2
1982 *ABC News/Washington Post* Exit Poll Sample Characteristics (%)

| Characteristic | Full Sample | Non-Freeze States | Freeze States |
| --- | --- | --- | --- |
| **Sex** | | | |
| Male | 43.74 | 43.55 | 44.30 |
| Female | 43.50 | 43.71 | 42.89 |
| **Race** | | | |
| White | 81.79 | 81.37 | 82.97 |
| Black | 9.19 | 10.11 | 6.58 |
| Other race | 2.04 | 1.69 | 3.01 |
| **Age** | | | |
| 18–24 | 9.49 | 9.47 | 9.56 |
| 25–29 | 11.51 | 11.03 | 12.86 |
| 30–39 | 22.51 | 22.76 | 21.82 |
| 40–49 | 16.63 | 16.89 | 15.89 |
| 50–59 | 15.77 | 15.81 | 15.65 |
| 60 or over | 17.00 | 17.18 | 16.48 |
| **Education** | | | |
| Eight grade or less | 3.62 | 3.85 | 2.98 |
| Some high school | 7.49 | 7.84 | 6.50 |
| High school | 26.04 | 26.54 | 24.60 |
| Some college | 24.84 | 24.27 | 26.45 |
| College graduate | 17.10 | 17.07 | 17.19 |
| Postgraduate | 12.78 | 12.41 | 13.85 |
| **Party identification** | | | |
| Democrat | 39.04 | 39.90 | 36.58 |
| Republican | 24.14 | 23.93 | 24.74 |
| Independent | 28.60 | 28.55 | 28.74 |
| Something else | 3.61 | 3.07 | 5.15 |
| **Ideology** | | | |
| Liberal | 21.02 | 20.16 | 23.47 |
| Conservative | 35.62 | 36.17 | 34.07 |
| Moderate | 35.64 | 35.75 | 35.34 |

*Note:* Percentages may not sum to 100 due to missing data.

## AGENDA-SETTING IN HOUSE ELECTIONS

One of the defining characteristics of House elections is that voters are largely uninformed about the candidates and campaign messages in these races (Jacobson 2001; Mann and Wolfinger 1980; Stokes and Miller 1962; Wolak 2004). Voters typically have a difficult time recalling the names of House candidates, especially challengers, and cannot identify issues from House campaigns. Although this lack of visibility provides the opportunity for issues in House races to be defined by outside sources, my expectation is that the lack of candidate visibility diminishes the strength of the association between agenda issues and House candidates. In short, I expect that freeze ballot measures will influence the standards of candidate evaluation for House candidates, but because House candidates are not highly visible, I also expect to find a modest effect. Unfortunately, the exit poll did not ask voters comparable questions about their voting decisions for governor or senator to make direct comparisons.

To test the agenda-setting hypothesis, I examine whether freeze ballot measures increase the probability that respondents will mention the freeze issue as important to their vote choice for House candidates. In particular, I examine whether voters residing in states with freeze ballot measures were more likely to consider it important in voting for House members. The question used to evaluate this hypothesis was: "Were any of the items below very important to you in choosing which candidate to vote for today in the race for the U.S. House of Representatives from your district?" Two of the answers to this question, "My candidate's support for an immediate freeze on nuclear weapons" or "My candidate's opposition to an immediate freeze on nuclear weapons," were combined to form the dependent variable. The variable is coded one (1) if respondents mentioned their candidate's support or opposition to the freeze and zero (0) for no mention.[3] Overall, 12 percent of respondents checked one of these two items. Of these respondents, almost 4 percent (N = 909) mentioned that they voted for a candidate if the candidate took a position against the freeze and close to 8 percent (N = 1847) of voters did the same if their candidate supported the freeze.

Dummy variables are used to indicate whether states (combined and individually) had a freeze initiative or referendum.[4] I also control for a variety of factors that might account for respondents' mentioning the freeze as important to their House vote. Given the partisan dimensions of the freeze issue, I control for voters with strong partisan attachments. A voter's opinion of Reagan's foreign policy agenda may also increase the probability that he or she mentions the freeze as important to voting for House candidates. In particular, since Reagan's tough stance toward the

Soviet Union was central to his foreign policy, individuals who disapproved of his position would be more likely to mention the freeze as important to their vote. Finally, considering the importance of the economy in the 1982 elections, I control for voters who mentioned this issue as the most important problem facing the nation. Although some voters might have been concerned with both economics and the freeze, most voters who mentioned economics as the most important problem facing the nation were probably less likely to base their vote for House of Representatives on the freeze.[5] (The appendix at the end of the chapter includes the coding for these variables as well as the other variables in this chapter.)

## RESULTS

Table 5.3 reports the results of the probit analysis for the agenda-setting effect. Column 1 presents the results from the freeze campaign model and column 2 presents the results by state. The first column shows that freeze ballot measures had a statistically significant effect on voters mentioning the freeze issue as important to their vote for House. Similarly, the statistically significant coefficients for each of the state dummy variables with a freeze initiative or referendum in the next column indicate that this effect is present in each state with a freeze ballot measure rather than one or two of these states driving the effect. Taken together, these results suggest that the freeze did play a role in voting for House candidates in states with an initiative or referendum on the subject.

To assess the magnitude of these effects, figure 5.1 depicts changes in probabilities of mentioning the freeze issue across groups of voters in states with and without freeze ballot measures, holding all other variables at their mean value. Freeze ballot measures increase the probability that voters mentioned the freeze as important to their vote by .04, an effect nearly comparable to that of holding strong partisan dispositions. All else equal, voters in states with freeze ballot measures had a probability of .14 of mentioning the freeze as important to the vote for House whereas voters in states without freeze ballot measures had a probability of .10 (not shown). Admittedly, this is not a big change. However, given the small changes in probability generated by the other predictors such as holding strong partisan dispositions, the change for freeze ballot measures is notable. Although there is not a baseline for comparison with another type of office, the modest effect suggests that the lack of candidate visibility dampens the linkage between agenda issues and House candidates.

In the state-by-state analysis, the influence of freeze campaigns varied across states. For example, compared to states without freeze ballot measures, living in Oregon increased the probability of using the freeze as an

TABLE 5.3
Probit Analysis of the Agenda-Setting Effect of Freeze Ballot Measures in the 1982
U.S. House Elections

| Variable | Freeze Ballot Measure | |
| --- | --- | --- |
| | Grouped | By State |
| Ballot measure | .20***<br>(.025) | — |
| Arizona | — | .22*<br>(.129) |
| California | — | .29***<br>(.042) |
| Massachusetts | — | .29***<br>(.080) |
| Michigan | — | .09*<br>(.053) |
| New Jersey | — | .11**<br>(.048) |
| Oregon | — | .35*<br>(.172) |
| Wisconsin | — | .20***<br>(.046) |
| Partisan | .24***<br>(.029) | .23***<br>(.029) |
| Foreign policy | −.33***<br>(.023) | −.34***<br>(.023) |
| Economic voter | −.30***<br>(.025) | −.30***<br>(.025) |
| Constant | −.92***<br>(.026) | −.92***<br>(.026) |
| N | 21,973 | 21,973 |
| Chi-square | 472.61*** | 506.78*** |
| % Predicted correctly | 89 | 89 |
| Proportional Reduction in Error | .43 | .44 |

*Note:* Estimates are probit coefficients with standard errors in parentheses. Dependent variable = 1 if mentioned freeze, 0 if otherwise.
  * $p < .05$ (one-tailed test)
  ** $p < .01$ level (one-tailed test)
  *** $p < .001$ level (one-tailed test)

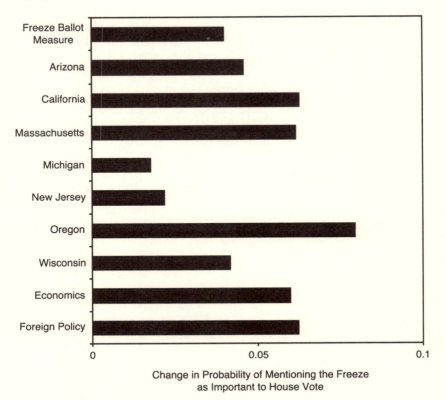

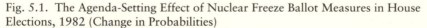

Change in Probability of Mentioning the Freeze
as Important to House Vote

Fig. 5.1. The Agenda-Setting Effect of Nuclear Freeze Ballot Measures in House
Elections, 1982 (Change in Probabilities)
   *Note*: Quantities represent changes in probabilities (based on Clarify simulations) calculated by looking at a minimum to maximum change in an independent variable holding all other variables at their mean values. Absolute values
reported.

important consideration in a House race by about .08, while being a resi-
dent of California or Massachusetts increased the probability by about
.06. Similar to the findings on abortion, environmental, and tax ballot
measures from chapter 4, freeze ballot questions had a significant agenda-
setting effect.

## (INDISCRIMINATELY) PRIMING THE VOTE

In this section, I investigate whether freeze ballot measures had voters
assign greater weight to the freeze issue in voting for congressional or

gubernatorial candidates. The obstacles hindering priming effects for freeze ballot measures range from heavy reliance on cues other than agenda issues (e.g., incumbency) to candidates' neglecting the issue in their campaigns. Characteristics of the electoral environment such as these provide a demanding test of indiscriminate priming effects.

To evaluate the priming effects of the freeze ballot measures and campaigns, I provide two distinct analyses. First, I analyze individual voting decisions for House, Senate, and gubernatorial candidates by comparing the effects of supporting the freeze issue on vote choice by whether or not voters lived in a state with a freeze ballot measure. The second analysis considers the ability of freeze ballot measures to tie together voting decisions across offices by inducing voters to choose multiple Democratic candidates.

In the analyses below, a vote for the Democratic candidate is coded one (1) and a vote for the Republican candidate is coded zero (0). A question on the exit poll asking respondents to check a box to indicate whether they were for or against an immediate freeze on nuclear weapons was used to measure support for the freeze, and a dummy variable measures whether a state had a ballot measure on the freeze. Since the 1982 elections were about much more than the nuclear freeze, I control for a variety of alternative explanations of the vote. Scholars have used this election as a critical test case concerning the influence of national conditions (e.g., Abramowitz 1984; Jacobson and Kernell 1983) so I control for major issues, economic and presidential evaluations, party identification and ideology (see the appendix at the end of the chapter for coding).[6] I begin with an analysis of voting for House candidates in an election year in which Republicans lost twenty-six seats in the House of Representatives.[7]

## FREEZE BALLOT MEASURES AND VOTING FOR HOUSE CANDIDATES

As mentioned above, voters frequently know very little about the choices that confront them in House elections. Indeed, House races in which voters recall the challenger's name often indicate competitive contests (Jacobson 2001). The case for spillover effects, therefore, is relatively strong for these races given the relatively little amount of information available. But the small amount of information about these races also creates strong incumbent and partisan effects. The heavy reliance on these cues, therefore, may leave a small role for agenda voting when compared to more visible races. Indeed, as mentioned, my expectation is that the freeze will have a smaller effect in House races as compared to Senate and gubernatorial races.

TABLE 5.4
The Priming Effect of Nuclear Freeze Ballot Measures on the Vote Choice for
Democratic House Candidates, 1982

| Variable | Full Sample | Freeze Ballot Measure | No Freeze Ballot Measure |
|---|---|---|---|
| Freeze supporter | .08* | .18* | .04 |
| | (.024) | (.048) | (.028) |
| Democrat | .58* | .56* | .59* |
| | (.016) | (.032) | (.019) |
| Ideology | .13* | .14* | .13* |
| | (.017) | (.032) | (.019) |
| Presidential approval | −.56* | −.55* | −.57* |
| | (.033) | (.063) | (.038) |
| Economy | .23* | .24* | .22* |
| | (.018) | (.035) | (.021) |
| Social security | −.27* | −.38* | −.23* |
| | (.029) | (.058) | (.034) |
| Constant | .54* | .48* | .56* |
| | (.027) | (.053) | (.031) |
| N | 16,532 | 4,351 | 12,181 |
| Chi-square | 6,983* | 1,989* | 5,015* |
| % Predicted correctly | 79 | 79 | 79 |
| Proportional Reduction in Error | .49 | .49 | .49 |

Note: Estimates are probit coefficients with standard errors in parentheses. Dependent
variable = 1 if voted for Democratic candidate, 0 if Republican.

* $p < .001$ level (one-tailed test)

Table 5.4 reports the probit results for the House voting models. To test the priming hypothesis, I compare voters who lived in states with freeze ballot measures to voters who did not.[8] Column 1 presents the results for all voters, and columns 2 and 3 report the results for voters in states with and without freeze issues, respectively.

The results from the first column show that supporting the freeze had a positive and statistically significant effect on voting for Democratic House candidates. Yet, the results reported in columns 2 and 3 demonstrate that the impact of freeze attitudes was determined by the presence or absence of freeze ballot measures. The size of the coefficient for freeze supporter is much larger for voters living in states with freeze ballot measures. Not only does the size of the coefficient for freeze supporter become much smaller in states without freeze ballot measures, but also it is not statistically distinguishable from zero. Thus, the analyses indicate that attitudes about the freeze did not have any impact on House voting in states without a freeze ballot measure but had a positive impact on House voting in states where a freeze measure appeared on the ballot. The important thing to note about the control variables is that their coefficients are stable across different model specifications. With the exception of social security, which might be a more important issue in states with freeze ballot measures, these estimates suggest that most of the other political factors in 1982 had a similar effect across states.

Formal tests of coefficient differences for freeze attitudes across states with and without freeze measures support the above interpretations. In so doing, I account for potential differences in residual variation (unobserved heterogeneity) across groups (Allison 1999; Hoetker 2002).[9] Following Allison's (1999) recommendations, I performed a series of tests culminating in the examination of whether the impact of attitudes about the freeze differs significantly across voters in freeze and non-freeze ballot measure states.[10] Both the Wald chi-square test (p = .00) and the log likelihood test (p = .01) indicate significant differences.[11] The direct comparisons, a conservative approach for testing differences, as well as the less formal comparisons involved in comparing coefficients across equations, suggest that freeze ballot measures and their accompanying campaigns and media coverage primed voters to use the issue in voting for Democratic House candidates.

The predicted probabilities for a hypothetical Independent voter show how potent the freeze measures were for House voters. In results not shown, holding all other variables at their mean, an Independent voter who lived in a state with a freeze ballot measure but did not support the freeze had a probability of voting for a Democratic House candidate of .54. Changing this hypothetical voter's profile so that he or she supported the freeze increased the probability of voting for a Democratic House candidate to .61. As shown in figure 5.2, the changes in probability for an average voter—all variables held at their mean values—show the relative importance of freeze attitudes across states with and without freeze ballot measures. Supporters of the freeze who lived in states with freeze ballot measures had a probability of voting for Democratic House candidates that was .07 greater than that of freeze opponents, a difference that is more than four times greater than for citizens living in states without freeze ballot measures (.016). Although this change in probability is smaller than that for party identification (.43) or economic evaluations (.17) (not shown), it is impressive that the freeze campaigns had any influence on voting for House candidates given the strong pull of incumbency and the major focus on the economy and President Reagan.

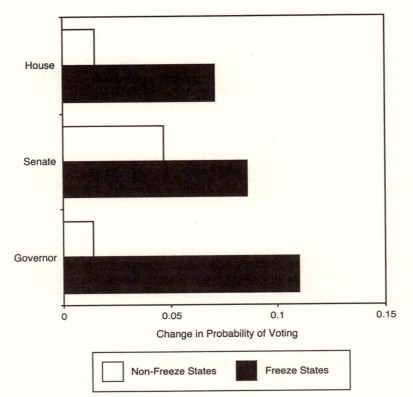

Fig. 5.2. The Priming Effect of Nuclear Freeze Ballot Measures on Voting for House, Senate and Gubernatorial Candidates (Change in Probabilities)

*Note*: Quantities represent changes in probabilities (based on Clarify simulations) of voting for a Democratic candidate calculated by looking at a change in freeze attitudes (from opposition to support) holding all other variables at their mean values.

The results suggest that the freeze was an important consideration for voters in states with ballot measures on the subject. Controlling for competing explanations, freeze ballot measures primed voters to place a greater weight on the issue as compared to voters in non-freeze states. However, because voters have little issue information about House elections it might be that the freeze shaped the standards of candidate evaluation in these races more than other types of elections, such as those for senator or governor, where voters are exposed to higher levels of information about the candidates and issues from the campaign. On the other hand, as I argue in chapter 2, House races might be less susceptible to agenda effects given the lack of candidate visibility and the heavy reliance on cues such as party identification and incumbency. To explore these possibilities, I consider voting decisions for both Senate and gubernatorial elections, beginning with the former.

## FREEZE BALLOT MEASURES AND VOTING FOR SENATE CANDIDATES

Voting for U.S. Senate candidates typically takes place in an environment richer in information than that of House races. With greater visibility, Senate candidates are better able to inform voters about themselves and the issues they deem important to their campaigns. However, as mentioned, this visibility makes Senate candidates more susceptible to agendas. Despite Senate candidates' greater ability to shape the agenda, the opportunity for voters to see, hear, and read about them creates opportunities for salient issues to become attached to their candidacies.

The 1982 Senate elections were relatively uneventful. While several elections were decided by very close margins, the partisan makeup of the Senate remained the same after the election. Two seats on each side were lost. Otherwise, this was an election year where Senate incumbents did very well.[12]

Overall, ten states with Senate elections were included in the sample: California, Connecticut, Michigan, New Jersey, New York, Ohio, Pennsylvania, Texas, Virginia, and Wisconsin. Of these states, four had freeze campaigns: California, Michigan, New Jersey, and Wisconsin. California and New Jersey featured open-seat contests, and Michigan and Wisconsin had incumbent Democrats running for reelection.

Although the freeze figured prominently in states with freeze ballot measures, its visibility in Senate campaigns varied. According to Tidmarch, Hyman, and Sorkin (1984), the freeze was a top issue in media coverage of the Massachusetts, New York, and Washington Senate contests. Although Massachusetts had a freeze measure, it was not included in the poll. As for the other states with freeze ballot measures, the authors found that the freeze was the second most covered story in California's Senate contest and the third most covered story in Michigan, whereas in New Jersey it was not ranked among the top three Senate stories (Wisconsin was not included in their study). Wisconsin's Senate election appeared to have little issue content at all. Putting little effort into his reelection campaign, William Proxmire reported spending nothing to the Federal Elections Commission in his race against challenger Scott McCallum. Some Senate candidates in states without freeze ballot measures made it central to their campaigns. While only suggestive, the *New York Times* reported on October 19, 1982, that the issue might be decisive in Senate races in Maine, New Mexico, and Missouri. Taken together, the freeze

TABLE 5.5

The Priming Effect of Nuclear Freeze Ballot Measures on the Vote Choice for Democratic U.S. Senate Candidates, 1982

| Variable | Full Sample | Freeze Ballot Measure | No Freeze Ballot Measure |
|---|---|---|---|
| Freeze supporter | .17** | .23** | .12* |
| | (.032) | (.051) | (.042) |
| Democrat | .55** | .56** | .55** |
| | (.022) | (.035) | (.029) |
| Ideology | .16** | .12** | .18** |
| | (.022) | (.034) | (.029) |
| Presidential approval | −.54** | −.55** | −.54** |
| | (.044) | (.068) | (.057) |
| Economy | .24** | .23** | .25** |
| | (.024) | (.038) | (.032) |
| Social security | −.37** | −.37** | −.36** |
| | (.040) | (.062) | (.053) |
| Constant | .40** | .44** | .38** |
| | (.035) | (.057) | (.045) |
| N | 9,130 | 3,830 | 5,300 |
| Chi-square | 6,983** | 1,989** | 2,402** |
| % Predicted Correctly | 80 | 80 | 80 |
| Proportional Reduction in Error | .54 | .54 | .54 |

*Note:* Estimates are probit coefficients with standard errors in parentheses. Dependent variable = 1 if voted for Democratic candidate, 0 if Republican.

   * $p < .01$ level (one-tailed test).

  ** $p < .001$ level (one-tailed test).

did appear to play some role in the Senate contests for candidates in freeze states but also did so in states without freeze ballot measures.

Table 5.5 reports the probit results for the Senate voting models. As found in the House models, supporters of the nuclear freeze had varying levels of support for Democratic Senate candidates according to whether or not they lived in states with freeze ballot measures. The coefficient for freeze supporter is significantly different from zero for all three models, but its effect is larger in states with freeze ballot measures compared to states without them. The size of the coefficient grows by almost a third in freeze states when compared to the full model, and it shrinks to almost half the size in states without freeze ballot measures. In contrast to the

House models, however, the freeze issue had a statistically significant effect on voting for Democratic Senate candidates, even in states without freeze measures.

Direct comparison of the coefficients for freeze attitudes across freeze and non-freeze ballot measure states suggests that the effect of the freeze is the same across the groups.[13] Both the likelihood ratio test (p = .12) and the Wald chi-square test (p = .12) suggest no difference across groups for this coefficient. However, since this method is limited in its ability to detect differences for a specific coefficient across groups, I examine the effect of one variable relative to another across groups, rendering any difference in residual variation irrelevant (see Hoetker 2002). Given that partisan identification is the strongest predictor in the model, I compare the effects of freeze attitudes relative to partisan identification across freeze and non-freeze ballot measure states. The Wald test (chi-square of 28.6, $p$-value of .00) indicates a strong difference. This suggests that, at least relative to partisan identification, freeze attitudes had a greater effect in states with freeze ballot measures.

Figure 5.2 depicts the changes in probabilities. As seen in the cluster of bars in the middle of the graph, the probability of voting for a Democratic Senate candidate shifts by .09 between freeze opponents and supporters for voters in states with freeze ballot measures, and the difference shrinks to .05 for voters in states without freeze ballot questions. Further, consider a hypothetical Independent voter living in a state with a freeze initiative or referendum (results not shown). In states with ballot measures on the freeze, this voter had a .53 probability of voting for a Democratic senator if he or she opposed the freeze. If this hypothetical voter supported the freeze, on the other hand, he or she had a .62 probability of voting for a Democratic senator.

The differences across freeze and non-freeze ballot measure states are not as substantial as those for the House model, but they suggest that freeze initiatives and referenda primed voters to give greater weight to the freeze issue in judging Senate candidates. The magnitude of the effects for Senate voting, however, are larger than those for the House, suggesting that the issue had a greater effect on more visible candidates.

## THE CRUCIAL TEST OF VOTING FOR GUBERNATORIAL CANDIDATES

To this point, I have shown that freeze campaigns had a priming effect on voting for congressional candidates. I now consider gubernatorial elections. Recall that priming happens regardless of whether candidates address an issue in their campaign (campaign-specific effects approach) or whether they are running for a federal or state office (the institutional

responsibilities approach) (see chapter 1). Gubernatorial contests constitute the most demanding test of the three types of elections because foreign policy issues are not germane to the institutional responsibilities of
governors, and none of the gubernatorial candidates campaigned on the
freeze issue.

How can we be reasonably sure that it is priming rather than campaign
effects or institutional responsibilities? In looking at campaign effects,
gubernatorial candidates did not link the freeze issue to their candidacies.
Drawing on Beyle's (1985, 1986) extensive research and collaboration
with numerous other scholars on the 1982 gubernatorial elections, candidates running for the statehouse did not make the freeze an important
issue in their campaigns. In all thirty-six gubernatorial elections, the key
issues typically involved the economy or the candidates themselves while
the freeze was not mentioned as important to any of these races (Beyle
1985, 1986). Similarly, the freeze was not an issue priority in newspaper
coverage of the 1982 gubernatorial races (Tidmarch, Hyman, and Sorkin
1984).

Turning to the institutional responsibilities theory, it is reasonable to
assume that voters considered the freeze a national (or international)
issue. If voters reason in this manner they would be less likely to evaluate
gubernatorial candidates based on the freeze because it is not an issue
relevant to state governance. Taken together, these approaches predict
that the freeze should have no effect on voting behavior in gubernatorial
elections. On the other hand, if the freeze had an effect, it is strong evidence of spillover effects. It is also further confirmation that depending on
the magnitude of the effect, the visibility of candidates drives the linkage
between candidates and agenda issues.

The 1982 gubernatorial elections included 36 races, 24 of which pitted
incumbents against challengers and 12 of which were open-seat contests.
In contrast to the Senate elections, the Democrats made impressive gains
by picking up seven seats. Overall, eleven states with gubernatorial elections were included in the sample: Alabama, California, Connecticut, Illinois, Iowa, Michigan, New York, Ohio, Pennsylvania, Texas, and Wisconsin. Of these states, three had freeze ballot measures: California,
Michigan, and Wisconsin. Each of the gubernatorial races featured open
seats. In the Michigan and Wisconsin races, the Democratic candidates
won by strong margins while in California the Democrat narrowly lost
to the Republican. Although economic issues were central to many of
these races, freeze ballot measures were also on the minds of many state
voters. Although gubernatorial candidates did not discuss the freeze and
the freeze did not appear in news coverage of these campaigns, it appears
that candidates running for governor in states with freeze campaigns
could not hide from the issue.

TABLE 5.6
The Priming Effect of Nuclear Freeze Ballot Measures on the Vote Choice for Democratic Gubernatorial Candidates, 1982

| Variable | Full Sample | Freeze Ballot Measure | No Freeze Ballot Measure |
|---|---|---|---|
| Freeze supporter | .10* | .29* | .04 |
| | (.030) | (.059) | (.035) |
| Democrat | .57* | .58* | .57* |
| | (.020) | (.040) | (.024) |
| Ideology | .23* | .26* | .21* |
| | (.020) | (.040) | (.024) |
| Presidential approval | −.60* | −.61* | −.61* |
| | (.040) | (.078) | (.047) |
| Economy | .26* | .19* | .28* |
| | (.022) | (.045) | (.026) |
| Social security | −.38* | −.36* | −.38* |
| | (.037) | (.072) | (.043) |
| Constant | .38* | .46* | .35* |
| | (.033) | (.066) | (.038) |
| N | 10,958 | 2,930 | 8,028 |
| Chi-square | 5,472* | 1,523* | 3,978* |
| % Predicted correctly | 81 | 81 | 81 |
| Proportional Reduction in Error | .60 | .59 | .60 |

Note: Estimates are probit coefficients with standard errors in parentheses. Dependent variable = 1 if voted for Democratic candidate, 0 if Republican.
  * $p < .001$ level (one-tailed test).

The models used to test the influence of freeze issues on gubernatorial elections are identical to those used for Senate and House elections. Table 5.6 reports the results of the probit analyses.

Voter support for the nuclear freeze in the full model has a statistically significant effect on voting for Democratic gubernatorial candidates. The separate models for voters living in states with and without freeze ballot measures, however, show that freeze ballot measures are driving this effect. The coefficient for freeze supporter almost triples in size for voters in freeze ballot measure states. In states without freeze initiatives and referenda, the effect of freeze support is dramatically reduced. Furthermore, the coefficient is statistically insignificant for voters in states without freeze ballot measures. Direct comparisons between the freeze and non-freeze ballot measure models support these comparisons.[14] Both the Wald test (p = .00) and the likelihood ratio test (p = .00) validate rejecting the hypothesis that there is no significant difference for freeze supporters across freeze and non-freeze ballot measure states. In addition, comparing the effects of freeze attitudes relative to partisan identification (ratio) indicates significant differences across freeze and non-freeze ballot measure states (p = .00).

The cluster of bars at the bottom of figure 5.2 depicts the changes in probability for voting for Democratic gubernatorial candidates. For voters in states with freeze ballot measures, support for the freeze increased the probability of voting for Democratic gubernatorial candidates by .11. In contrast, the effect is minuscule in states without freeze ballot measures (.01) and, of course, it is not statistically distinguishable from zero. To further explore these effects, consider a hypothetical Independent voter in a state with a freeze initiative or referendum who opposed the freeze (results not shown). All else equal, this voter had a .52 probability of voting for a Democratic gubernatorial candidate. The same hypothetical voter had a .63 probability of voting for a Democratic governor if he or she supported a nuclear freeze. On the other hand, holding all else equal, an Independent voter who opposed the freeze and lived in a state without a freeze ballot question had a .46 probability of voting for a Democratic governor. If this voter supported the freeze he or she had a probability of voting for the Democratic gubernatorial candidate of .48, a much smaller effect. Again, as found in the congressional races, the freeze had a meaningful effect on voting for Democratic candidates.

As with the House and Senate races, voters' evaluations of gubernatorial candidates were influenced by freeze ballot measures. With the greater availability of information about the freeze, voters made candidate evaluations based on this issue. This evidence indicates that priming effects—driven by agendas—influence voters across different choices and electoral environments. In addition, the comparable results for the Senate and gubernatorial contests suggest that candidate visibility rather than institutional responsibilities or campaign issues from a given race account for the association between agenda issues and candidates.

## Freeze Ballot Measures and Voting for Teams of Democratic Candidates

In the previous sections, I found that freeze ballot measures had a priming effect across different types of elections. In this section, I examine whether freeze ballot measures—via priming—tie voting decisions together across different offices. Specifically, I examine whether freeze ballot measures primed voters to choose teams of Democratic candidates. The analyses proceed in two waves. I first examine pairings of voting decisions for Democratic candidates: House and Senate; Senate and governor; and House and governor. Next, I examine voting for all three offices in those states where all three offices were on the ballot.

These analyses constitute a demanding test of priming voting decisions indiscriminately. Moving beyond a single office, these analyses test whether the freeze primed voting decisions across offices with different institutional responsibilities and different campaign circumstances. This is no easy task considering the many forces producing split-ticket votes, especially the power of incumbency (Box-Steffensmeier 1996; Burden and Kimball 2002; Mann and Wolfinger 1980). Overall, ticket-splitting among congressional and gubernatorial elections was common in 1982. For example, 58 percent of voters who lived in a state with a gubernatorial, senatorial, and House contest cast a split ticket.

A primary tenet of agenda voting is that voting decisions across offices are interrelated. In contrast to a standard probit model where voting decisions are assumed to be independent, bivariate (two equation) and trivariate (three equation) probit models treat voting decisions across offices as separate but interrelated decisions by estimating equations for each office simultaneously (see Greene 2000).[15] Although I am looking at the common effects of freeze attitudes across offices, multiple voting decisions likely share other factors in common that are unmeasured (omitted variables). Multivariate probit models depend not only on the independent variables but also on the omitted variables or error terms. Not accounting for omitted variables may produce inefficient coefficient estimates. Using this family of probit models, I examine joint probabilities of voting for more than one office. Examining the effects of freeze attitudes and other variables on voting for multiple offices allows a specific test of whether freeze attitudes increase the probability of voting for teams of Democratic candidates. In addition to looking at the joint probability of voting for two or three offices, I examine probabilities of voting for individual offices to validate the previous results where I examined voting for each office individually.

I first examine voting for House and Senate, then voting for Senate and governor, and finally voting for House and governor. In the following section I examine voting for all three offices. The use of two and three equation models is necessary because not all states included opportunities for voting for all three offices in the 1982 elections.

Table 5.7 reports the bivariate probit results for priming voting decisions for Democratic candidates across different pairings of offices. The results for freeze attitudes across freeze and non-freeze ballot measure states largely mirror those of the office-by-office analyses. In each of the

TABLE 5.7
Bivariate Probit Estimates of the Priming Effect of Freeze Ballot Measures on Voting for Democratic Candidates

| | House & Senate Bivariate Probit | | | | Governor & Senate Bivariate Probit | | | | Governor & House Bivariate Probit | | | |
|---|---|---|---|---|---|---|---|---|---|---|---|---|
| | Freeze Ballot Measure | | No Freeze Ballot Measure | | Freeze Ballot Measure | | No Freeze Ballot Measure | | Freeze Ballot Measure | | No Freeze Ballot Measure | |
| Variable | House | Senate | House | Senate | Governor | Senate | Governor | Senate | Governor | House | Governor | House |
| Freeze supporter | .17*** (.052) | .21*** (.052) | .02 (.043) | .12** (.043) | .27*** (.061) | .30*** (.059) | -.00 (.048) | .08* (.046) | .31*** (.061) | .12* (.060) | .04 (.035) | .01 (.035) |
| Democrat | .53*** (.035) | .54*** (.035) | .60*** (.030) | .56*** (.030) | .59*** (.040) | .57*** (.040) | .58*** (.032) | .55*** (.031) | .57*** (.040) | .53*** (.039) | .57*** (.024) | .62*** (.024) |
| Ideology | .13*** (.035) | .13*** (.035) | .14*** (.030) | .17*** (.029) | .25*** (.040) | .14*** (.040) | .20*** (.032) | .12*** (.031) | .26*** (.041) | .09* (.040) | .21*** (.024) | .11*** (.024) |
| Presidential approval | -.60*** (.069) | -.54*** (.069) | -.50*** (.059) | -.57*** (.059) | -.62*** (.080) | -.59*** (.079) | -.55*** (.064) | -.52*** (.064) | -.64*** (.080) | -.57*** (.078) | -.61*** (.048) | -.57*** (.048) |
| Economy | .22*** (.039) | .24*** (.039) | .25*** (.033) | .23*** (.033) | .18*** (.046) | .19*** (.045) | .28*** (.036) | .23*** (.036) | .20*** (.046) | .25*** (.044) | .28*** (.027) | .20*** (.026) |
| Social security | -.38*** (.063) | -.37*** (.063) | -.31*** (.053) | -.37*** (.054) | -.38*** (.073) | -.36*** (.072) | -.46*** (.060) | -.37*** (.059) | -.39*** (.075) | -.43*** (.073) | -.37*** (.044) | -.25*** (.043) |
| Constant | .53*** (.058) | .45*** (.058) | .51 (.047) | .39*** (.047) | .49*** (.067) | .49*** (.066) | .42*** (.052) | .38*** (.050) | .48*** (.068) | .52*** (.066) | .35*** (.039) | .58*** (.039) |
| N | 3,681 | | 5,048 | | 2,836 | | 4,262 | | 2,810 | | 7,726 | |
| rho | .489*** | | .416*** | | .527*** | | .537*** | | .511*** | | .425*** | |
| Log likelihood | -3204.68 | | -4558.68 | | -2326.68 | | -3743.59 | | -2324.15 | | -6900.14 | |

Note: Estimates are bivariate probit coefficients with standard errors in parentheses.
* p < .05 level (one-tailed test)
** p < .01 level (one-tailed test)
*** p < .001 level (one-tailed test)

bivariate probit models, the coefficient for freeze supporter is larger for voters in states with freeze ballot measures compared to voters in states without them. Furthermore, the coefficients obtain statistical significance for voters in states with freeze ballot measures but do not in states without them. Note that the rho coefficient for each model is statistically significant, indicating that the equations are interrelated.

Figure 5.3 depicts changes in probability of voting for Democratic candidate pairings. In each set of bars, the change in bivariate probability (with all other variables set at their mean values) in response to a change in freeze attitudes is greater in states with freeze initiatives and referenda. Among these states, the largest change in probability is .12 for voters choosing both a Democratic governor and senator while the change in probability for voters choosing both a Democratic House member and governor and both a Democratic member of the House and Senate is .09 and .08, respectively. The smaller effects for the dyads with House candidates likely represent differences in the electoral environments of House races. Candidates in House races are much less visible than candidates in Senate and gubernatorial contests, all else equal. Since the average House candidate is not visible, especially challengers, many voters in these contests likely used partisan or incumbency cues that dampened the effects of the freeze, thus weakening the dyadic relationship with Senate and gubernatorial candidates.

Although these changes in probability are smaller than presidential approval (−.24), for example, they represent meaningful differences (results not shown). For example, all else equal, a hypothetical Independent voter who opposes the freeze and lives in a state with a freeze initiative or referendum has a probability of .51 of voting for both a Democratic senator and governor. Switching this hypothetical voter's opinion on the freeze from opponent to supporter increases the probability of voting for both Democratic candidates to .62. Looking at these same first differences in states without freeze ballot measures produces no change in probability. Thus, the ability of freeze ballot measures to tie together voting decisions for different offices suggests that voters use common issues to evaluate candidates running for different offices despite the fact that issue responsibilities and/or campaign messages differ.

In addition, the changes in probability for voting for a single office from the bivariate probit estimates are nearly identical to those depicted in figure 5.2 for the single equation models. For example, the change in probabilities computed from the single equation models shown in figure 5.2 for the House and Senate are .07 and .09, respectively. In the bivariate probit model for the House and Senate these same probability changes are .07 and .08. Other changes in probability across different bivariate probit

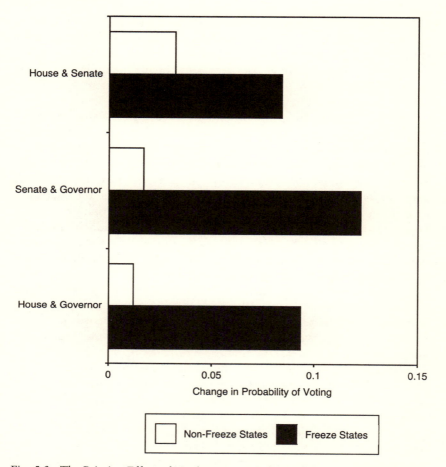

Fig. 5.3. The Priming Effect of Nuclear Freeze Ballot Measures on Voting for Multiple Democratic Party Candidates in the 1982 Midterm Elections (Change in Probabilities)

*Note*: Quantities represent changes in bivariate probabilities (voting for two Democratic candidates) of voting for a Democratic candidate calculated by looking at a change in freeze attitudes (from opposition to support) holding all other variables at their mean values.

models (e.g., House and governor) exhibit these types of negligible differences between the probabilities from the single equation probit models.

Table 5.8 presents the multivariate (or trivariate) probit results of voting for all three Democratic candidates running for House, Senate, and governor.[16] The statistically significant correlation coefficients for rho indicate that the equations for each office are interrelated. The pattern of

TABLE 5.8
Trivariate Probit Estimates of the Priming Effects of Freeze Ballot Measures on Voting
for Democratic House, Senate, and Gubernatorial Candidates

| Office / Variable | Freeze Ballot Measure | | No Freeze Ballot Measure | |
|---|---|---|---|---|
| | Coefficient | Standard Error | Coefficient | Standard Error |
| **House** | | | | |
| Freeze supporter | .12* | .061 | −.01 | .048 |
| Democrat | .53** | .040 | .61** | .032 |
| Ideology | .08* | .040 | .11** | .033 |
| Presidential approval | −.57** | .080 | −.53** | .066 |
| Economy | .24** | .045 | .22** | .037 |
| Social security | −.44** | .074 | −.31** | .060 |
| Constant | .53** | .067 | .52** | .053 |
| **Senate** | | | | |
| Freeze supporter | .30** | .060 | .08* | .047 |
| Democrat | .55** | .041 | .55** | .032 |
| Ideology | .14** | .041 | .12** | .032 |
| Presidential approval | −.58** | .081 | −.54** | .065 |
| Economy | .20** | .046 | .22** | .037 |
| Social security | −.37** | .073 | −.40** | .060 |
| Constant | .49** | .067 | .39** | .052 |
| **Governor** | | | | |
| Freeze supporter | .30** | .062 | .01 | .049 |
| Democrat | .58** | .041 | .59** | .033 |
| Ideology | .25** | .041 | .19** | .033 |
| Presidential approval | −.65** | .081 | −.55** | .066 |
| Economy | .19** | .047 | .27** | .037 |
| Social security | −.41** | .075 | −.47** | .061 |
| Constant | .51** | .069 | .43** | .053 |
| rho12 (House & Senate) | .41** | .033 | .34** | .027 |
| rho13 (House & Governor) | .45** | .032 | .34** | .027 |
| rho23 (Senate & Governor) | .47** | .031 | .51** | .024 |
| N | 2,730 | 4.064 | | |
| Log likelihood | −3340.06 | −5365.09 | | |
| Wald Chi-square | 2195** | 3153** | | |

*Note:* Coefficients are simulated maximum-likelihood estimates using the GHK smooth recursive
simulator. Dependent variable = 1 if voted for Democratic candidate, 0 if Republican.
  *$p < .05$ level (one-tailed test)
  **$p < .001$ level (one-tailed test)

results from the earlier analyses recurs—freeze attitudes play an important role in voting for all three types of offices in states with freeze initiatives and referenda, but do not do so for voters in states without freeze ballot measures. The size of the coefficients for freeze supporter in states with ballot questions are, at minimum, several times larger than that found for non-freeze ballot question states. Not only are the coefficients for freeze supporter minuscule in non-freeze states but with the exception of voting for Senate, they also cannot be statistically distinguished from zero.

Figure 5.4 depicts the probability of voting for Democratic candidates in freeze states, both individually and collectively. Holding all other variables at their mean, opponents of the freeze are mildly inclined toward Democratic candidates, but supporters of the freeze show a demonstrably stronger inclination. Moving from freeze opponent to supporter in states with a freeze initiative or referendum increases the joint probability of voting for all three Democratic candidates by .06. In contrast, all else equal, the change in the joint probability of voting for all three Democratic candidates in states without freeze ballot measures is −.03 (not shown). For voters in states with freeze ballot measures, the probability of voting for a Democratic House candidate shifts by .05 between freeze opponent and supporter. Changes in probability of voting for a Democratic Senate or gubernatorial candidate increase by .11 for both offices between freeze opponents and supporters. The same probability changes for voters in states without freeze ballot measures for Democratic House, Senate, and gubernatorial candidates are −.003, .03, and −.002, respectively (not shown).

As found in previous analyses, the impact of the freeze did not play as large a role as other factors that explained voting in the 1982 midterm elections (see Abramowitz 1984). For example, in states with freeze initiatives and referenda, presidential approval produced a change in probability of −.29, but this is not unexpected given the political climate of the 1982 elections. Although the impact of the freeze was less than that of other variables, freeze attitudes played a significant role in states with freeze initiatives or referenda.

## CONCLUSION

Taken together, the results in each of the above analyses indicate that voters make few distinctions among offices and campaign messages when voting. Instead, well-known issues cut across electoral domains and tie together voting decisions. The common thread that ran through each of these analyses was nuclear freeze ballot measures and campaigns. Voters

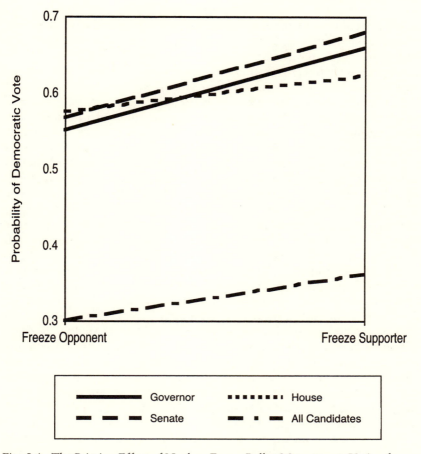

Fig. 5.4. The Priming Effect of Nuclear Freeze Ballot Measures on Voting for Democratic Party Candidates in the 1982 Midterm Elections (Predicted Probabilities)

*Note*: Quantities represent predicted probabilities of voting for a Democratic candidate calculated by looking at the difference between freeze opponents and supporters holding all other variables at their mean values.

in states with freeze initiatives and referenda were likely to consider the freeze issue when making voting decisions for a given office or across offices, while voters in states without them were not likely to do so.

In addition to differentiating the basis of candidate judgments across electoral environments, the impact of freeze ballot measures demonstrates that agendas may tie together voting decisions across offices. Freeze ballot measures, their campaigns, and accompanying media coverage indiscriminately primed voters to choose various Democratic candidates. This effect occurred across different offices, overriding concerns such as institutional responsibilities or the absence of candidate dialogue about the issue. Voters did not seem to care which office they were voting for insofar as they applied their attitudes about the freeze issue toward the vote.

The results also suggest that spillover effects happen more than commonly recognized. In the low-information environment of House elections, for instance, it is unlikely that many voters received campaign messages about the freeze from the candidates. Despite the fact that voters are more aware of Senate elections, few Senate candidates bothered to campaign on the issue. Furthermore, none of the gubernatorial candidates mentioned the freeze in their campaigns. Nevertheless, voters in states with freeze campaigns consistently gave the freeze issue greater weight in their candidate evaluations across these offices. Ignoring the broader electoral environment of voting may lead researchers to misread when and where information effects occur.

The differences in the impact of freeze attitudes across offices lend insight into how agendas affect voting decisions across information environments. Overall, the results show that the freeze likely had the least potent effect in House races and had nearly comparable effects in the Senate and gubernatorial races, although the effect was slightly larger in voting for governor. These differences suggest that despite the lower levels of information voters have in House races, issues from outside a House contest do not override the effects of incumbency and party identification. The greater effects for the higher visibility races for Senate and governor suggest that the ingredients of candidate choice in these contests might be more susceptible to spillover effects.

The results also undermine the notion that voters assess institutional responsibilities when voting for candidates. Although we might expect that voters would use the freeze when voting for federal offices, this argument would deny such use when voting for gubernatorial candidates. This finding is especially persuasive in the case of gubernatorial elections, given that we would not expect voters who make decisions in this manner to hold these particular candidates responsible for foreign policy issues. The fact that the freeze influenced both offices by the same quantity or nearly the same quantity in the above analyses suggests that votes for governor and senator, at least by the standards of the freeze issue, may share more in common than votes for House and Senate candidates. Overall, when looking at this question of whether voters make voting decisions according to institutional responsibilities, we see that voter evaluations of President Reagan and his economic program had a similar effect across all three types of elections. These results alone would be evidence contrary to the claim that voters make distinctions between federal and state offices.

In sum, voters are not finicky consumers of issues. For the most part, they do not bother themselves about institutional criteria or the specific content of the candidates' campaigns. Voters are, however, influenced by heavy exposure to political information. In particular, agendas—through priming—shape evaluations for multiple candidates. They may differentiate the criteria voters use to evaluate candidates across political environments but they also infuse electoral choices with common meaning within an electoral environment.

## VARIABLE CODING FOR AGENDA-SETTING ANALYSIS

*Ballot measure*
Coded one (1) if a state had a nuclear freeze ballot measure and zero (0) otherwise.

*Arizona, California, Massachusetts, Michigan, New Jersey, Oregon, Wisconsin*
Coded one (1) if the state had a nuclear freeze ballot measure and zero (0) otherwise.

*Foreign policy*
Coded one (1) if respondents disapproved of Reagan's handling of foreign affairs and zero (0) otherwise. This item was coded from an open-ended question.

*Economics most important*
Coded one (1) if respondents mentioned an economic item and zero (0) otherwise. This item was coded from an open-ended question.

*Partisan*
Coded one (1) if respondents mentioned that party was important to their vote for House of Representatives and zero (0) otherwise. This item was coded from an open-ended question.

## VARIABLE CODING FOR THE PRIMING ANALYSES

*Ballot measure*
Coded one (1) if a state had a nuclear freeze ballot measure and zero (0) otherwise.

*Freeze supporter*
Coded one (1) if voters checked that they were for an immediate freeze and zero (0) if they checked that they were against it.

*Job approval*
Coded one (1) if respondent approved of the president's job performance and zero (0) otherwise.

| | |
|---|---|
| *Economic evaluation* | Coded one (1) if voters believed the economy was getting worse, negative one (−1) if they thought that the economy was getting better, and zero (0) if they thought it was staying the same. |
| *Social security* | Coded one (1) if voters approved of Reagan's handling of social security and zero (0) if they disapproved. |
| *Party ID* | Coded one (1) if voters identified as Democrat, zero (0) if they identified as Independent, and negative one (−1) if they identified as Republican. |
| *Ideology* | Coded one (1) if voters identified as liberal, zero (0) if moderate, and negative one (−1) if conservative. |

*Chapter 6*

TAKING THE INITIATIVE: ILLEGAL IMMIGRANTS,

AFFIRMATIVE ACTION, AND STRATEGIC

POLITICIANS IN CALIFORNIA'S 1994

AND 1996 ELECTIONS

No candidate single-handedly controls the agenda. With competition from opponents, other campaigns, and the media, it is often remarkable that some candidates are able to get their messages through to voters. Although candidates running for higher-level offices have a greater degree of control over the agenda than do their counterparts running for lower-level offices, it is far from complete. To gain some advantage in this undertaking, political parties and candidates have increasingly turned to initiatives as a means of setting the agenda.

In this chapter, I will examine ballot initiatives as agenda-setting tools of political parties and candidates. Taking a page from the national GOP playbook, California's Republican Party in the 1994 and 1996 elections sought to win over Democratic and Independent voters by using ballot initiatives involving racial issues. Using data from Voter News Service and the California Field Poll, I investigate the effect of two ballot initiatives—Propositions 187 and 209—across myriad offices: president, U.S. Senate, U.S. House, governor, state senate, and state assembly. In so doing, I evaluate whether the agenda-setting efforts of GOP strategists were successful in priming voters to choose Republican candidates.

## THE STRATEGIC USE OF BALLOT INITIATIVES

Agenda formation is not a simple task. A cornucopia of interest groups, issue entrepreneurs, candidates, parties, and events, to name a few sources, compete for limited issue space on an agenda. Although the sponsorship and support of ballot initiatives are generally the purview of interest groups (Gerber 1999), political parties and candidates have increasingly supported ballot measures to provide themselves with popular issues to win elections (Schrag 1998, 226; Smith and Tolbert 2001). Indeed, some observers of the California initiative process claim that candidates use initiatives as a "magic carpet ride" to win elected office (Bell and Price 1988, 383).

In earlier chapters, I depicted candidates (or parties) as subject to agenda forces. Most of the time this is the case—influencing the flow of information is largely outside the control of most nonpresidential candidates due to limited issue space on the agenda and scarce financial resources. Because of this, and coupled with an inattentive electorate, candidates are often unable to get their messages effectively communicated and thus may often be evaluated by voters based on issues outside their contest.

Since agendas shape voting, politicians seek to shape agendas. In so doing, candidates attempt to prime the considerations voters bring to bear in making candidate judgments (Druckman, Jacobs, and Ostermeier, 2004; Jacobs and Shapiro 1994). As discussed in chapter 2, parties and candidates sometimes attempt to define the agenda with issues on which they have a strong reputation. With the initiative process, parties and candidates attempt to do this through several activities: providing money and resources to qualify and advertise an initiative; emphasizing an initiative in campaigns; and stressing an opponent's unpopular or noncredible position on an initiative issue. If convincingly done, the choice of candidate or party is mapped onto the issue dimension. In this way, candidates hope to *constrain* their opponents to address issues that help themselves but hurt their opponents.

Despite the agenda-setting potential of direct legislation, most candidates and parties choose not to invest in the process given its high costs (e.g., getting an initiative qualified, the burden of running multiple campaigns) and the risk associated with choosing a winning issue (also see chapters 2 and 3). California Democrats, for example, chose to align themselves with Proposition 128, or Big Green, in the 1990 elections but undoubtedly regretted it after the measure was defeated by a 64 percent to 36 percent margin. Therefore, it is critical for parties and candidates to choose an initiative issue that voters support by a large margin, and the more solid the support behind it the better. If a substantial amount of the leg work is already done on what appears to be a popular issue, candidates and parties can free-ride or, if need be, contribute resources to ensure the initiative's success.

Even so, the payoffs associated with the initiative strategy are risky compared to directing resources into candidate efforts such as turnout and advertising. The costs incurred by individual politicians for sponsoring initiatives are largely prohibitive because they bear the costs and thus have fewer resources available for their own campaigns. The most frequently cited example of a candidate spreading his or her resources too thinly is John Van de Kamp's failed bid to become the Democratic Party's nominee in California's 1990 gubernatorial election. Going into the Democratic primary, Van de Kamp sponsored three initiatives to give his campaign an added boost and strong policy angle (Lubenow 1991). Ulti-mately, however, this strategy failed and he lost the nomination.

Political parties, on the other hand, are more likely to use initiatives as agenda-setting tools since they can disperse the costs through economies of scale.[1] Similar to an economic firm, political parties benefit from econo-mies of scale by spreading the cost of advertising across all party candi-dates, thereby lowering the cost of initiative sponsorship. When the Re-publican Party promoted Propositions 187 and 209, they were using common resources to provide a collective good for all their candidates—winning issues.

## RACE AS A PARTISAN WEDGE ISSUE

A wedge issue divides a party or candidate's coalition. "Used effectively, a wedge issue can divide supporters of the opposing candidate, either persuading them to switch or to just sit out the election" (Baer 1995, 58). The success of direct legislation as a wedge issue is contingent on four factors: whether voters deem the issue important; whether it is widely supported, especially by voters who ordinarily would not vote for a given party; whether it is easily understood; and whether it is identifiable as belonging to one of the two parties (issue ownership). Depending on the degree to which these ingredients are present, ballot measures vary in their ability to prime voters in a way that advantages or disadvantages a party.

Choosing the correct issue is not an easy undertaking. Riker (1986) refers to this choice and others like it as the art of "heresthetics." In mass elections, heresthetics involves the manipulation of issue dimensions through bringing in new or reinforcing old issues that result in "structur-ing the world so you can win" (ix). If successfully done, the redefinition of choice changes losing issues into winning ones. Choosing the correct initiative as a means of setting the agenda for candidate races, then, can help candidates and political parties win elections. As I will demonstrate shortly, Republicans had a lot of success by helping qualify Proposition 187 for the ballot.

Race is the quintessential wedge issue in American politics. Racial is-sues are highly emotive, understandable, and have opposing sides, each strongly identified with one of the two major parties. Identified as one of the strongest "symbolic predispositions" an individual can hold, racial prejudice involves affective and unthinking responses rather than cogni-tion or self-interest (Sears, Huddy, and Schaffer 1986). Furthermore, these attitudes are relatively stable over time as compared to attitudes on most other issues (Converse and Markus 1979). Although race has a long his-tory in U.S. politics, its role in contemporary electoral politics began after the early 1960s (Carmines and Stimson 1989; Pomper 1972). In a dramatic reversal of long-held positions, the Democratic Party became the home of racial liberalism and the Republicans took on a social conservatism that, like their position on New Deal social welfare policies, advocated a restricted role for an active national government. Carmines and Stimson (1989, 117) argue that in contrast to the overt racism of Jim Crow segregation, this "new issue species" of racial politics allowed Republicans to take an opposing position on racial questions that is not overtly racist. In so doing, Republicans have effectively used racial issues to capture white votes from Independents and Democratic Party identifiers.

Beginning with the candidacy of Barry Goldwater in 1964, race became strongly identified with the political parties (Carmines and Stimson 1989; Kinder and Sanders 1996; Mendelberg 2001; Pomper 1972). Since then, Republican politicians have sometimes used the "race card" as a wedge issue (Mendelberg 2001). From Nixon's 1968 law-and-order campaign to the infamous Willie Horton ad intended to help George Bush's 1988 presidential campaign, the GOP has effectively used racial appeals to win white Democratic and Independent votes. Using a variety of approaches, scholars have found ample evidence that racial attitudes affect the voting decisions of white voters (Kinder and Sanders 1996; Mendelberg 2001; Sears 1988; Sears et al. 1980; Valentino 1999; Valentino, Hutchings, and White 2002).

Mendelberg's (2001) theory of racial priming is especially helpful in understanding the role that subtly racist appeals might have played in the initiative campaigns. In her theory, the norm of racial equality governs white voters' reactions to racial appeals. If candidates offer explicitly racist messages, white voters reject them as violations of the norm of racial equality. Thus, it is unwise for candidates to run explicitly racist campaigns. However, although the norm of racial equality is firmly embedded in the American creed, racial stereotypes, fears, and resentments persist. Candidates that make implicitly racist appeals prime these negative racial predispositions. By receiving less scrutiny, implicit messages activate negative racial stereotypes. Thus, overtly racist campaign messages may not work (they may backfire), but subtly racist communications may significantly affect the voting decisions of white voters.

## Initiatives as Partisan Wedge Issues

As I will detail shortly, the campaigns behind Propositions 187 and 209 conform to Mendelberg's account of how candidates play the race card in modern campaigns. Both initiatives likely invoked racial resentment or racist/negative stereotypes, but the advocates of these propositions eschewed explicitly racist rhetoric. In 1994, Proposition 187, or the self-titled "Save Our State" (SOS) initiative, sought to restrict public benefits to illegal immigrants. The illegal immigrants in question, without doubt, were Mexican and portrayed as causing economic harm to California— stealing the jobs of legal residents and siphoning off the vitality of the state through welfare "freeloading." In the 1996 elections, Proposition 209 or, as its creators dubbed it, the California Civil Rights Initiative (CCRI), sought to end racial and gender preferences in government hiring and access to higher education. The campaign for CCRI avoided using the term *affirmative action* and instead employed the rhetoric of "equal treatment" and "ending race- and gender-based preferences." Race was present but only insofar as it was connected to "reverse discrimination" or an "unfair advantage," criticisms that implicitly highlighted a zero-sum game between racial minorities and whites.

## The Problem of Assessing Racial Attitudes

Racial attitudes likely influenced opinion on the illegal immigration and affirmative action initiatives and by extension the effect these issues had on candidate evaluations. Studies of voting on both initiatives demonstrate that racial threat was a primary factor explaining white voter support for Propositions 187 (Tolbert and Hero 1996) and 209 (Ramirez 2002; Tolbert and Grummel 2003). In the aftermath of these initiatives, Latino political behavior and opinion in California also changed by increasing voter participation (Barreto and Woods 2005; also see Pantoja, Ramirez, and Segura 2001), political knowledge levels (Pantoja and Segura 2003), and Democratic Party identification (Bowler, Nicholson, and Segura 2004).

In the case of Proposition 209, research on attitudes toward affirmative action further suggests that racial attitudes are the leading predictor of white citizens' opinions on these policies, controlling for nonracial predispositions (Alvarez and Brehm 2002, chap. 6; Kinder and Sanders 1996; Sears et al. 1997). But, it would be careless to argue that racial attitudes explain *all* opinion on these issues. For example, even though Kuklinski et al. (1997) demonstrate that blatant racial prejudice is a significant predictor of attitudes toward affirmative action, they find that it is not the only factor accounting for these attitudes and that many whites dislike affirmative action policies for reasons other than ill feelings toward African Americans. Similarly, in the case of Proposition 187, it would be misguided to attribute all opinion on illegal immigration to race. For example, Alvarez and Butterfield (2000) find that nativist feelings—the favoring of native-born citizens over immigrants—brought on by California's ailing economy was a major determinant of opinion on Proposition

187. Although racial attitudes likely accounted for some nativist sentiment, it is difficult to say how much.

Since opinion on illegal immigration and affirmative action includes both racial and nonracial considerations, how do I assess the impact of racial priming? Studying the impact of racial attitudes in most election surveys is elusive because many surveys do not include the type of questions or experimental manipulations required to find such effects. This is especially true of exit polls where relatively few questions are included. In short, although studies of these initiatives and issues suggest an important role for racial attitudes, I cannot state precisely their exact role.

## THE GOP AND PROPOSITION 187

The history of Proposition 187, or the SOS initiative, is inextricable from GOP campaign politics. Like two other conservative proposals on illegal immigration that folded in early 1994, the chances that the SOS initiative would qualify for the November ballot looked slim in the fall of 1993 (Schultz 1996, 87–88). The most extreme of these proposals, SOS sought to bar illegal immigrants from public schooling, non-emergency health care, public assistance, and social services. Further, it required that local government officials report any suspected illegal immigrants to the INS. Although it survived longer than its counterparts did, "In mid-March, with less than six weeks to go, the campaign reported having collected just 150,000 signatures of the more than half million they would need to qualify for the November ballot" (Schultz 1996, 88). It looked as if the SOS initiative would fade from California's political landscape.

The California Republican Party saved SOS. "The party rolled out a 200,000 piece fundraising mailing for the initiative and helped field an army of paid signature gatherers to finish the task of qualification" (Schultz 1996, 88). Ronald Prince, one of the founders of SOS, recalled that the GOP helped qualify the initiative but that the GOP also used it as a fund-raising vehicle for its candidates.[2] Not only did it serve as a good issue to use in the November election, but Republicans also used it to solicit funds for their candidates.

Against the backdrop of a lagging economy and a growing concern among a segment of white voters about California's changing demographic patterns, the timing of the initiative as a solution to these problems was ideal (Cain, MacDonald, and McCue 1996). Both Proposition 187 campaigns—for and against—were instrumental in feeding this growing frustration. While opponents of the initiative argued that it would have an adverse effect on crime and the economy, proponents of SOS, along with Republican candidates, framed the debate in terms of "cheating" and "breaking the rules" but used images and symbols that featured Mexicans.[3]

An enormous march by its opponents fueled Proposition 187's visibility and its racial significance. On Sunday, October 17, over 70,000 protesters staged the largest march in the history of Los Angeles. At home, televisions and newspapers displayed images of Latinos marching underneath a sea of Mexican flags. The march may have done Proposition 187 opponents more harm than good: "In the end, the photo of 70,000 mostly nonwhite faces, marching under foreign flags, became precisely the image of 'invasion' that Governor Wilson and other Proposition 187 boosters had been trying to conjure up for months" (Schultz 1996, 78).

Coupled with high exposure from the elections for governor and U.S. senator, Proposition 187 became the single most important event of California's 1994 elections. Awareness of Proposition 187 was unusually high: 91 percent of Californians reported that they had heard or read about it (Nicholson 2003, 406). Speaking after the election, Republican pollster Paul Holm found that when voters were asked, "What's the most important race or issue in the election," 40 percent of voters mentioned Proposition 187, while 25 percent of voters said the governor's race (Lubenow 1995, 124).

Voters consistently supported Proposition 187. Although SOS showed signs of declining support over the course of the campaign, its support never dipped below a 12 percent lead in the Field Poll. For most of the campaign, its support hovered around 60 percent. In July, support among registered voters was 64 percent to 27 percent. Moving into October, support for it declined: 53 percent were in favor and 39 percent were opposed. On election day, Prop. 187 passed with 59 percent voting for it and 41 percent voting against it. Group support for Proposition 187 divided along racial lines (Alvarez and Butterfield 2000; Tolbert and Hero 1996). For example, Tolbert and Hero (1996) report that a majority of white (nonethnic) voters supported the initiative (63 percent) whereas support among Latinos was less forthcoming (23 percent).

## Pete Wilson and Proposition 187

The campaigns for and against Proposition 187 were also fought in the governor's race. Although Republican incumbent Pete Wilson did not endorse Proposition 187 at the onset of the election season, he became its strongest proponent and made it the cornerstone of his reelection bid against Democrat Kathleen Brown. In the Wilson campaign's television commercials, conspicuous images of the problem—illegal immigrants— were tied to the solution—Proposition 187 and Pete Wilson as governor. Early in the campaign, his ads showed Mexican immigrants illegally crossing California's border with a voice-over saying, "They keep coming." Race was not explicitly mentioned, but the faces were unquestionably brown. Less than three weeks before the election, the Wilson campaign aired another illegal immigration ad featuring the Statue of Liberty with a voice-over declaring, "There is a right way and a wrong way."

Wilson's efforts to integrate his candidacy with Proposition 187 were highly effective. From September 1 to election day, four of the state's largest newspapers featured Proposition 187 as a top story in the gubernatorial election (Collet 1995, 267–68).[4] Public opinion polls also showed that immigration was the key issue in the governor's race. In a *Los Angeles Times* exit poll, a majority of voters, 39 percent of the sample, mentioned illegal immigration as the most important issue in the governor's race. When California voters were asked in September about "what they liked or disliked about each of the candidates in their own words," Mark Di-Camillo of the Field Poll found that they "could easily play back Wilson's two major campaign themes; he's going to be tough on crime, and he's going to be tough on illegal immigration" (Lubenow 1995, 119). Speaking after the election, Dick Dresner of the Wilson campaign summed up the effect their efforts had on the campaign:

> At the end, the immigration issue seemed to catch everybody's imagination to such a degree that at one point we asked what was the governor's position on Prop. 187, was he for it or against it. It's the only time in the 25 years I've been polling where we got better than 90 percent of the people knowing the answer to a question like that. We got 94 or 95 percent saying that Wilson favored Prop. 187. More people knew that than people know that Sacramento is the capital of California, to put it in perspective. (Lubenow 1995, 122)

Linking his candidacy to this initiative, Wilson appeared to be successful at making a vote for Proposition 187 and a vote for Pete Wilson nearly identical choices (see Alvarez and Butterfield 2000; Tolbert and Hero 1996, 815).

Kathleen Brown, Wilson's Democratic opponent, avoided discussing Proposition 187 for most of the campaign. Although Brown opposed the initiative from the beginning, she said little about it until the final weeks of the race. The *Los Angeles Times* reported that "State Treasurer Brown, 49, changed the focus of her campaign in the final two weeks to reflect her belief that the initiative would be defeated—and Wilson, a supporter, would go down with it" (Decker and Stall 1994). With little money left in the final days of her campaign, Brown aired two new ads criticizing Wilson's position on Proposition 187. Brown's strategy failed: on election day she lost whereas Prop. 187 and Pete Wilson won. Despite trailing Brown by 20 points a year before the election, Wilson defeated Brown by a 14-point margin. Proposition 187 was widely considered by campaign analysts and strategists for both sides as a critical element in Wilson's decisive victory (Lubenow 1995).

## Michael Huffington and Proposition 187

Michael Huffington was virtually unknown in California before running against Diane Feinstein for U.S. Senate. With a thin record of legislative accomplishments, the one-term House member from Santa Barbara had a difficult task ahead of him. Feinstein was well liked in California and had high name recognition due to her incumbent status and the fact that she had run for statewide offices in both 1990 (unsuccessfully for governor) and 1992 (she had won a special election for U.S. senator). Despite his deficits, Huffington's candidacy was viable because of his great personal wealth and the Republican-friendly climate of the 1994 elections.

Outspending Feinstein by more than two to one, Huffington ran a media campaign that increased his name recognition and decreased Feinstein's strong level of support. By the end of the campaign, Huffington had spent $30 million to Feinstein's $14.4 million. This spending advantage helped him get out a message that voters were receptive to hearing. Working with a conservative agenda both within the state and nationally, he was able to define his candidacy with conservative issues that gave him position and credibility advantages (Cain 1995). On the issue of crime, Huffington had a credibility advantage. Although Feinstein contended that she was "tough on crime," voters typically perceive Republican candidates as more credible on this issue. Furthermore, Huffington's enthusiastic support of Proposition 184, an anti-crime initiative dubbed "three strikes and you're out," bolstered his "tough on crime" credentials. Like Wilson, Huffington also had a position advantage on the issue of illegal immigration because Feinstein opposed Proposition 187. In addition to the issues of illegal immigration and crime in California, the backdrop of national issues in 1994 consisted of anti-tax, anti–big government, and anti–President Clinton sentiments. Taken together, Huffington had a stark agenda advantage over Feinstein.

In contrast to the gubernatorial candidates, Huffington and Feinstein spent much of the election ducking questions about Proposition 187. When asked about it, which happened often, both candidates declined to state a position. However, less than three weeks before the election with Feinstein comfortably ahead in the polls, Huffington endorsed Proposition 187 in a hastily arranged news conference (Krikorian and Lesher 1994). The following day, Feinstein came out against it, acknowledging the possibility that her position could cost her the election (McDonnell and Lesher 1994).

Huffington almost pulled even with Feinstein in the final two weeks of the campaign. In addition to the boost Huffington received from Prop. 187, he released a barrage of negative ads about Feinstein and her husband, Richard Blum. Since Huffington had an enormous war chest to spend on advertising, Feinstein could do little to stop her declining support in the polls. Just as Huffington had narrowed the gap, however, the *Los Angeles Times* broke a story about his employing an illegal immigrant as a nanny. Media coverage of the race quickly shifted to the "nannygate" scandal. Further intensifying the focus on the candidates and illegal immigration was a story about Feinstein's having employed an undocumented immigrant as a maid. Despite the fact that both candidates had a personal problem on this issue, Huffington's story was probably more damaging given his strong support of Proposition 187. Furthermore, it is likely that Huffington's initial denial and attempt to blame his wife troubled voters and could have neutralized the impact of Prop. 187 in the Senate race. On election day, the race was too close to call. Ultimately, Huffington lost to Feinstein by a 2 percent margin.

## DID PROPOSITION 187 AFFECT VOTING DECISIONS FOR GOVERNOR AND SENATE?

All else equal, I would expect Proposition 187 to have had the same effect in both the Senate and governor's races. However, there were two important differences that likely mattered. First, the Senate candidates discussed Proposition 187 much later in the election than did the candidates for governor. For much of the election, Huffington and Feinstein battled over other issues. In contrast, the gubernatorial candidates, especially Wilson, focused on Proposition 187 throughout the campaign. Thus, the linkage between Prop. 187 and the governor's race was likely stronger than that found between Prop. 187 and the Senate contest. The second important difference between the Senate and governor's races is that both Senate candidates had employed illegal immigrants. This news, which was a major story, might have dampened the effect of Proposition 187 on voting for Senate candidates. A third difference, one that I have argued is irrelevant to most voters, is that senators and governors have different institutional responsibilities. Even though a narrow interpretation of institutional responsibilities would posit that Proposition 187 is a state responsibility (ballot propositions only affect state law), it is difficult to partition responsibility because both the federal and state governments share responsibility for this issue. Nonetheless, I expect Proposition 187 to have played an important role in the Senate contest, especially among those with strong preferences. In the end, Proposition 187 was probably an effective wedge issue in both races, but more so in the gubernatorial race.

## Data and Research Design for the 1994 Gubernatorial and Senate Races in California

To evaluate the effect of Proposition 187 on the U.S. Senate and governor's races, I use Voter News Services (VNS) 1994 General Election Exit Polls for California (ICPSR 6520). This exit poll is well suited for evaluating voting behavior in these races because it includes questions about Proposition 187 and the issues that mattered most to voters for the Senate and governor's races, including illegal immigration. The dependent variable in each model is whether the respondent voted for the Republican candidate. If the respondent voted for the Republican candidate in the gubernatorial or Senate race, respectively, the dependent variable equals one (1), and it equals zero (0) if he or she voted for the Democratic candidate. In addition to examining the effects of Proposition 187, I control for a variety of variables important to explaining voting decisions such as issues, party identification, ideology, and presidential approval (see the appendix at the end of the chapter for coding). The analyses include all non-Hispanic respondents.

Table 6.1 shows the results of the probit analysis for the governor's race. The first column presents the results for the entire sample and the second and third columns report the results by whether voters indicated that immigration mattered to their vote or made no such indication—29 percent of voters indicated that immigration was an important issue in their vote for governor. In the model including all respondents, it appears that Wilson's strategy of highlighting Proposition 187 and crime worked—both variables obtain statistical significance and have a positive effect on voting for Wilson. In making these issues salient to voters, it appears that Wilson was able to walk away from evaluations about the economy and jobs—neither of these variables is statistically significant. Contrary to an institutional responsibilities approach, it also appears that national forces played an important role as well given that presidential approval is a statistically significant predictor of the gubernatorial vote.

Although several of the control variables in the model have a modest to large effect on the vote choice for governor, changes in probabilities in the model including all voters reveal that party identification, ideology, presidential approval, and Proposition 187 had the largest effects (results not shown). If a voter supported Proposition 187, his or her probability of voting for Wilson is .26 greater than a voter who did not support the initiative, holding all other variables at their mean. By comparison, if a voter approved of President Clinton's job as president, his or her probability of voting for Wilson is .34 less than a voter who disapproved of Clinton's job performance, holding all other variables at their mean. Crime and the state economy, on the other hand, had smaller first difference effects, changing the probability of voting for Wilson by .12 and -.19, respectively.

TABLE 6.1

The Priming Effect of Proposition 187 on Voting for the Republican Gubernatorial Candidate in California's 1994 Elections

| Variables | Immigration Issue Mattered to Vote | | |
| --- | --- | --- | --- |
| | All Voters | Mentioned | Not Mentioned |
| Proposition 187 | .69*** | 1.80*** | .39** |
| | (.147) | (.380) | (.160) |
| Party identification | .88*** | .78*** | .87*** |
| | (.091) | (.239) | (.103) |
| Ideology | .48*** | .62** | .51*** |
| | (.106) | (.260) | (.125) |
| Presidential approval | −.93*** | −.22 | −1.03*** |
| | (.155) | (.371) | (.182) |
| State economy | −.17 | .12 | −.25* |
| | (.116) | (.299) | (.134) |
| Economy & jobs | −.22 | .57 | −.18 |
| | (.154) | (.509) | (.174) |
| Crime | .33* | .18 | .38* |
| | (.158) | (.397) | (.181) |
| Constant | .70** | −.67 | .92** |
| | (.291) | (.671) | (.345) |
| N | 682 | 196 | 486 |
| Chi-square | 528*** | 144*** | 357*** |
| % Predicted correctly | 88 | 93 | 86 |
| Proportional reduction in error | 72 | 72 | 70 |

Source: Voter News Service 1994 General Election Exit Poll, California (ICPSR 6520).

Note: Entries in parentheses are standard errors. Dependent variable = 1 if voted for Pete Wilson, 0 if for Kathleen Brown.

*significant at the .05 level (one-tailed test)

**significant at the .01 level (one-tailed test)

***significant at the .001 level (one-tailed test)

Was Proposition 187 a wedge issue? Figure 6.1A shows the changes in probability by Democratic and Independent voters for the full sample according to whether they opposed or supported Proposition 187. All else equal, a Democratic voter who opposed 187 had a probability of voting for Wilson of .18 whereas a Democratic supporter of the initiative had a .41 probability of voting for Wilson. The effect of Proposition 187 on voting for Wilson was even greater among Independent voters. Independent voters opposed to Prop. 187 had a .49 probability of voting for

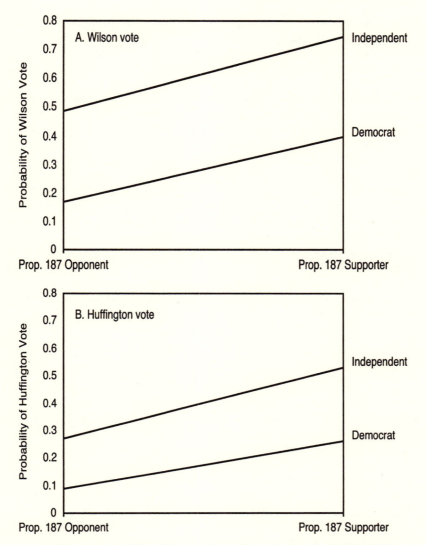

Fig. 6.1. The Priming Effect of Proposition 187 on Voting for the Republican Gubernatorial and Senatorial Candidates in California's 1994 Elections (Predicted Probabilities)

*Note:* Quantities represent predicted probabilities (based on Clarify simulations) of voting for the Republican candidate looking at differences between Proposition 187 opponents and supporters holding all other variables at their mean values.

Wilson. On the other hand, if an Independent voter supported Proposition 187, he or she had a .75 probability of voting for Wilson. The magnitude of these effects suggests that illegal immigration on the ballot induced many voters, both Independent and Democratic, to vote for the Republican governor.

The results in columns 2 and 3 of table 6.1 reveal that the segment of voters who indicated immigration mattered to their vote for governor (almost a third of voters) voted for Wilson, in large part, because of Prop. 187. Both the likelihood ratio test (p = .01) and Wald test (p = .00) reject the null hypothesis that the coefficient for Proposition 187 is the same across groups. The effect of the initiative is striking when comparing the immigration and non-immigration-minded voters. The coefficient for Proposition 187 is four times larger for voters who identified it as important to their vote. Among these voters, it is the most important predictor of the vote. Holding all other variables at their mean, if a voter supported Prop. 187 his or her probability of voting for Wilson is .46 greater than a voter who opposed the initiative. By comparison, the probability of a Republican voting for Wilson is .32 greater than a Democrat. The remaining variables produced smaller changes in probabilities: presidential approval (−.04); the state economy (.04); jobs (.07); and crime (.03).

### Proposition 187 and the Senate Contest

Table 6.2 presents the results of the probit analysis for the Senate contest. As mentioned, fewer respondents indicated immigration was important to their vote choice in the Huffington-Feinstein race than did respondents asked the same question with regard to the Wilson-Brown contest. In the model including all voters, Proposition 187 nonetheless appears to have played a role. The coefficient is statistically significant and positive, indicating that support for Proposition 187 was positively related to voting for Huffington. In addition, all of the other predictors in the model are statistically significant. This is the case even for state economic conditions, a finding contrary to an institutional responsibilities approach since a U.S. Senate candidate, much less a challenger, should not shoulder any responsibility for a state matter.

The changes in probability derived from the models presented in table 6.2 clarify the effects of the variables (results not shown). Holding all other variables at their mean, if a voter supported Proposition 187 his or her probability of voting for Huffington is .26 greater than a voter who opposed the initiative. The magnitude of this effect is comparable to that of state economic evaluations, an important consideration given California's bad economic times (−.26). As a basis of further comparison, a change in probability for party identification has the largest effect

TABLE 6.2
The Priming Effect of Proposition 187 on Voting for the Republican Senatorial
Candidate in California's 1994 Elections

| Variables | Immigration Issue Mattered to Vote | | |
| --- | --- | --- | --- |
| | All Voters | Mentioned | Not Mentioned |
| Proposition 187 | .69*** | 1.33*** | .56*** |
| | (.150) | (.421) | (.169) |
| Party identification | .72*** | .99*** | .63*** |
| | (.087) | (.218) | (.100) |
| Ideology | .32** | .08 | .48*** |
| | (.105) | (.257) | (.127) |
| Presidential approval | −1.08*** | −.45 | −1.24*** |
| | (.156) | (.431) | (.179) |
| State economy | −.23* | −.07 | −.26* |
| | (.112) | (.266) | (.129) |
| Economy & jobs | .43** | .26 | .54*** |
| | (.157) | (.503) | (.174) |
| Crime | .41** | −.37 | .67*** |
| | (.169) | (.429) | (.198) |
| Constant | .179 | −.14 | .15 |
| | (.274) | (.763) | (.312) |
| N | 662 | 124 | 538 |
| Chi-square | 483*** | 81*** | 398*** |
| % Predicted correctly | 87 | 88 | 88 |
| Proportional reduction in error | .72 | .64 | .70 |

Source: Voter News Service 1994 General Election Exit Poll, California (ICPSR 6520).
Note: Entries in parentheses are standard errors. Dependent variable = 1 if voted for Michael Huffington, 0 if voted for Diane Feinstein.
    *significant at the .05 level (one-tailed test)
  **significant at the .01 level (one-tailed test)
***significant at the .001 level (one-tailed test)

(.52) followed by presidential approval (−.39). Given the central importance of these variables for models of voting behavior, Proposition 187 had a substantial effect in the Senate contest.

To get a better sense of whether Proposition 187 was a wedge issue, figure 6.1B depicts the probability of Independents and Democrats voting for Huffington by whether they opposed or supported Proposition 187.

Compared to Wilson (see figure 6.1A), Independents and Democrats had a lower probability of voting for Huffington. However, as with voting for Wilson, the initiative helped Huffington with both Democrats and Independents, especially the latter. Holding all other variables at their mean, a Democrat opposed to Proposition 187 had a .09 probability of voting for Huffington whereas a Democrat who supported it had a .26 probability of voting for him. In results not shown, if a Democrat who supported Prop. 187 also disapproved of Clinton's job performance, he or she had a probability of voting for Huffington of .46. In figure 6.1, Independents opposed to Prop. 187 had a probability of voting for Huffington of .26 whereas Independents who supported 187 had a .53 probability of voting for Huffington. For these voters, all else equal, Proposition 187 was a crucial issue that gave Huffington a slight edge over Feinstein.

Turning to columns 2 and 3 of table 6.2, the analysis of voters for whom immigration was important to their vote—about 18 percent—shows that Proposition 187 had a substantial effect. The coefficient for Proposition 187 is more than twice as large for voters who mentioned immigration mattered compared to voters that did not make such an indication. However, whether the coefficient differs significantly across groups is uncertain. Although the Wald test is significant (p = .00), the likelihood ratio test is not (p = .95). Again, I calculated changes in probability to better interpret the results from columns 2 and 3 of table 6.2 (results not shown). The change in probability of voting for Huffington is substantially different for Proposition 187, comparing voters who mentioned immigration as important to their vote to voters who did not. Second only to party identification, Proposition 187 increased the probability of voting for Huffington by nearly .46 for voters who indicated immigration was important to their Senate vote. By way of comparison, for this same group the change from a Democratic Party identifier to a Republican Party identifier increased the probability of voting for Huffington by .62 while approval of Clinton's job performance lowered the probability of voting for Huffington by .14 compared to disapproval. The effects of Proposition 187 are less than half the size for voters who did not mention immigration as important to their vote for senator. If a voter in this group supported Proposition 187, his or her probability of voting for Huffington is .19 greater than a voter who opposed the initiative. Overall, the results indicate that Proposition 187 played a substantial role in the Senate race. But, it played a smaller role for Huffington than it did for Wilson. As mentioned, the "nannygate" scandal may have discounted Huffington's position on Proposition 187, and both Senate candidates' late position taking on the initiative could have also diluted its effects.

## Proposition 187 and Voting for Governor and Senate

The above analyses demonstrate that Proposition 187 was a salient issue for voters choosing Senate or gubernatorial candidates. Yet, as discussed in chapter 5, a primary tenet of agenda voting is that agendas tie voting decisions together by infusing them with a common evaluative basis. As before, testing this theory requires methods that treat voting decisions as interrelated. To evaluate the joint probability of voting for Wilson and Huffington, I use seemingly unrelated bivarate probit analysis. This method is similar to bivariate probit by accounting for the correlation among errors between equations, but differs slightly because seemingly unrelated models permit the inclusion of different independent variables in each equation. This is a desirable attribute since the equations for the gubernatorial and Senate races above included independent variables specific to each office (the variables for the economy, jobs, and crime asked about whether an issue mattered for a specific office).

Table 6.3 presents the results of the seemingly unrelated probit analysis for governor and senator. The estimated correlation coefficient, rho, assesses the interrelatedness of voting decisions. Rho is statistically significant, indicating a positive relationship between voting decisions for both offices. Thus, similar to the bivariate probit analyses from chapter 5, voting decisions across federal and state offices share a common evaluative basis.

The coefficient estimates for Proposition 187 in both the Senate and gubernatorial equations are both statistically significant and nearly equal in size. This finding indicates that Proposition 187 had similar effects on voters choosing Senate and gubernatorial candidates, likely because both candidates discussed the issue and were highly visible. To better interpret the effects of the variables from table 6.3, I calculated changes in probabilities (results not shown). Holding all other variables at their mean, the probability of voting for Wilson or Huffington individually yields nearly identical first differences (.27 for each office individually), and these quantities are nearly the same as those found in the single equation models reported in the previous sections. The multivariate probit verifies that the effect of the SOS initiative on voting for senator is not a statistical artifact of cross correlation.

The substantive purpose for estimating the two equations together is to examine the effect of Proposition 187 on voting for both Republican candidates (jointly). If a voter supported Proposition 187, his or her probability of voting for both Republican candidates is .26 greater than a voter who opposed the initiative, holding other variables at their mean. This effect is nearly comparable to the individual effects reported above. Although Proposition 187 had a large effect on voting for these candidates separately and jointly, it did not eclipse the other predictors in the model

TABLE 6.3
Seemingly Unrelated Bivariate Probit Estimates of the Priming Effect of
Proposition 187 on Voting for Senatorial and Gubernatorial Candidates

| Variable | Senate | Governor |
|---|---|---|
| Proposition 187 | .72\*\*\* | .71\*\*\* |
| | (.153) | (.156) |
| Party identification | .69\*\*\* | .88\*\*\* |
| | (.088) | (.096) |
| Ideology | .34\*\*\* | .45\*\*\* |
| | (.107) | (.110) |
| Presidential approval | −1.00\*\*\* | −.93\*\*\* |
| | (.162) | (.169) |
| State economy | −.26\*\* | −.20\* |
| | (.115) | (.122) |
| Economy & jobs | .47\*\*\* | −.13 |
| | (.154) | (.160) |
| Crime | .37\*\* | .37\*\* |
| | (.164) | (.162) |
| Constant | .20 | .68\*\* |
| | (.284) | (.311) |
| N | 620 | |
| Log likelihood | −370.72 | |
| rho | .549\*\*\* | |

Source: Voter News Service 1994 General Election Exit Poll, California (ICPSR 6520).
Note: Estimates are seemingly unrelated bivariate probit estimates with standard errors
in parentheses. Dependent variables = 1 if voted for Republican, 0 if voted for Democrat.
   \*p < .05 (one-tailed test)
   \*\*p < .01 level (one-tailed test)
   \*\*\*p <. 001 level (one-tailed test)

when looking at other changes of probabilities. The probability of casting
a vote for both Wilson and Huffington (jointly) shifts by .50 moving from
Democrat to Republican and by -.37 moving from voters who disapproved of President Clinton's job performance to those who approved.
Although these factors played a larger role, it is striking how substantial
an effect Proposition 187 had in these races given the strong influence of
national forces in the 1994 elections.

## Proposition 187 and Voting for Governor, Senate, and House

The seemingly unrelated bivariate probit analysis indicates that Proposition 187 primed voters to choose both a Republican Senate and guberna-

torial candidate. Using multivariate probit, I expand the analysis to include House races. While the analysis of Senate and gubernatorial elections lent insight into whether agendas bridge the apparent gap between federal and state offices, this analysis moves beyond that question by examining whether agendas prime voting decisions across electoral contests with varying amounts of electoral information.

Although I expect Proposition 187 to effect voting decisions for all three contests, its effect on House races will likely be smaller than its effect on Senate or gubernatorial contests. As discussed in chapter 2, the lower visibility of down-ballot races provides less opportunity for voters to think about these candidates. Consequently, the connection between an agenda issue and House candidates will not be as strong as it might in higher-information races. The information-poor environment of a typical House race dampens agenda effects and promotes heavy reliance on incumbency and party identification.

Further diluting the link between the initiative and voting for House was the near absence of House candidates campaigning on illegal immigration or Proposition 187. Descriptive accounts of California's House races from the *California Journal* and the *Almanac of American Politics* suggest that illegal immigration or Proposition 187 was an issue in about ten of these contests.[5] Like many House contests, the descriptions of these races indicate that many were lopsided contests where the challenger was unknown.

In most House contests between an incumbent and a weak challenger, it is not in the incumbent's interest to campaign heavily, much less campaign for or against a controversial issue. For example, a safe incumbent like Robert Matsui from California's Fifth Congressional District had little incentive to discuss the ballot proposition since he was, like most Democrats, a member of the political party on the "wrong" side of this issue. On the other hand, Orange County Republican Dana Rohrabacher from the Forty-fifth Congressional District campaigned for Proposition 187. Running in a highly conservative district, Rohrabacher did not place himself at risk by enthusiastically supporting Proposition 187. In either case, most voters probably never heard much of what Matsui or Rohrabacher said in their campaigns given that neither was likely heard above the din of voices in California's electoral marketplace.

Despite the absence of campaign talk in House races about Proposition 187, voters were thinking about the initiative a lot. The campaigns for and against the initiative, media coverage, and the gubernatorial and Senate contests discussing the initiative placed it firmly on the agenda. In contrast to the campaign messages from and about most House contests, issues on the agenda are available to most voters. Riding a conservative tide in 1994, taxes, big government, and an unpopular Democratic president combined with the issue of illegal immigration to help Republican House candidates in California. In California's 1994 House elections, these issues helped Republicans steal three Democratic seats and almost take control of several others from veteran Democratic incumbents such as Vic Fazio and Anthony Beilenson. Furthermore, Republicans took control of the state assembly for the first time in over twenty years and made considerable gains in the state senate. Although Proposition 187 likely played a larger role in the gubernatorial and senatorial contests because of the higher visibility of these candidates and the fact that the initiative appeared in the Senate and gubernatorial campaigns, voters likely evaluated California's House candidates in 1994, at least in part, according to Proposition 187.

Since the 1994 VNS exit polls from the Senate and gubernatorial analyses did not include any items about vote choice for House, I use the California Field Poll taken before the election (October 12–30). In addition to questions about intended vote choice for House, Senate, and governor, the survey included items about vote intentions on ballot propositions, opinions of President Clinton, party affiliation, and ideology (the coding for these variables are in the appendix). The dependent variable is coded one (1) if the respondent intended to vote for the Republican candidate and zero (0) otherwise.

Table 6.4 reports the trivariate probit estimates of voting for Republican gubernatorial, Senate, and House candidates in California's 1994 elections. The statistically significant rho coefficient for each dyad of offices indicates that decisions to vote for candidates across each of these offices are interrelated. For each office, support for Proposition 187 had a statistically significant and positive effect on voting for Republican candidates. The coefficients for Wilson and Huffington provide further evidence that Proposition 187 played an important role in shaping voting decisions for these candidates. Although Proposition 187 had a significant effect on voting decisions for House candidates as well, the coefficient is considerably smaller for them, suggesting that the initiative played a lesser role in House contests. Thus, as found in the results for the nuclear freeze ballot measures, the obscurity of many House candidates, especially challengers, dampens the effects of agendas.

With the exception of Proposition 184, the "three strikes and you're out" initiative, all the control variables have statistically significant effects in each equation. As the other major initiative in California's 1994 elections, it is peculiar that Proposition 184 did not exhibit statistically significant effects across offices. Proposition 184 mandated increased penalties for felons convicted of a third crime. The initiative had attracted little attention until the abduction and murder of a twelve-year-old, Polly Klaas. The Klaas murder became a major news story that roused public attention. In the aftermath of the Klaas story, Republican Senate hopeful Michael Huffington made Proposition 184 the cornerstone of his cam-

TABLE 6.4

Trivariate Probit Estimates of the Priming Effects of Proposition 187 on Voting for Republican Gubernatorial, Senate, and House Candidates

| Office / Variable | Coefficient | Standard Error |
|---|---|---|
| Governor | | |
|   Proposition 187 | .79*** | .157 |
|   Republican | .97** | .174 |
|   Conservative | .54*** | .173 |
|   Elect Clinton | −.93*** | .164 |
|   Proposition 184 | .24 | .161 |
|   Constant | −.59*** | .174 |
| Senate | | |
|   Proposition 187 | .77*** | .149 |
|   Republican | .78*** | .164 |
|   Conservative | .50** | .159 |
|   Elect Clinton | −.80*** | .169 |
|   Proposition 184 | .39** | .155 |
|   Constant | −1.17*** | .182 |
| House | | |
|   Proposition 187 | .41* | .176 |
|   Republican | 1.57*** | .177 |
|   Conservative | .74*** | .179 |
|   Elect Clinton | −.108*** | .174 |
|   Proposition 184 | .11 | .181 |
|   Constant | −.74*** | .183 |
| rho (Governor & House) | .40*** | .102 |
| rho (Governor & Senate) | .36*** | .088 |
| rho (Senate & House) | .35*** | .099 |
| N | 497 | |
| Log likelihood | −515.22 | |
| Wald Chi-square | 505*** | |
| Likelihood ratio test Chi-square | 33.33*** | |

Source: Field Poll (October 12–30).

Note: Coefficients are simulated maximum-likelihood estimates using the GHK smooth recursive simulator. Dependent variables = 1 if voted for Republican, 0 if otherwise. Likelihood ratio test examines rho (Governor & House) = rho (Governor & Senate) = rho (Senate & House) = 0.

  *p < .05 (one-tailed test)

  **p < .01 level (one-tailed test)

  ***p <.001 level (one-tailed test)

paign, funded it, and became its cochair. Wilson also made crime a major issue in his campaign, and research suggests it played a significant role in his reelection (A. Simon 2002). Yet, voter support for Proposition 184 had a statistically significant effect on voting for senator but not governor or representative. These results suggest that Prop. 184 was not a major issue affecting voting decisions across the ballot in 1994.

The results from table 6.4 suggest that Proposition 187 had a significant effect on voting decisions across offices, but they do not convey the impact of the initiative on jointly voting for all three Republican offices. Figure 6.2 depicts changes in probability associated with voting for all three offices jointly as well as individually. Holding all other variables constant at their mean values, if a voter supported Proposition 187, his or her probability of casting a Republican vote for all three offices is .19 greater than a voter who opposed Proposition 187.

Figure 6.3 shows that voting for Proposition 187 moved the "average" voter to choose all three Republican candidates from .10 to .29. Not surprisingly, the effects of Proposition 187 on voting for each office individually were even more substantial. Whereas opponents of Prop. 187 had a probability of voting for Wilson of .43, supporters had a .73 probability of supporting him. For Huffington, voters who opposed Prop. 187 had a .24 probability of voting for him and voters who supported Prop. 187 had a .52 probability of supporting him. Hence, as shown in figure 6.2, the change in probability of voting for Wilson increased by .30 when moving from Proposition 187 opponent to supporter and the same quantity for Huffington is .29. Both of these changes in probability are very similar to those reported for the bivariate probit models even though the analyses are based on different samples.

Support for Proposition 187 also had a substantial effect on the change in probability of voting for House candidates. Specifically, a voter against Proposition 187 had a probability of voting for a Republican House candidate of .45 whereas a voter who supported the initiative had a .61 probability. The increase in probability of .16 is substantial, but as expected, less so when compared to the Senate and gubernatorial candidates. This is likely due to the lower visibility of House candidates and the diminished opportunity for their candidacies to be linked to Proposition 187. Taken together, these results suggest that Proposition 187 was an important issue in the 1994 elections across the ballot.

## THE GOP AND PROPOSITION 209

Financially, Proposition 209's beginnings were similar to those of Proposition 187. The initiative proposal, dubbed the California Civil Rights

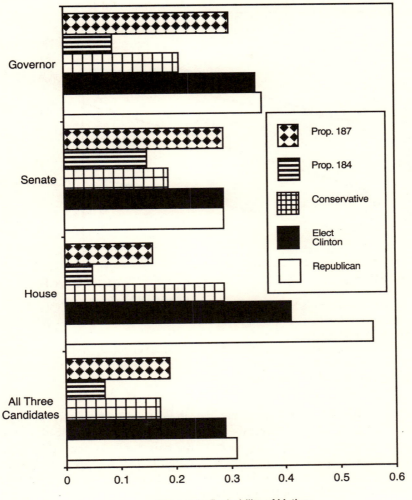

Fig. 6.2.  The Priming Effect of Proposition 187 on Voting for Republican Candidates in California's 1994 Elections (Change in Probabilities)

*Note*: Quantities represent changes in probabilities of voting for the Republican candidate calculated by looking at a minimum to maximum change in an independent variable holding all other variables at their mean values. Absolute values reported.

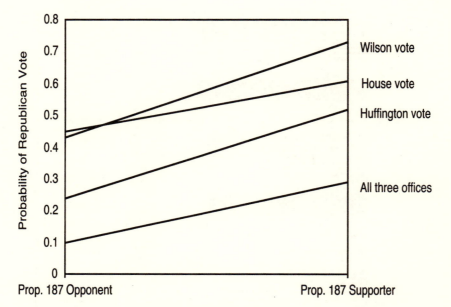

Fig. 6.3. The Priming Effect of Proposition 187 on Voting for Republican Gubernatorial, Senate, and House Candidates in California's 1994 Elections (Predicted Probabilities)

*Note*: Quantities represent predicted probabilities of voting for the Republican candidate looking at differences between Proposition 187 opponents and supporters holding all other variables at their mean values.

Initiative (CCRI) by its supporters, was in financial trouble and at risk of not qualifying for the November ballot. A year before the election, the signature-gathering effort to put it on the ballot was suspended because the campaign had run out of funds (Mendel 1995). With few businesses willing to contribute to such a controversial proposal, it appeared that CCRI would fade from the political scene.

Likely fearing the initiative would not qualify for the November ballot, California's Republican Party became CCRI's chief patron. Following an infusion of $480,000 to its committee on February 21, 1996, the CCRI campaign turned in 1.1 million signatures, almost twice the number of signatures needed to qualify it. The motive behind this contribution, according to the *Los Angeles Times*, was to give Republican candidates in the state, and possibly beyond, a winning issue (Lesher 1996). Later, various Republican Party organizations contributed funds to boost the initiative's popularity (Smith and Tolbert 2001).

Both sides of the debate tried to frame the initiative in terms favorable to their respective positions. Opponents of Proposition 209 tried to frame it as a women's issue. Hoping to focus the debate away from a racial interpretation of the issue—a sure loser with many white voters—opponents stressed that Proposition 209 included a loophole that would hurt women and girls through weakening current legal protections and allowing discrimination. Fighting the proposition on this front, opponents hoped that many women would consider the issue harmful. Also taking a gender approach to fighting CCRI were Democrats and women's organizations such as the National Organization of Women (NOW).

Later in the campaign, opponents turned to racial images and symbols that depicted Prop. 209 advocates as racists—a violation of the norm of racial equality. With Proposition 209 leading in the polls during the closing days of the election, opponents unleashed a $1 million advertising campaign that featured former Ku Klux Klan leader David Duke speaking in favor of the initiative at a California State University–Northridge debate on Proposition 209 sponsored by the student body (*San Diego Union Tribune* 1996). Obviously, opponents hoped that Duke's support of the proposition would be important enough to persuade voters that CCRI was racist.

The Yes on 209 committees' advertisements emphasized values such as "fairness" and "equity" and soundbites such as "set asides" and "quotas." Proponents of CCRI used advertisements that featured catchphrases such as "bring us together," "prohibit discrimination," and "equal chance to compete." In the first television advertisement in support of Prop. 209, CCRI Chairman Ward Connerly, an African American, said, "[W]hat is important is that we all have an equal chance to compete" (Lesher and Stammer 1996). In a later radio advertisement, the Yes on 209 campaign featured a woman who claimed to have been told to leave a freshman English class that was intended for African American students (Nakato 1996). The shift in strategy from campaign ads that featured norms of equality to the zero-sum politics of racial preferences tracked public support for the initiative.

Public opinion polls showed that support for CCRI was generally high throughout the campaign. Early in the election, a mid-July *Los Angeles Times* poll found that voters supported CCRI 59 percent to 29 percent (Stall 1996). But, support for the initiative fluctuated over the course of the campaign. An early October Field Poll found that it was supported 47 percent to 32 percent and a late October Field Poll found the margin had dwindled to 5 percent—46 percent to 41 percent (Mendel 1996a). In a Field Poll taken one week later, support for the initiative had rebounded, amounting to a 14 percent lead (Mendel 1996b). Whether the movement in the polls was due to sampling error or responses to campaign stimuli, the initiative won by an impressive 10 percent vote margin—55 percent to 45 percent.

Democrats and Republicans were involved on both sides of the Proposition 209 debate. In particular, the Republican Party assisted the CCRI effort from beginning to end. Less than two weeks before the election, *Sacramento Bee* columnist Dan Walters commented that Republicans "have taken over the campaign entirely" (Walters 1996). In addition to the $997,034 the California Republican Party gave to the CCRI committee (Jones 1996), the *Washington Post* reported that the state and national Republican Parties were planning to spend at least $2 million on commercials for Prop. 209 (Harden 1996). In contrast, the state Democratic Party and the Democratic National Committee contributed $275,169 and $100,000, respectively, to the Campaign to Defeat 209 (B. Jones 1996). Although Republicans typically have deeper pockets than do Democrats, the difference in spending suggests that the initiative was critical to the Republican strategy in California.

Pete Wilson and Newt Gingrich discussed the strategic importance of CCRI to Republican electoral fortunes in California in an early September "confidential" conference call to a group of business leaders. Speaking of Proposition 209, Wilson reportedly said, "This, I think, has every bit the potential to make a critical difference in the race for (GOP presidential nominee) Dole and House members." Furthermore, he said, "CCRI is very much an issue in legislative and congressional races. And it is one that works strongly to our advantage." Gingrich, the Republican Speaker of the U.S. House of Representatives, was reported to have said, "I believe as Speaker of the House, from my vantage point, the California Civil Rights Initiative is vital because we have to be competitive in California to keep control of the House" (Orlov 1996).

The national Republican Party also saw Proposition 209's strategic importance and endorsed it for inclusion in the party platform. Foremost in the minds of Republican strategists was using Proposition 209 as a means to set the electoral agenda with affirmative action in California and perhaps nationwide. In so doing, they hoped to give their candidate, Bob Dole, a strong issue to use against Bill Clinton. To the chagrin of many Republican strategists, the Dole campaign was reluctant to use the initiative until the closing weeks of the campaign.

## WAITING FOR DOLE

Although Dole had endorsed CCRI in March 1996, he did not discuss the initiative until the final weeks of the election. In large part, Dole's reluctance to discuss affirmative action and Proposition 209 was probably due to his vice presidential running mate choices. His initial aversion was tied to wooing Colin Powell—a supporter of affirmative action programs—onto the ticket (Chavez 1998). Later in the campaign after it became apparent that Powell would not accept the position, Dole's hesitation to campaign on CCRI might have been due to his selection of Jack Kemp as his running mate.

Before joining Dole on the Republican ticket, Kemp had come out against Republicans using race as a campaign issue in 1996. He said, "If '96 is run on dividing the races, I will not participate" (Broder 1995). Kemp, however, appeared to have changed his mind around the time of the Republican National Convention in San Diego when he accepted Dole's offer to be his vice presidential running mate. Not long after his selection, Kemp backtracked on his support for affirmative action and endorsed CCRI. After both he and Dole backed the initiative, the ticket's campaign manager suggested that both candidates stump for its passage. This possibility was short-lived, at least for Kemp, who publicly stated that he would not campaign for the initiative in late September. Dole continued to be silent on the issue.

Dole's neglect of CCRI elicited criticism from many Republicans. Clinton's opposition to CCRI focused Republican energy on the initiative since it was one of the few important issues on which the candidates held opposing positions and Dole had an advantage. Furthermore, CCRI was an issue that worked to the advantage of Republicans since it had popular support. CCRI Chairman Ward Connerly recognized Dole's neglect as a lost opportunity as early as July and criticized him for it (Novak 1996). In early August, Lyn Nofziger also criticized Dole for neglecting the initiative. Nofziger was alarmed that Dole had distanced himself from CCRI and urged him to use it as a campaign issue (Marelius 1996b). By far, the most outspoken critic of Dole's neglect of CCRI was Governor Wilson. Wilson was CCRI's earliest and most vociferous supporter. The governor had planned to use it in his bid for the Republican presidential nomination, but for a variety of reasons, his campaign was unsuccessful. Recognizing CCRI's importance to Republican candidates in lower offices and his own long-term political ambitions, Wilson repeatedly urged Dole to use it as a means to winning the state's valuable electoral college votes.

With three weeks remaining in the campaign, the Field Poll showed Dole had closed Clinton's lead in California to ten points. At this time, Dole was still ignoring CCRI, and Wilson publicly denounced him for neglecting California and the issues that could win him the state's electoral college votes—affirmative action and illegal immigration. Although Dole supported Propositions 187 and 209, Wilson claimed the "drumbeat of repetition" needed to influence voters was missing (Marelius 1996a). Encouraged by the Field Poll numbers and having ready-made wedge issues available, Dole began to campaign vigorously in the state and used CCRI as a defining issue. Coming out strongly for CCRI, he began to discuss the issue with greater frequency and at greater length. Indeed, in a three-day swing through the state in the closing days of the election, Dole said he would emphasize both issues because they are "very important. They're wedge issues" (Harden 1996). Citing president Clinton's opposition to the measure, Dole tied himself to the initiative more explicitly, asserting that Proposition 209's passage "will require two votes—one for the measure itself and one for an American president who will not undermine it after it is passed" (Harden 1996). In the remaining two weeks of the campaign, the Republican Party also waged an expensive run of political advertisements criticizing President Clinton for opposing Propositions 209 and 187.

In the end, however, Dole's campaign and the issues he discussed were relatively unimportant against an incumbent president sitting on top of a healthy economy (Abramson, Aldrich, and Rohde 1998; Herrnson and Wilcox 1997). Furthermore, while Clinton focused on the economy and micro-issues such as school uniforms and themes that revolved around his "bridge to the future" metaphor, Dole flitted from issue to issue (Ceaser and Busch 1997, 152-53). More important, both the media and voters found the election dull. Both voter interest and media coverage were substantially lower than in the 1992 election (Ceaser and Busch 1997, 155; Just 1997, 97). Incessant polling likely contributed to this disinterest since neither candidate's standing showed significant movement throughout the election. Despite Dole's last-minute California strategy with CCRI as the centerpiece, he lost the state, receiving 38 percent of its popular vote to Clinton's 51 percent.

## DID PROPOSITION 209 HELP DOLE?

During and after California's 1996 elections political analysts commented that Proposition 209 had little effect on the presidential vote. Nothing that Dole or Clinton did during the campaign appeared to influence the polls. Furthermore, Proposition 209 never became the political event of the election season. Clinton ignored the issue and Dole did the same until the final weeks of the campaign. Given this neglect, Proposition 209 did not achieve center stage in the presidential election. In addition, Proposition 209 did not have the economic discontent behind it that fueled Proposition 187. Indeed, Proposition 187's nickname, "Save Our State," declared that California was in big trouble. For many Californians, the state did not seem as though it was in need of saving in 1996.

Nonetheless, Proposition 209 was a leading issue in California and, toward the end of the election, it became the key to Dole's California strategy. Of all the propositions on the ballot during this election, CCRI was the best known, with 86 percent of voters reporting that they had heard or read about it (Nicholson 2003, 406). Although CCRI did not work as its Republican supporters had intended, it likely played an important role among a segment of voters strongly committed to it.

## Data and Research Design for the 1996 Presidential Race in California

Hoping to evaluate what effect, if any, CCRI might have on the presidential contest in California, Edmond Costantini and I wrote several questions for the early October 1996 Field Poll conducted October 1–9. To assess the effect of CCRI on the presidential vote choice we asked voters, "In deciding how you will vote for president, how important is each candidate's stand on Proposition 209—very important, somewhat important, not too important, or not at all important?" By comparing respondents who claimed it was important to those who said it was not, I evaluate the effect Proposition 209 had on the presidential vote—a vote for Dole equals one (1), and zero (0) otherwise. In so doing, I control for a variety of factors important to explaining voting decisions in presidential elections (see the appendix to this chapter for variable coding).

## Results and Discussion of the 1996 Presidential Race in California

Table 6.5 shows the probit estimates for the 1996 presidential race in California. The first column of the table reports the results for all voters regardless of whether they claimed Proposition 209 was important to their presidential vote choice. The results suggest that voters who supported Proposition 209 intended to vote for Dole, but the split-sample analysis suggests that the association between presidential vote choice and CCRI is driven by respondents who said that Proposition 209 was important to their presidential vote choice. The coefficient for Proposition 209 among voters who said that the initiative was important is positive and significant whereas for voters who claimed the initiative was unimportant it is negative and not statistically different from zero. Directly comparing the coefficients for Proposition 209 across groups indicates that the difference is statistically significant. Both the likelihood ratio test (p = .04) and Wald chi-square test (p = .05) indicate significant differences between voters who mentioned Proposition 209 as important to their presidential vote choice and those who did not.

The changes in probability clarify the effects of the results from table 6.5 (results not shown). Holding all other variables at their mean, if a voter intends to vote yes on Proposition 209, his or her probability of

TABLE 6.5
The Priming Effect of Proposition 209 on Voting for the Republican Presidential
Candidate in California's 1996 Elections

| Variables | All Voters | Prop. 209 Is Important | Prop. 209 Is Not Important |
|---|---|---|---|
| Proposition 209 | .27** | .66** | −.10 |
| | (.117) | (.211) | (.281) |
| Republican | .89** | .81** | 1.00** |
| | (.122) | (.217) | (.288) |
| Conservative | .57** | .57* | .86** |
| | (.121) | (.221) | (.279) |
| Clinton opinion | −1.83** | −1.88** | −1.74** |
| | (.122) | (.218) | (.276) |
| White | .31* | .50* | −.28 |
| | (.139) | (.224) | (.342) |
| Constant | −.51** | −.82* | −.10 |
| | (.168) | (.295) | (.392) |
| N | 978 | 328 | 178 |
| Chi-squared | 721** | 247** | 126** |
| % Predicted correctly | 88 | 90 | 87 |
| Proportional reduction in error | .66 | .69 | .63 |

Source: Field Poll (October 1–9).
Note: Entries in parentheses are standard errors. Dependent variable = 1 if voted for Dole, 0 if otherwise. Number of respondents in the split-sample analyses does not equal the number of respondents in analysis for all voters because of missing data.
*significant at the .01 level (one-tailed test)
**significant at the .001 level (one-tailed test)

voting for Dole is .20 greater than a voter who intends to vote no on the initiative. To give a better sense of this quantity, all else equal, holding a favorable opinion of Clinton lowers that probability of voting for Dole by .58 compared to voters holding an unfavorable opinion of Clinton. Republican Party identification produces the next largest change in probability. A shift from Independent or Democratic Party identifier to Republican Party identifier increases the probability of a Dole vote by .26. The difference between opposing and supporting 209 increases the probability of voting for Dole from .15 to .35, a substantial change. So, did Proposition 209 help Dole among any voters? Holding all else equal, a white conservative who intended to vote against Proposition 209 had a probability of voting for Dole of .29 whereas this same voter had a probability of .54 of voting for Dole if he or she supported CCRI. Thus, it seems that Proposition 209 may have been more effective for Dole in shoring up his base than peeling votes away from Clinton or winning over undecided voters.

In contrast, the change in probability for voters who said that Proposition 209 was unimportant to their presidential vote is negative (−.04) and the effect is not statistically different from zero. Changes in probability for these voters suggests that voters relied more heavily on party identification (.35) and ideology (.32) since these quantities are considerably larger than those for voters who mentioned Prop. 209 as important to their presidential vote.

Many Republicans had probably recognized before the 1996 elections that Clinton was likely to defeat Dole in California and that Proposition 209 would not likely alter this outcome. However, much more was at stake given that the Republicans wanted to protect their new majorities in the House and Senate. Furthermore, California Republicans wanted to protect their new majority in the state assembly and add seats to their growing numbers in the state senate.

## Proposition 209 and Down-Ballot Races

Moving toward the 1996 elections, Republican Party officials were likely concerned with down-ballot races, especially those for U.S. House of Representatives. In 1994, Republicans had taken control of the House for the first time in forty-two years and were concerned about keeping their new majority status. In addition, for the first time since 1970, the 1994 elections brought Republicans a thin majority in the California State Assembly (41 Republicans, 37 Democrats). Because of this, coupled with a strong desire to erode the Democrats' thin majority in the California State Senate (22 Democrats, 16 Republicans, 2 other), 1996 represented a crucial election year.

But, 1996 did not look as if it would be a great year for Republican candidates, at least insofar as the top of the ticket was concerned. The 1996 Republican presidential candidate, Robert Dole, did not look as if he was going to defeat President Clinton much less provide Republican down-ballot candidates any boost. Indeed, Clinton's commanding lead for most of the campaign suggested that if any party's down-ballot candidates would do well they would be Democrats. As mentioned, the state Republican Party helped qualify Proposition 209 and fund campaign ads in hopes of defining the agenda with a winning issue. Did it work? On election day, Dole lost in California and three Republican House incumbents in California were defeated. In the state legislative races, Republicans lost seats in both chambers. Democratic gains in the assembly races were especially vital given that Democrats regained majority party status. Although the election returns suggest that Proposition 209 did not have the effect that Republican strategists had hoped, it still might have diminished the loss of seats for down-ballot Republican candidates.

Studying the impact of Proposition 209 on voting for House and state legislative candidates lends insight into the effects of agendas down the ballot. Although I argue that agendas affect voting for offices similarly, their ability to do so depends on the visibility of candidates. By examining presidential, House, California State Senate, and California State Assembly races, I test the hypothesis that agenda effects diminish with less visible offices. As elaborated in chapter 2, the link between an issue and a candidate is less likely to develop or be strengthened with an unknown candidate. In other words, agendas are less potent for obscure offices.

Of the down-ballot offices examined, I assume House candidates are the most visible, assembly candidates the least visible, and that the visibility of state senate candidates falls someplace in between. This ranking follows the conventional wisdom about the relative importance or influence of elected offices. All else equal, pundits consider a seat in the House of Representatives more important than a seat in the California state legislature. In the California state legislature, all else equal, many consider a seat in the assembly less important than a seat in the senate because the former has eighty members who serve two-year terms and the latter has a membership half as large that serves four-year terms.

Campaign expenditures are another way of looking at the relative visibility of candidates. Jacobson (2001, chap. 5) shows that voters' ability to recognize or recall the name of a House challenger rises with increases in campaign spending. Working from the assumption that campaign spending translates into candidate visibility, the average (median) campaign expenditure by district for each office suggests that candidates in House contests are the best known among the down-ballot offices. The average House contest witnessed spending of $598,520.[6] In addition, the average state senate candidate was more visible than the average assembly candidate, at least insofar as campaign expenditures heighten visibility. The average state senate contest witnessed total spending of $423,346, whereas the average assembly contest witnessed total spending of $353,551.[7] Despite the variability of spending for a given office type, these figures suggest that awareness of down-ballot candidates varies across offices.

While the amount of information about candidates varies across offices, the content of candidates' campaigns did not include much discussion of Proposition 209. Descriptive accounts of the races suggest that CCRI was not a major campaign issue for many of the down-ballot candidates. For the House races, descriptive accounts of the candidates' campaigns from the *California Journal* and the *Almanac of American Politics* reveal that only three House contests emphasized Proposition 209 or affirmative action. The descriptive account of the state legislative races from the *California Journal* shows that the initiative might have played an even smaller role since only one assembly race, and none of the state senate races, emphasized affirmative action or Proposition 209. If Proposition 209 played a significant role in the down-ballot races, then, it is likely due to spillover effects given the absence of the initiative from candidates' campaigns.

Although candidate visibility and agenda effects explain the role of agendas in nonpresidential elections, they do not do the same for presidential contests. Presidential candidates command much more attention. These contests provide voters with a large amount of individuating information that may diminish the spillover potential of agendas. Dole made an effort to attach his candidacy to Proposition 209, but because there are so many more potential considerations that voters may draw on in presidential races (e.g., the national economy), the effect of a visible issue, especially one that is not a defining issue, is necessarily less. Had Dole emphasized CCRI throughout his campaign, my expectation is that it would have had a greater effect on presidential vote choice than in any of the down-ballot contests. However, since Dole did not make it a defining issue early in the campaign and because the poll was taken prior to his emphasizing the issue, I have no clear expectation about its effect on presidential voting as compared to the down-ballot offices.

Given my expectation about the interrelatedness of voting decisions across offices, I use multivariate probit analysis. Table 6.6 presents the estimates of a multivariate probit analysis of voting for a Republican presidential, House, state senate, and assembly candidate using the same predictors as before. The rho coefficients suggest that voting decisions for these offices are statistically related and thus share a common evaluative base. The sizes of the coefficients vary considerably across different pairings of offices, indicating varying degrees of interrelatedness. The size of the rho coefficients among voting decisions for down-ballot offices are much larger (e.g., House and state senate) than those pairing a vote for president with a down-ballot race (e.g., president and assembly). Thus, despite institutional arrangements demarcating federal and state policy responsibilities (voting decisions for House and president should be highly related because they are both federal offices and share responsibility over national policymaking), the rho coefficients indicate that voting decisions for House have more in common with voting decisions for state senate and assembly. In short, these results suggest that information differences among offices, not institutional arrangements, structure voting decisions.

TABLE 6.6
Multivariate Probit Estimates of the Priming Effect of Proposition 209 on Voting for Republican Presidential, House, and State Legislative Candidates

| Variables | Coefficient | Standard Error |
|---|---|---|
| President | | |
| Proposition 209 | .39* | .176 |
| Republican | .77*** | .189 |
| Conservative | .51** | .186 |
| Clinton opinion | −2.02*** | .185 |
| White | .30 | .199 |
| Constant | −.32 | .238 |
| House | | |
| Proposition 209 | .39** | .155 |
| Republican | 1.10*** | .169 |
| Conservative | .74*** | .164 |
| Clinton opinion | −1.00*** | .172 |
| White | .28 | .178 |
| Constant | −1.08*** | .246 |
| State Senate | | |
| Proposition 209 | .32* | .155 |
| Republican | 1.07*** | .168 |
| Conservative | .59** | .166 |
| Clinton opinion | −1.18*** | .172 |
| White | .33* | .176 |
| Constant | −.94*** | .239 |
| Assembly | | |
| Proposition 209 | .13 | .152 |
| Republican | .82*** | .168 |
| Conservative | .71*** | .163 |
| Clinton opinion | −1.21*** | .169 |
| White | .33* | .169 |
| Constant | −.62** | .233 |
| rho (president & House) | .48*** | .086 |
| rho (president & state senate) | .41*** | .094 |
| rho (president & assembly) | .45*** | .087 |
| rho (House & state senate) | .78*** | .046 |
| rho (House & assembly) | .78*** | .047 |
| rho (state senate & assembly) | .80*** | .045 |
| N | 454 | |
| Log likelihood | −476.83 | |
| Wald Chi-square | 434*** | |

Source: Field Poll (October 1–9).
Note: Coefficients are simulated maximum-likelihood estimates using the GHK smooth recursive simulator. Dependent variables = 1 if voted for Republican, 0 if otherwise.
    *p < .05 (one-tailed test)   **p < .01 level (one-tailed test)
  ***p < .001 level (one-tailed test)

What role did Proposition 209 play in these elections? The coefficients for Proposition 209 are statistically significant for three of the four offices. Thus, although CCRI infiltrated most of the significant down-ballot contests, its effect on voting for the least visible office, the assembly, is not statistically distinguishable from zero. The size of the coefficients across the down-ballot offices also suggests that the effects of Proposition 209 diminished with candidate visibility. The coefficient for Proposition 209 is more than twice as large in the state senate race as it is the assembly race. Although the difference is not as great, the coefficient for Proposition 209 in the state senate race is considerably smaller than the coefficients for the House or presidential contests.

Figure 6.4 shows the effects of Proposition 209 on voting for these offices by depicting changes in probabilities. Examining the probability of voting for each office individually, a voter in favor of Proposition 209 has a probability of voting for a Republican House candidate .14 greater than a voter opposed to the initiative, holding other variables at their mean. The effect is the same for the presidential contest. Moving down the ballot, the same change for state senate and state assembly is .11 and .05, respectively. Thus, among the down-ballot races, decreasing candidate visibility dampened the impact of Proposition 209. Collectively, the effect of Proposition 209 on voting for all four GOP candidates was modest but not surprising given the large impact of partisan identification and incumbency cues in the down-ballot contests. If a voter supported Proposition 209, his or her probability of voting for all four candidates is .05 greater than a voter who opposed CCRI.

To gain a better sense of the range over which these changes occur, observe Figure 6.5, which depicts the predicted probabilities of voting for Republican candidates by support for Proposition 209. As shown in figure 6.5A, Proposition 209 had similar effects on voting for Dole and Republican House candidates. An opponent of Proposition 209 had a probability of voting for the Republican House candidate of .27 whereas a supporter had a .41 probability. The amount of the change is identical for Dole, moving from .25 to .39 between Proposition 209 opponents and supporters. Figure 6.5B depicts the same changes for state legislative offices. These changes are very similar to those of the federal offices. A voter opposed to Proposition 209 had a probability of voting for a Republican state senate candidate of .26 whereas a supporter of the initiative had a .38 probability. The same change for the assembly ranges from .34 to .39 between opponents and supporters of CCRI, respectively. In addition, the probability of voting Republican for all four candidates was .09 among voters opposed to Proposition 209 and .15 among supporters of the initiative. For the "average" California voter in 1996, then, Proposition 209 was not much of a wedge issue in voting for Republican candidates separately or together.

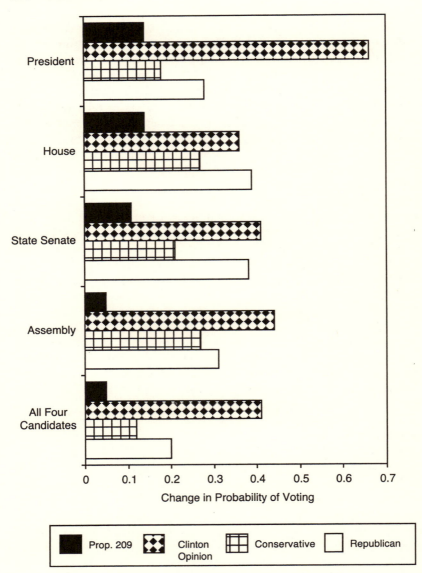

Fig. 6.4.  The Priming Effect of Proposition 209 on Voting for Republican Candidates in California's 1996 Elections (Change in Probabilities)

*Note*: Quantities represent changes in probabilities of voting for the Republican candidate calculated by looking at a minimum to maximum change in an independent variable holding all other variables at their mean values. Absolute values reported.

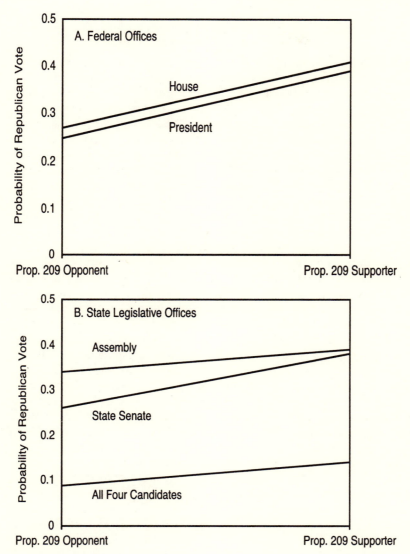

Fig. 6.5. The Priming Effect of Proposition 209 on Voting for Republican Candidates in California's 1996 Elections (Predicted Probabilities)

*Note*: Quantities represent predicted probabilities of voting for the Republican candidate looking at differences between Proposition 209 opponents and supporters holding all other variables at their mean values.

## CONCLUSION

The Republican Party's strategy of using ballot initiatives to set the agenda in California met with mixed results. In 1994, Proposition 187 helped Republican gubernatorial, Senate, and House candidates. The issue appeared to sway Independent, and to a lesser extent Democratic, voters to choose Republican candidates. In 1996, on the other hand, Proposition 209 had lesser effects. It did little to move the average voter to choose Republican candidates. Yet, despite Proposition 209's inability to move the average voter, it nonetheless affected voting decisions across offices and may well have dampened GOP losses in what was a strong year for Democrats. In each type of race, with the exception of the less visible assembly races, ballot propositions on illegal immigration and affirmative action primed voting decisions across offices.

The more influential of the two initiatives, Proposition 187, had the greatest effect on its biggest supporter, Pete Wilson. Michael Huffington also benefited from Proposition 187, but it had a lesser effect on his candidacy. These findings are consistent with the visibility hypothesis: all else equal, agenda issues are more likely to prime voting decisions for visible candidates. Yet, because both candidates campaigned on Proposition 187, it is difficult to say how much of the initiative's influence is due to a traditional campaign effect (e.g., a voter evaluates a candidate on the basis of an issue the candidate campaigned on) or a spillover effect (e.g., a voter evaluates a candidate on the basis of a salient issue regardless of whether the candidate campaigned on it). The former represents a conventional application of priming in political science research in which the prime is explicitly linked to the target of evaluation, whereas the latter represents an indiscriminate priming effect in which the two need not be explicitly linked, but both need to be visible. Thus, despite evidence of priming effects, I cannot disentangle which of the two processes—direct or indiscriminate priming—is responsible.

The down-ballot races enabled me to better evaluate these processes since the candidates have low or, in some cases, minuscule visibility. In these contests, it does not matter much if candidates did or did not campaign on an issue because most voters will not have heard anything they had to say. Thus, if the issue had an effect on voters in these contests it is likely the product of an agenda issue's indiscriminately priming voters—a spillover effect. The results from this chapter suggest that ballot initiatives influenced voting for down-ballot candidates. Both propositions affected voting decisions for House candidates, even though most voters probably did not hear much from these candidates and many of them avoided any campaign talk about these initiatives. In the case of Proposition 209, I found that it breached state senate races but not state assembly races. These results are consistent with the visibility hypothesis that agenda issues have diminishing effects as the visibility of offices diminish. Indeed, among the down-ballot races, the effect of Proposition 209 was greatest for House races, the most visible of these offices. In comparison, Proposition 209 had the least effect on voting decisions in assembly races, the least visible of these offices. And its effect on voting for state senate candidates, races that are typically more visible than those for assembly but less than those for House, fell between contests for these other offices.

The results from this chapter clearly demonstrate that issues on the ballot affect voting decisions across offices. Nevertheless, why these initiatives? My argument, in brief, was that Propositions 187 and 209 primed racial attitudes. In so doing, they heightened racial resentments and these attitudes were partly, if not mostly, responsible for why these initiatives mattered. Furthermore, consistent with Mendelberg (2001), the likely reason that these initiatives were effective in shaping voting decisions was that racial attitudes were implicitly primed—had the initiatives been blatantly racist, voters would have rejected them as a violation of the norm of racial equality. Neither ballot initiative was explicitly about race, but implicitly race was likely the reason voters cared about them. However, because the initiatives were not blatantly racist, it is difficult to say how much race mattered. Thus, whereas my results demonstrate clearly the effects of ballot initiatives, my claim of racial priming rests more on qualitative grounds.

Finally, these results speak to whether voters use institutional responsibilities in reaching voting decisions. Sorting out whether institutional responsibilities might account for these differences is confusing and may even illustrate the futility of such an approach for most issues. As governor, Wilson clearly had responsibility for dealing with the issue of illegal immigration since illegal immigrants consume public goods and influence the state's economy. Yet Wilson also made the case that the federal government should shoulder some of the burden placed on the state by illegal immigrants. In other words, the issue had both state and federal dimensions. The line separating state and federal functions is probably clearer in the case of Proposition 209. Proposition 209 was clearly a state issue. The initiative dealt with state public policy, and the federal government had no responsibility for its implementation. Nevertheless, voters did not seem to care about this distinction when voting for president or U.S. House of Representatives. While voters linked Proposition 209 to candidates running for federal offices, they did not do so uniformly for state offices. California voters evaluated state senate candidates in light of Proposition 209, but they did not do the same for state assembly candidates. The dividing line between whether voters link issues to candidates turns on candidate and issue visibility rather than institutional responsibilities.

## APPENDIX

### Proposition 187 Analyses, VNS Exit Poll (Tables 6.1, 6.2, and 6.3)

| | |
|---|---|
| *Proposition 187* | Coded one (1) if respondents indicated that they voted yes on Proposition 187 and zero (0) otherwise. |
| *Party identification* | Coded one (1) for Republican, zero (0) for Independent, and negative one (−1) for Democrat. |
| *Ideology* | Coded one (1) for conservative, zero (0) for moderate, and negative one (−1) for Democrat. |
| *Presidential approval* | Coded one (1) if respondents approved of President Clinton's job performance and zero (0) otherwise. |
| *State economy* | Coded three (3) if respondents believed the condition of California's economy was poor, two (2) if they believed it was not so good, one (1) if they believed it was good, and zero (0) if they believed it was excellent. |
| *Crime* | Coded (1) one if respondents checked that crime mattered most in voting for an office and zero (0) otherwise. Since the question was asked separately for each office, this variable takes on different values depending on whether the dependent variable is for the Senate or gubernatorial contest. |
| *Economy and jobs* | Coded one (1) if respondents checked that the economy or jobs mattered most in voting for an office and zero (0) otherwise. Since the question was asked separately for each office, this variable takes on different values depending on whether the dependent variable is for the Senate or gubernatorial contest. |

### Proposition 187 Analysis, Field Poll Survey (Table 6.4)

| | |
|---|---|
| *Proposition 187* | Coded one (1) if respondents indicated they intended to vote yes on Proposition 187 and zero (0) otherwise. |
| *Republican* | Coded one (1) for Republican, zero (0) otherwise. |
| *Conservative* | Coded one (1) for conservative, zero (0) otherwise. |

| | |
|---|---|
| *Elect Clinton* | Coded one (1) if respondents said they would be strongly inclined or somewhat inclined to vote for President Clinton if the election were held today and zero (0) if they were not inclined or had no opinion. |
| *Proposition 184* | Coded one (1) if respondents indicated they intended to vote yes on Proposition 184 and zero (0) otherwise. |
| *Crime* | Coded one (1) if respondents checked that crime mattered most in voting for an office and zero (0) otherwise. Since the question was asked separately for each office, this variable takes on different values depending on whether the dependent variable is for the Senate or gubernatorial contest. |
| *Economy and jobs* | Coded one (1) if respondents checked that the economy or jobs mattered most in voting for an office and zero (0) otherwise. Since the question was asked separately for each office, this variable takes on different values depending on whether the dependent variable is for the Senate or gubernatorial contest. |

## *Proposition 209 Analyses, Field Poll Data (Tables 6.5 and 6.6)*

| | |
|---|---|
| *Proposition 209* | Coded one (1) if respondents indicated they intended to vote yes on Proposition 209 and zero (0) otherwise. |
| *Republican* | Coded one (1) for Republican, zero (0) otherwise. |
| *Conservative* | Coded one (1) for conservative, zero (0) otherwise. |
| *Clinton opinion* | Coded one (1) if respondents said they had a favorable opinion of President Clinton and zero (0) otherwise. |
| *White* | Coded one (1) if respondents indicated they were non-Hispanic white and zero (0) otherwise. |

## Chapter 7

## DIRECT DEMOCRACY: THE PEOPLE'S AGENDA?

In this book, I have shown that agendas affect voting decisions. Specifically, I have demonstrated that the issues raised by direct legislation affect voters' candidate evaluations for a variety of offices regardless of the institutional responsibilities associated with an office or whether the issue is somehow a part of the campaign for an office. Ballot measures on topics such as abortion, the nuclear freeze, or affirmative action define voting decisions by increasing the salience of issues. By infusing politics with common concerns, agendas tie voting decisions together across elected offices.

What does this mean for democratic theory? On the one hand, voting for candidates based on policy issues is helpful to democracy. Among the reasons a voter may choose candidates, democratic theorists favor issue voting above all others. Voting for candidates based on policy issues thus meets democratic objectives. On the other hand, democracy is undermined when voters do not participate in deciding on what issues matter. If voters are not involved in constructing the agenda, popular control is subverted and so is democracy. The question of agenda control, then, is crucial to understanding the democratic implications of agendas. However, since I have shown that direct legislation sets the agenda in candidate races, it is important to explore whether issues moved onto the agenda by direct legislation differ meaningfully from those that move onto the agenda through traditional campaign means. If direct legislation enhances or hinders agenda control by the people, my results have important implications for representative democracy.

According to Dahl (1989, chap. 8), a *fully* democratic system should include, among other things, *final* agenda control by the people or, to use Dahl's term, *demos*. In his words, *"The demos must have the exclusive opportunity to decide how matters are to be placed on the agenda of matters that are to be decided by means of the democratic process"* (113, emphasis original). This does not mean that the people need to be involved in every agenda decision but only that they have an opportunity for final control over the agenda should they find it necessary. To illustrate the implications of agenda control, Dahl conceives of a country in which an antidemocratic movement seizes power and modifies the constitution so that the people can only address nonsignificant issues such as traffic control. Such a change, he concludes, is "a travesty of democracy" because the people are no longer sovereign in setting the agenda. For Dahl, final agenda control by the people is as important as other democratic requisites such as effective, informed, and equal participation.

Barber (1984, 180–81) is equally insistent about the role of agendas in democracy. He observes that "a people that does not set its own agenda, by means of talk and direct political exchange, not only relinquishes a vital power of government but also exposes its remaining powers of deliberation and decision to ongoing subversion. What counts as an 'issue' or a 'problem' and how such issues and problems are formulated may to a large extent predetermine what decisions are reached" (181). Thus, both Dahl and Barber recognize the crucial importance of agenda control: agenda-setters establish the dialogue and the procedures for voting that shape political outcomes.

Despite Dahl and Barber's recognition that agendas matter, they underestimate their importance. Both theorists conceive of agenda deliberation narrowly, primarily focusing on a given public policy proposal. While not wrong, this view is incomplete in that it neglects *electoral settings*. In elections, deliberation on an issue means more than simply deciding the outcome of a given policy proposal. It is about problems the people want their elected leaders to solve. In this way, the agenda determines what politics is about and implicitly what voting means. Thus, agendas have sweeping effects on representative government and important implications for democratic control.

## WHO CONTROLS THE AGENDA?

Who controls the agenda? Barber would say that the people should be the primary impetus for policy proposals in a "strong democracy," but he, like Dahl and other contemporary democratic theorists, recognizes that citizens do not play such a role. Indeed, Barber and other contemporary democratic theorists correctly understand agenda-setting as a top-down process wherein leaders place issues before the people. One variant of this view held by Schumpeter (1976) is that the people have no meaningful say in setting the agenda.[1] He argues that elites "fashion and . . . create the will of the people" (263). If Schumpeter is correct in arguing that the will of the people is "manufactured," democracy is a sham. But, there is good reason to believe Schumpeter is wrong. Empirical work on voting and elections suggests that campaigns activate voters' latent predispositions about which issues are important (Berelson, Lazarsfeld, and McPhee 1954; Gelman and King 1993; Hutchings 2003; also see Zaller 1992). Thus, electoral agendas are democratic in the sense that the people play arbiter concerning which issues belong and which issues do not. If the people do not find an issue important, there is little that elites can do to persuade them otherwise.

While agenda control in democratic elections may be top-down, the public retains a crucial role. To set the agenda, candidates and parties appeal to voters' latent attitudes about what is politically important. This is no easy task since the issues that resonate with voters vary across time and space. Even popular policy proposals do not resonate with voters all the time. Ronald Reagan had success capturing voter attention with tax cut proposals in 1980, but Bob Dole did not in 1996. Access to voters, then, is insufficient for shaping their priorities—voters must agree, at least implicitly, that an issue is important. In this regard, the people are at least "semi-sovereign" because they play the important role of arbiter in the democratic process (Schattschneider 1960). Since voters have an implicit say in what is on the agenda in democratic elections, agenda control does not subvert the democratic process. Thus, even if only the few have access to the agenda, the many reside over its content by vetoing issues. In this way, agenda control in mass elections conforms to Dahl's democratic ideal—the people retain final agenda control.

Given that the people ultimately decide which issues matter, elections in the United States have an unquestionably democratic character to them. Central to the people's (implicitly) deciding what is important is the absence of institutional arrangements for agenda-setting. Absent institutions, agendas are preference induced—the people may not have put an issue on the agenda, but they decide whether it belongs. Thus, in contrast to agenda-setting in a legislative body where actors use institutional rules for manipulating agendas, candidates and parties in mass elections prime issues. In order for these issues to make it onto the agenda, they must resonate with voters. Sometimes this works but often it does not. Because the people ultimately preside over what is acceptable fodder for agendas, democratic elections simply do not lend themselves to the intricate maneuverings of the legislative setting where rules and procedures often thwart majoritarian preferences.

## Direct Legislation and Agenda Control

Ironically, direct legislation may diminish agenda control by the people. Born a tool of the people, direct legislation is supposed to empower the people to set their own agenda should their representatives fail to address issues important to them. While this happens some of the time (e.g., California's tax revolt), interest groups mostly use direct legislation in furthering their own goals. Despite its populist roots and ill-deserved reputation as a tool of the people, then, direct legislation dampens popular control of the agenda. Over twenty years ago Magleby warned how "the agenda of issues to be decided by voters is determined by proponents' capacity to hire professional signature gathering firms or by the dedication of issue-activists or single-issue groups who desire to place measures on the ballot" (1984, 182). Little has changed. If anything, the process is less accessible to the people today (see Broder 2000; Ellis 2002, chap. 3; McCuan et al. 1998). As a matter for public decision, there is little or no debate over whether a proposed issue for the ballot is politically important. Of course, many issues on the ballot do not capture public attention (e.g., denturism), but given the right issue and the right circumstances, the legitimacy bestowed by direct legislation may heighten an issue's importance. Thus, in contrast to criticisms of direct legislation's being overly responsive to majority preferences, it is more likely the case that at least insofar as agenda control is concerned, the process gives greater weight to minority preferences.

Although I do not wish to push this point too far, the institutional "legs" given an issue by direct legislation may undermine the public's role in elections. In this way, direct legislation may be more destructive of democratic aims than previously recognized. Although wealthy interests cannot "dupe" voters to pass laws they do not like (Bowler and Donovan 1998; Gerber 1999; Lupia 1994), money buys legitimacy for an issue simply by virtue of getting it on the ballot. Since direct legislation removes the question of whether issues are politically relevant, it can alter voters' predispositions about an issue's importance and, in doing so, may dampen the implicit gatekeeping role the people play in deciding which issues are worthy of agenda status.

The loss of agenda control has significant implications for representative democracy since direct legislation shapes the agenda for candidate races. I found that ballot measures on the nuclear freeze, abortion, taxes, the environment, illegal immigration, and affirmative action primed the evaluative criteria voters used to choose candidates, irrespective of whether an issue was relevant to the duties of an office or whether the issue was discussed by candidates in a particular contest. In my analyses, the major divide between whether or how much a ballot measure influenced candidate voting was the visibility of candidates. The less visible the candidates, the less likely that an association between candidates and ballot measures would form. Otherwise, candidate evaluations shared the same basis of evaluation. Although many democratic theorists would embrace the idea of voters using shared policy considerations for voting decisions up and down the ballot, they would admonish such behavior if voters had no role in choosing the issues. While it is difficult to speculate about such matters, it seems unlikely that illegal immigration would have been the major issue it was in California's 1994 elections had it not been on the ballot.[2] The fact that the issue was on the ballot directed attention toward illegal immigrants and away from California's ailing economy. Wilson and other Republican candidates, of course, cultivated the illegal immigration issue, but had it not been on the ballot, Wilson's opponent, Kathleen Brown, could have argued that the economy was the important issue. Voters then could have decided (implicitly) which candidate's agenda made sense. Proposition 187 helped erase this possibility.

None of this discussion about the importance of ballot measures in setting the agenda is new to party strategists. As I made clear in chapter 3, both Democrats and Republicans have used direct legislation as a tool for shaping the agenda. Despite the costs and risks involved, I expect this process to continue in California and beyond. For the 2004 elections, state legislatures in Georgia, Kentucky, Mississippi, Oklahoma, and Utah have approved placing state constitutional amendments on the ballot for voters to decide whether to ban gay marriages. At the time I write this, signatures are being gathered in Arkansas, Massachusetts, Michigan, Montana, North Dakota, Ohio, and Oregon to place initiatives on the ballot proposing to ban gay marriage (Peterson 2004). Although Republican state party organizations are not backing these ballot measures explicitly, the partisan dimensions are unmistakable.

In Georgia, for example, Republican state legislators were the driving force behind the constitutional amendment proposal. Despite the fact that the Georgia legislature had passed a law in 1996 prohibiting gay marriage, Republican backers of a ban on gay marriage and civil unions insist that the state's constitution must be amended to ensure that judges do not circumvent the law. The presence of this issue on the ballot during the presidential election year is not lost on Democrats. Ryan Lee, a reporter for the *Southern Voice*, wrote the following with regard to State Senator Vincent Fort (D-Atlanta): "Republicans hope to use the issue [gay marriage] as a wedge issue to turn out the conservative vote, a tactic that may impact his Democratic colleagues" (Lee 2004). None of this is to say that the backers of the resolution are not sincere in their beliefs and values on this issue (they certainly are), only that they and their political opponents understand the strong electoral implications of ballot measures for setting the electoral agenda.

This discussion underscores the tension between direct (or popular) and representative democracy. On the one hand, direct legislation is the most democratic of institutions in the United States since it allows the people to decide matters of public policy directly. In addition, many scholars have found that it enhances the quality of democratic life by increasing political efficacy (Bowler and Donovan 2002; Gilens, Glaser, and Mendelberg 2001), participation (M. Smith 2001; Tolbert, Grummel, and Smith 2001), and knowledge (M. Smith 2002). Direct legislation thus helps promote Barber's notion of "strong democracy" since it promotes democratic engagement. On the other hand, as I have argued, direct legislation diminishes the role of the people in deciding what issues matter in an election. Because any person or group with ample financial resources may qualify an issue for the ballot, direct legislation lessens the people's prerogative for deciding what is politically important. In this way, direct legislation brings us closer to Schumpeter's notion of a "manufactured will," a subversion of rule by the people. Since I have shown that what is politically important influences the people's choice of candidates, a "manufactured" agenda has significant and negative implications for representative democracy. The character of *representative democracy* in states with direct legislation may be of lesser quality than that found in states without direct legislation.

This creates something of a democratic dilemma. Is it more desirable for the people to choose elected representatives under an agenda in which they had a role in constructing but cannot directly decide matters of public policy, or is it more desirable to let them choose elected representatives and decide directly matters of public policy where the agenda was chosen for them? Which is better for democracy? Since final agenda control by the people is an essential feature of representative democracy, I tentatively conclude that it is more desirable for the people to have agenda control. But, I am hesitant to draw strong conclusions without further empirical research on the prevalence of "manufactured" agendas by direct legislation. I have asserted that most issues placed on the agenda by direct legislation would not have been on the agenda absent placing the matter on the ballot. However, further research on this matter will have to answer this question and doing such research would be most difficult.

It is unfeasible, of course, to suggest getting rid of direct legislation for a seemingly undistorted agenda because citizens overwhelmingly support the ability to vote on matters of public policy and because people view agendas "as fixed and self-evident, almost natural, and in this sense incidental to such vital democratic processes as deliberation and decision-making" (Barber 1984, 180–81). Thus, direct legislation is a tangible thing whereas an agenda is not; making an argument for getting rid of the former to preserve the integrity of the latter would be unpalatable to many citizens.

## IMPLICATIONS FOR EMPIRICAL RESEARCH

The implications of my research for the empirical study of voting and elections are significant as well. Here, I elaborate on areas that could usefully be addressed in future research.

One area for future research concerns the heterogeneity of agenda effects, for both voters and issues. In this book, I argue that agendas have blunt effects, but I also show that they have a greater effect on some voters. Compared to partisans, for example, agendas had a greater effect on shaping the votes of Independents. Yet agendas may also affect voters differently across levels of political knowledge (e.g., Zaller 1992) or social groups (e.g., Hutchings 2003). Although I did not focus on these distinctions, they may lend insight into how agendas affect voters differentially. As with voters, issues exhibit heterogeneity as well. For this reason, future research might examine the varying effects of agenda issues across varying levels of salience. Here, I defined an issue on the agenda simply by whether it appeared on the ballot. Obviously, as the results in chapter 4 suggest, not all ballot measures are equally well-known. Although it is typically safe to assume that abortion ballot measures are salient, it is probably not safe to assume that all tax and environmental ballot measures have the same stature. As a highly charged issue, abortion typically captures the attention of the electorate whereas tax and environmental issues likely vary significantly in the voter attention they receive. Further research might uncover greater agenda effects if analysts distinguish lesser-known issues from better-known issues.

National issues often dominate the agenda, and one could apply my theory of agenda voting here as well. Some of the most commanding issues in this study hailed from national issues in the 1982 and 1994 midterm elections. For example, although the *Contract with America* did not appear much in individual campaigns for the House and Senate in the 1994 midterm elections, some of its components nationalized political discourse and affected many races. My theory of agenda voting would predict that the most visible candidates running for House and Senate had elements of the *Contract with America* spill over into their contests even if candidates ignored them. Since the visibility of candidates plays a crucial role in attaching issues to candidates, it may help explain why some issues from the *Contract* had such a big effect in 1994 despite their absence from many House and Senate campaigns. All of this suggests that while I have made exclusive use of states in this book, the theory is applicable beyond them.

My results strongly suggest that students of voting behavior should include the most salient information found in voters' information environments, which in practice oftentimes means state electoral environments. Beneath the surface of national politics, even in midterm elections with a strong national pulse, lives a neglected world of electoral issues. These issues stem from the efforts of candidates, political parties, interest groups, and media working within distinct electoral environments and they contribute in significant ways to what voters think is politically important. Although scholars have done substantial work in defining issues for particular contests in states (e.g., Kahn and Kenney 1999), work on nonpresidential elections needs to pay attention to the significance of other statewide campaigns as an important repository of agenda issues.

Beyond agendas, my study has important implications for the role of information in elections. Most studies of low-information contests neglect the electoral environment beyond the type of race under the analyst's microscope. But this is a limited approach. In contrast, I found that voters rely heavily on the information most accessible to them carried by the political environment. Sometimes the political environment will carry a sufficient amount of information about a contest so that voters may draw on the campaign issues found in that race or institutional requirements associated with an office. On other occasions the issues voters use in making candidate judgments for a given office will arrive from other sources such as campaigns for a different contest or, as documented here, ballot initiatives and referenda.

To gain a better sense of why this is so, one need not build a new theory of voting but only use what scholars have known for some time about the role of information in voter decision making. Given the large body of research that shows voters are uninformed about politics, conventional approaches assume a great deal of sophistication. In so doing, however, the implications of "low-information rationality" or "cue-taking" do not receive full consideration. The departure I make questions the practice of placing voters into neat boxes (by office) and assuming they only use information from within that box without regard to what is happening outside that box.

None of this is to suggest that we abandon the study of elections and voting by office. Rather, my research suggests that scholars should not make too much of these distinctions because voters do not care about them all that much. In my view, voters see candidates as very similar political objects and do not expend energy differentiating them by office or campaign messages. The political environment, especially agenda issues, infuses voting decisions with common meaning in this way. Agendas thus tie voting decisions together. Unfortunately, many approaches neglect the rich and diverse information environment that epitomizes U.S. elections (see Huckfeldt and Sprague 1995 for a discussion). I hope that this book helps move scholars toward organizing the study of voting decisions around the most salient morsels of information found in the electoral environment.

# NOTES

CHAPTER 1
KINDRED VOTES: AN INTRODUCTION

1. In all fifty states, citizens may vote on measures that state legislatures place on the ballot. In about half the states, citizens may vote on measures that citizens qualify for the ballot, the initiative and referendum.

2. The notable exception is the influence of presidential campaigns on voting decisions for lower offices (W. Miller 1955–1956; Mondak 1990).

3. Although it makes sense to distinguish voting for school board and Congress, it makes less sense to distinguish offices with broad policymaking powers.

4. Although one can define a campaign issue broadly to include almost any matter discussed in an election (e.g., character), I use the term in a narrower sense, focusing exclusively on policy issues.

5. Representation, of course, makes up the between-election interaction of legislators and constituents and thus provides important insight into how citizens view the institutional roles of House and Senate members.

6. The scholarly debate over the origins of divided government also speaks to whether voters draw on institutional distinctions. Some scholars argue that voters with moderate policy preferences intentionally engage in ticket-splitting to "balance" the parties (Fiorina 1996) while others argue that ticket-splitting is unintentional, a by-product of factors that shape voting behavior such as candidates, partisanship, and campaigns (Burden and Kimball 2002; also see Nicholson, 2005). Although this debate is beyond the scope of the book, my argument is consistent with unintentionalist accounts of divided government since intentionalist approaches presume a sophisticated understanding and application of institutional knowledge.

7. Proponents of on-line models of voter evaluation (e.g., Lodge, McGraw, and Stroh 1989) might argue that such confusion does not demonstrate that voters have not properly linked candidates to issues. More likely, according to the on-line account, voters would incorporate policy issues into their overall impression of a candidate and subsequently discard the information after the evaluation is updated. I address this criticism in chapter 2.

8. To be sure, other forces were, and are, at work in influencing voter decision making. At the time the authors of *The Changing American Voter* wrote, candidate-centered campaigns and longstanding partisan orientations worked to the advantage of Democratic candidates. However, agendas also influence voting behavior indirectly. For instance, we know that the dynamics of both candidate-centered campaigns (Jacobson and Kernell 1983) and partisan identification (Fiorina 1981) are structured in part by the "big" issues of the day.

CHAPTER 2
A THEORY OF AGENDA VOTING

1. Although it is a matter of debate whether media set the agenda or follow political elites, I do not address this debate. For a discussion of who leads public

opinion, see Bartels (1996), Behr and Iyengar (1985), Page and Shapiro (1992), Kuklinski and Segura (1995), and Zaller (1992).

2. Since I am more concerned with how agendas highlight the issues that the public considers politically relevant to voting decisions, I take a big tent approach to discussing where these issues come from by acknowledging that many different actors, of which the media may be foremost, are responsible for setting the agenda.

3. Although priming influences the information individuals bring to bear on political choices, it is important to keep in mind that its effects do not persuade individuals to take one position on an issue over another. As Miller and Krosnick (1996) point out, "[P]riming can be provoked simply by a news story devoting attention to an issue without advocating a position."

4. More generally, B.D. Jones (1994) argues that these types of approaches to political decision making can be subsumed under theories of selective attention in which shifts in context and salience produce shifts in choices but not underlying preferences.

5. For example, individuals who desire to make a social judgment independent of prior context may avoid priming effects (Martin 1986).

6. One thing that might inhibit such a linkage, of course, is the voter. If voting decisions are made with high levels of cognition, issues that are not relevant to a specific contest might be screened out. However, this type of screening is likely uncommon. As mentioned, most voters are unlikely to put this much effort into sorting and filtering electoral information.

7. Schmidt (1989, 27–28) uses the term *spillover effect* to refer to instances where a ballot proposition affects turnout and thus influences candidate races by mobilizing voters with a bias for conservative or liberal candidates. Although I do not directly examine this type of spillover effect, turnout generated by ballot propositions is likely an important factor in shaping the outcomes of some candidate races.

8. Kahn and Kenney (1999) report similar results, noting that about only one-fifth of voters could name an issue from their state's Senate contest.

9. Proponents of the on-line model of political judgment would likely argue that it is irrelevant whether voters correctly identify issues (e.g., Lodge, McGraw, and Stroh 1989; Lodge, Steenbergen, and Brau 1995). For these models, voters process information to form an impression but do not retain it. Later recalling the information is irrelevant because after the voter updates the impression the information is discarded. As discussed, I assume a memory-based model of candidate evaluation wherein voters store information in memory that may be recalled for making a judgment. Although both on-line and memory-based processes are likely at work in the vote decision (Redlawsk 2001), memory-based models provide a more satisfying account of how agenda issues affect candidate evaluation because it is unlikely that salient issues are discarded from memory as the on-line model would predict.

10. Of course, in some instances issue ownership will not influence voting decisions. On issues where neither party has clear ownership, an opponent may decrease an issue's ability to divide the electorate through support for it. Issues such as political reform likely fall into this category.

11. Atkeson and Partin also claim that voters understand these differences, but the evidence they present is not persuasive. In three of the six issues they investigate, the modal response to which office was responsible for handling it was "shared equally" between governor and senator. The responses for the other three questions also show that many citizens believe both governors and senators are jointly responsible.

12. The manner in which a ballot measure can focus attention on an issue is somewhat analogous to the manipulation of rules in a legislature. Therefore, in contrast to elections without ballot issues, legislative politics and direct legislation have equilibria induced through structure rather than (strictly) preference. Although ballot measures are *not* Structure-Induced-Equilibria (SIE), the emphasis on institutions is similar. Shepsle defines a structure-induced equilibrium "as an alternative (status quo ante) that is invulnerable in the sense that no other alternative, allowed by the rules of procedure, is preferred by all the individuals, structural units, and coalitions that possess distinctive veto or voting power" (1989, 137). The essential concepts are procedure and structure. In the U.S. House of Representatives, for example, committees (structure) and rules of debate (procedure) produce equilibria that might not exist in their absence.

CHAPTER 3
STUDYING AGENDAS AND DIRECT LEGISLATION IN U.S. ELECTIONS

1. The manner in which a ballot measure can focus attention on an issue is akin to the manipulation of rules in a legislature (see Shepsle 1989). Therefore, in contrast to elections without ballot measure issues, legislative politics and direct legislation have equilibria induced through structure rather than (strictly) preference. Although ballot measures are *not* technically speaking SIE, the emphasis on institutions is similar.

2. California's Proposition 5 on Indian gaming accounted for over $92 million of the total spending (http://www.Ballotfunding.org).

3. Although the vast majority of voters have little appreciation for the differences, initiatives differ with respect to type and process. There are two types of initiatives: the statutory initiative and the constitutional initiative. Twenty-one states allow the statutory initiative, eighteen states allow initiatives to amend the constitution, and fifteen allow both (Waters 2003). The statutory initiative allows citizens to enact or amend a statute, and the constitutional initiative permits citizens to amend the state constitution, although this distinction is moot for most voters. How an initiative becomes a law, however, directly concerns whether a ballot will be voted on in an election. Specifically, the initiative process can be direct, indirect, or both. Although the process can differ among states with either procedure, the critical difference between them is that the direct initiative requires the issue to be directly voted on and the indirect initiative requires the state legislature's involvement. In most states with the indirect initiative, the legislature is required to consider the legislation before it is placed on the ballot. Should the legislature consider the initiative and reject it, the legislation is placed on the ballot to be decided in the next election. However, if the legislature approves the legislation without substantive change, voters do not consider it. States also differ with

regard to the percentage of signatures required to place an initiative on the ballot and the number of votes to pass an initiative into law. In most states, the number of signatures required to place an initiative on the ballot is some percentage of the vote from the last gubernatorial election. To pass an initiative into law, states typically require a simple majority vote. For a more detailed description of initiatives, see Dubois and Feeney (1998) and Waters (2003).

4. In contrast to the initiative, the referendum allows the electorate to approve or disapprove of statutes proposed or enacted by a legislature. A referendum can be placed on the ballot through citizen petition, referral by the legislature, or constitutional requirement. As with initiatives, the number of signatures required to place a referendum on the ballot is often a specified percentage of the vote in the last gubernatorial election, and a simple majority is typically required to pass a referendum into law. For a more detailed description of referenda, see Waters (2003).

5. Nevertheless, using states as laboratories is still a natural experiment since we cannot randomly assign individuals to treatment groups.

CHAPTER 4
BALLOT MEASURES AND CONGRESSIONAL ELECTION AGENDAS

1. By only including tax propositions that do not include reference to another policy issue, I do not eliminate the possibility that opponents of the measure might attempt to define it along another issue dimension. Although they were unsuccessful, opponents of California's Proposition 13, the (in)famous property tax initiative, attempted to define it as an issue that would be harmful to the state's public school system. Without public opinion data on each issue, something that does not exist, I rely on descriptions of the measures.

2. For example, I include ballot measures affecting homeowners but exclude those targeted at smaller groups such as smokers, drinkers, widowers, or renters. I also exclude ballot measures that target small tax cuts such as those pertaining to food.

3. The first question asked respondents if there was anything in particular they liked or disliked about each candidate. For example, each respondent was asked, "Was there anything in particular you liked about the Democratic candidate for the U.S. Senate?" as well as a similar question regarding dislikes. The same questions were asked about House candidates. In the NES Senate study, up to five mentions for each question are coded. The other question asked of respondents was, "In your state, what issue did the candidates talk about most during the campaign for the Senate (House of Representatives in Washington)?"

4. According to Sigelman, "To the extent that the marginals are skewed, calculation of lambda and/or Goodman and Kruskal's tau seems to be a prerequisite to any meaningful assessment of classificatory accuracy" (1984, 79). The difference between the two statistics is that lambda assigns all the cases to the modal category in order to minimize the expected number of errors. In contrast, Goodman and Kruskal's tau better accounts for the distribution of the dependent variable. When deciding between the two statistics, Sigelman argues that "Goodman and Kruskal's tau is preferable to lambda because tau is sensitive to the distribution of non-modal cases" (1984, 79). Given that the dependent variable used in this

analysis is negatively skewed, I use Goodman and Kruskal's tau to account for this problem.

5. The codebook states, "Themes were culled from accounts of Senate elections in CQ's Special Report on the 1988 elections, Roll Call (10/30/88), CBS's briefing book," noted as unpublished, "The GRC Cook Political Report (10/28/88), the Presidential Campaign Hotline (Daily) from 10/1/88 to 11/8/88, and all issues of the Political Report (weekly) from 9/1/88 to 11/8/88."

CHAPTER 5
PRIMING THE FREEZE: NUCLEAR FREEZE BALLOT MEASURES
AS A COMMON BASIS OF CANDIDATE VOTING IN STATE
AND FEDERAL ELECTIONS

1. Many activists within the freeze movement wanted to link the issue with other peace causes or discussions of how money saved from a freeze would be used (Meyer 1990, 112).

2. One type of endogeneity concerns the potential for a nonrecursive relationship between voting for candidates and the nuclear freeze. In other words, not only might attitudes about the freeze inform voting for candidates, but preferences for candidates may also affect voting for the freeze (e.g., projection or persuasion effects). Unfortunately, data limitations preclude a two-stage estimation to account for endogeneity. The other items from the poll are related to both support for candidates and freeze opinion, thus eliminating the possibility of identifying an equation to purge the effects of candidate preference on freeze attitudes. Although I cannot statistically account for endogeneity, research by Markus and Converse (1979) and Page and Jones (1979) suggests that alternative explanations to issue voting such as persuasion and projection play a relatively minor role in models examining the effect of issues on candidate choice. Furthermore, Page and Jones suggest that projection and persuasion effects may be absent for salient issues, which, of course, means that issues on the agenda such as the nuclear freeze likely influence votes for candidates but not the reverse.

3. Voters could also choose Reagan's handling of the economy, candidate experience, partisanship, or none of the above.

4. Although Montana was included in the sample, it was dropped from the agenda-setting analysis because of the small number of cases (N = 68).

5. Unfortunately, the nuclear freeze was not among the eight choices given so I cannot directly test voters' perceptions of its importance.

6. Climbing interest rates and soaring unemployment figures made economics the dominant issue of the 1982 elections (Mann and Ornstein 1983). Although the economy was the dominant issue, social security was also purported to be on the minds of some voters (Mann and Ornstein 1983). For instance, in the week prior to the election Democrats made public an unpopular House Republican Campaign Committee fund-raising letter that suggested social security should be transformed into a voluntary program (Hunt 1983). Often characterized as a referendum on the president's performance, a voter's approval (or disapproval) of the way presidents handle their job has a significant effect on voting for House candidates at the midterm (Kernell 1977). However, in the 1982 elections scholars

questioned whether President Reagan was held wholly accountable for national conditions (Abramowitz 1984; Petrocik and Steeper 1986).

7. Breaking this down, one Republican challenger defeated a Democratic incumbent while Democratic challengers defeated twenty-two Republican incumbents. In open seats previously held by Democrats, the Republicans won three while in the reverse situation Democrats stole five seats from Republicans.

8. An alternative way of looking at the effects of the freeze ballot measures on voter choice is to use multiplicative interaction terms. Although Nagler (1991) states that either splitting the sample or including an explicit interaction term is appropriate, I use split samples because I am primarily interested in examining within and across group effects of the freeze issue on voting for candidates across states according to whether a state had a freeze measure. In contrast to using multiplicative interaction terms, a split-sample analysis allows me to examine the effect of a covariate on each group of voters as opposed to only looking across group differences. Furthermore, split-sample analyses allow me to test for differences in residual variation that may produce misleading coefficient estimates (Allison 1999; Hoetker 2002). Using a split-sample analysis, the coefficients and standard errors are consistent within each group. Multiplicative interaction terms, on the other hand, may produce misleading coefficient estimates because they force observations to have the same residual variation (Allison 1999; Hoetker 2002). Gomez and Wilson (2001, 907n.11) note that using a single-pooled model with a multiplicative interaction term requires calculating conditional standard errors and point estimates, a method for which they find no reliable Monte Carlo evidence in the literature. I found that grouping the data and including multiplicative interaction terms support the primary conclusions of my research.

9. If one does not test for unequal residual variation, one may draw false conclusions about the effects of coefficients across groups (Allison 1999; Hoetker 2002).

10. I use Hoetker's complogit program for these analyses in STATA 8.0 (see Hoetker 2002).

11. As recommended by Allison (1999), I first examined whether the residual variation of voters in states with freeze ballot measures varies significantly from voters in states without freeze ballot measures. The results of a Wald chi-square test ($p = .07$) and a log likelihood ratio test ($p = .02$) suggest that the residual variation of freeze ballot measure states is significantly different than that of non-freeze ballot states. I follow this procedure for all direct comparisons but typically restrict my discussion to formal tests of the coefficients.

12. In only two instances, Nevada and New Mexico, did incumbents lose their seats: a Democrat (Bingaman) unseated a Republican (Schmitt) in New Mexico, and a Republican (Hecht) unseated a Democrat (Cannon) in Nevada. Of the three open seats that year, Republicans held on to California, lost New Jersey, and won retiring Independent Harry Byrd's seat in Virginia.

13. Unlike the House model, there is mixed support for the hypothesis that residual variation across freeze and non-freeze ballot states is unequal. While the likelihood ratio test suggests unequal variation ($p = .00$), the Wald chi-square test ($p = .62$) indicates no difference between freeze and non-freeze ballot states.

14. The Wald test (p = .84) and likelihood ratio tests (p = .00) provide mixed support for the hypothesis of unequal residual variation across models, but the tests for directly comparing coefficients for freeze attitudes suggest a significant difference across freeze and non-freeze ballot states.

15. I estimate the bivariate probit models in STATA 8.0 using the biprobit command, a command that fits maximum-likelihood two-equation probit models. I estimate the trivariate probit model using mvprobit, a program written by Stephen Jenkins and Laurenzo Capelliari for STATA. This program estimates simulated maximum-likelihood multi-equation probit models using the Geweke-Hajivassiliou-Keane (GHK) smooth recursive simulator (see Greene 2000, 183–85).

16. The random process involved in the GHK simulator may lead to slightly different results. Thus, I also ran these models using Antoine Terracol's triprobit command that also makes use of simulated maximum likelihood using the GHK smooth recursive simulator. The results from the triprobit command are nearly identical to those for the mvprobit command.

CHAPTER 6
TAKING THE INITIATIVE: ILLEGAL IMMIGRANTS, AFFIRMATIVE ACTION, AND STRATEGIC POLITICIANS IN CALIFORNIA'S 1994 AND 1996 ELECTIONS

1. The expected "payoff" for parties is no more certain, so parties should also expect greater benefits from allocating money and resources to competitive seats. That said, the use of initiatives as an agenda-setting tool is becoming more widespread (Bell and Price 1988; Smith and Tolbert 2001).

2. Ronald Prince, telephone interview by the author, September 1996.

3. Although the campaign for Proposition 187 made no explicit mention of race, "SOS newsletters were peppered with overtly racist rhetoric such as, 'Wake up and smell the Refried Beans'" (Schultz 1996, 87).

4. The newspapers included in this research were the *Los Angeles Times*, *San Diego Union Tribune*, *Sacramento Bee*, and *San Francisco Chronicle*. Proposition 187 and immigration were listed as the most covered in the *San Diego Union Tribune* and the second most covered type of top story in the *Los Angeles Times*. It was tied for third with five other types of stories in the *Sacramento Bee*, and it was the tenth most covered issue in the *San Francisco Chronicle*.

5. However, it is possible that some House candidates discussed these issues and that the sources I have looked at failed to account for these instances.

6. These data are available at the Federal Elections Commission Web site: http://www.fec.gov/1996/states/ca_01.htm.

7. Campaign spending data for the state senate and assembly are available through the California secretary of state's Web site: http://www.ss.ca.gov/prd/cfund/ranksenexp.htm; http://www.ss.ca.gov/prd/cfund/rankassexp.htm.

CHAPTER 7
DIRECT DEMOCRACY: THE PEOPLE'S AGENDA?

1. In contrast to Dahl and Barber, Schumpeter argues that agenda control by elites is desirable since ordinary citizens are incapable of making informed decisions.

2. Dahl notes the difficulty of trying to distinguish between a distorted and an undistorted agenda but maintains that it is worth doing under certain circumstances. In his words, "[I]t would be a mistake to write off the idea of a distorted agenda as meaningless . . . for in some cases it is possible to furnish a convincing description of an alternative that (a) is excluded from serious consideration and (b) if it were seriously considered, would significantly alter the outcome of the decision-making process" (1982, 45). The economy in the 1994 California elections appears to meet both criteria.

# REFERENCES

Abbe, Owen G., Jay Goodliffe, Paul S. Herrnson, and Kelly D. Patterson. 2003. "Agenda Setting in Congressional Elections: The Impact of Issues and Campaigns on Voting Behavior." *Political Research Quarterly* 56:419–30.

Abramowitz, Alan I. 1980. "A Comparison of Voting for U.S. Senator and Representative in 1978." *American Political Science Review* 74:633–40.

———. 1984. "National Issues, Strategic Politicians, and Voting Behavior in the 1980 and 1982 Congressional Elections." *American Journal of Political Science* 28:710–21.

———. 1995. "It's Abortion, Stupid: Policy Voting in the 1992 Presidential Election." *Journal of Politics* 57:176–86.

Abramowitz, Alan I., and Jeffrey A. Segal. 1990. "Beyond Willie Horton and the Pledge of Allegiance: National Issues in the 1988 Elections." *Legislative Studies Quarterly* 15: 565–80.

———. 1992. *Senate Elections*. Ann Arbor: University of Michigan Press.

Abramson, Paul R., John H. Aldrich, and David W. Rohde. 1998. *Change and Continuity in the 1996 Elections*. Washington, DC: Congressional Quarterly Press.

Adams, Greg D. 1997. "Abortion: Evidence of an Issue Evolution." *American Journal of Political Science* 41:718–37.

Allison, Paul D. 1999. "Comparing Logit and Probit Coefficients across Groups." *Sociological Methods and Research* 28:186–208.

Alvarez, R. Michael. 1997. *Information and Elections*. Ann Arbor: University of Michigan Press.

Alvarez, R. Michael, and John Brehm. 2002. *Hard Choices, Easy Answers*. Princeton: Princeton University Press.

Alvarez, R. Michael, and Tara L. Butterfield. 2000. "The Resurgence of Nativism in California? The Case of Proposition 187 and Illegal Immigration." *Social Science Quarterly* 81:167–79.

Alvarez, R. Michael, and Jonathan Nagler. 1995. "Economics, Issues, and the Perot Candidacy: Voter Choice in the 1992 Election." *American Journal of Political Science* 39:714–44.

Ansolabehere, Stephen, and Shanto Iyengar. 1995. *Going Negative: How Political Advertisements Shrink and Polarize the Electorate*. New York: Free Press

Ansolabehere, Stephen, Roy Behr, and Shanto Iyengar. 1993. *The Media Game: American Politics in the Television Age*. New York: Macmillan.

Arceneaux, Kevin. 2003. "The Federal Face of Democratic Representation: The Effects of Responsibility Attribution on Cross-Level Voting Behavior and Government Responsiveness in the United States." Ph.D. diss., Rice University.

Arrow, Kenneth J. 1963. *Social Choice and Individual Values*. 2nd ed. New Haven: Yale University Press.

Arterton, F. Christopher. 1993. "Campaign '92: Strategies and Tactics of the Candidates." In *The Election of 1992*, ed. Gerald M. Pomper. Chatham, NJ: Chatham House.

Atkeson, Lonna Rae, and Randall W. Partin. 1995. "Economic and Referendum Voting: A Comparison of Gubernatorial and Senatorial Elections." *American Political Science Review* 89:99–107.

———. 1998. "Economic and Referendum Voting and the Problem of Data Choice: A Reply." *American Journal of Political Science* 42:1003–7.

———. 2001. "Candidate Advertisements, Media Coverage, and Citizen Attitudes: The Agendas and Roles of Senators and Governors in a Federal System." *Political Research Quarterly* 54:795–813.

Baer, Denise. 1995. "Contemporary Strategy and Agenda Setting." In *Campaigns and Elections American Style*, ed. James A. Thurber and Candice J. Nelson. Boulder, CO: Westview Press.

Barber, Benjamin. 1984. *Strong Democracy: Participatory Politics for a New Age*. Berkeley: University of California Press.

Bargh, John A. 1989. "Conditional Automaticity: Varieties of Automatic Influence in Social Perception and Cognition." In *Unintended Thought*, ed. John A. Bargh and James S. Uleman. New York: Guilford Press.

Bargh, John A., and Paula Pietromonaco. 1982. "Automatic Information Processing and Social Perception: The Influence of Trait Information Presented Outside of Conscious Awareness on Impression Formation." *Journal of Personality and Social Psychology* 43:437–49.

Barreto, Matt A., and Nathan D. Woods. 2005. "The Anti-Latino Political Context and Its Impact on GOP Detachment and Increasing Latino Voter Turnout in Los Angeles County." In *Diversity in Democracy: Minority Representation in the United States*. ed. Gary Segura and Shawn Bowler. Charlottesville: University of Virginia Press.

Bartels, Larry M. 1986. "Issue Voting under Uncertainty: An Empirical Test." *American Journal of Political Science* 30:709–28.

———. 1988. *Presidential Primaries and the Dynamics of Public Choice*. Princeton: Princeton University Press.

———. 1996. "Politicians and the Press: Who Leads, Who Follows?" Paper presented at the Annual Meeting of the American Political Science Association, San Francisco, September 1996.

Behr, Roy L., and Shanto Iyengar. 1985. "Television News, Real-World Cues, and Changes in the Public Agenda." *Public Opinion Quarterly* 49:38–57.

Bell, Charles, and Charles Price. 1988. "Lawmakers and Initiatives: Are Ballot Measures the Magic Ride to Success?" *California Journal* 19:380–86.

Berelson, Bernard R., Paul F. Lazarsfeld, and William N. McPhee. 1954. *Voting* Chicago: University of Chicago Press.

Berg, Larry L., and C. B. Holman. 1989. "The Initiative Process and Its Declining Agenda-Setting Value." *Law and Policy* 11:451–69.

Beyle, Thad L., ed. 1985. *Gubernatorial Transitions: The 1982 Elections*. Durham, NC: Duke University Press.

———. 1986. *Re-Electing the Governor: The 1982 Elections*. Lanham, MD: University Press of America.

Boehmke, Fredrick. 2002. "The Influence of Direct Democracy on the Size and Diversity of State Interest Group Populations." *Journal of Politics* 64:827–44.

Bowler, Shaun, and Todd Donovan. 1994. "Information and Opinion Change on Ballot Propositions." *Political Behavior* 16:411–35.

———. 1998. *Demanding Choices: Opinion, Voting, and Direct Democracy*. Ann Arbor: University of Michigan Press.

———. 2002. "Democracy, Institutions and Attitudes about Citizen Influence on Government." *British Journal of Political Science* 32:371–90.

Bowler, Shaun, Stephen P. Nicholson, and Gary M. Segura. 2004. "Earthquakes and Aftershocks: Tracking the Macropartisan Implications of California's Recent Political Environment." Paper presented at the Annual Meeting of the Western Political Science Association, Portland, Oregon, March 11–13.

Box-Steffensmeier, Janet M. 1996. "A Dynamic Analysis of the Role of War Chests in Campaign Strategy." *American Journal of Political Science* 40: 352–71.

Brace, Paul, and Aubrey Jewett. 1995. "The State of State Politics Research." *Political Research Quarterly* 48:643–81.

Branton, Regina P. 2003. "Examining Individual-Level Voting Behavior on State Ballot Propositions." *Political Research Quarterly* 56:367–77.

Broder, David S. 1995. "Kemp Says GOP Candidates Wrong on Affirmative Action." *Washington Post*, July 22, A2.

———. 2000. *Democracy Derailed: Initiative Campaigns and the Power of Money*. New York: Harcourt.

Burden, Barry C., and David C. Kimball. 2002. *Why Americans Split Their Tickets: Campaigns, Competition, and Divided Government*. Ann Arbor: University of Michigan Press.

Cain, Bruce E. 1995. "Lessons from the Inside Revisited." In *The 1994 Governor's Race: An Inside Look at the Candidates and their Campaigns by the People Who Managed Them*, ed. Gerald C. Lubenow. Berkeley, CA: Institute of Governmental Studies Press.

Cain, Bruce, John Ferejohn, and Morris P. Fiorina. 1987. *The Personal Vote*. Cambridge, MA: Harvard University Press.

Cain, Bruce, Karin MacDonald, and Kenneth F. McCue. 1996. "Nativism, Partisanship, and Immigration: An Analysis of Prop. 187." Paper presented at the Annual Meeting of the American Political Science Association, San Francisco, August 29–September 1.

California Commission on Campaign Financing. 1992. *Democracy by Initiative: Shaping California's Fourth Branch of Government*. Los Angeles: Center for Responsive Government.

Campbell, Angus, Philip. E. Converse, Warren E. Miller, and Donald Stokes. 1960. *The American Voter*. New York: John Wiley and Sons.

———. 1966. *Elections and the Political Order*. New York: Wiley.

Cappellari, Lorenzo, and Stephen P. Jenkins. 2003. "Multivariate Probit Regression Using Simulated Maximum Likelihood." *Stata Journal* 3:278–94.

Carmines, Edward G., and James A. Stimson. 1980. "The Two Faces of Issue Voting." *American Political Science Review* 74:78–91.

———. 1989. *Issue Evolution: Race and the Transformation of American Politics*. Princeton: Princeton University Press.

Carsey, Thomas M. 2000. *Campaign Dynamics: The Race for Governor.* Ann Arbor: University of Michigan Press.

Carsey, Thomas M., and Gerald C. Wright. 1998. "State and National Factors in Gubernatorial and Senatorial Elections." *American Journal of Political Science* 42:994–1002.

Ceaser, James W., and Andrew E. Busch. 1997. *Losing to Win: The 1996 Elections and American Politics.* Lanham, MD: Rowman and Littlefield.

Chavez, Lydia. 1998. *The Color Bind: California's Battle to End Affirmative Action.* Berkeley: University of California Press.

Chubb, John E. 1988. "Institutions, the Economy, and the Dynamics of State Elections." *American Political Science Review* 82:133–54.

Collet, Christian. 1995. "The 1994 Gubernatorial Campaign in the Newspapers." In *The 1994 Governor's Race: An Inside Look at the Candidates and Their Campaigns by the People Who Managed Them,* ed. Gerald C. Lubenow. Berkeley, CA: Institute of Governmental Studies Press.

Collins, Allan M., and Elizabeth F. Loftus. 1975. "A Spreading Activation Theory of Semantic Processing." *Psychological Review* 82:407–28.

Congressional Quarterly. 1982. *Congressional Quarterly Special Report: The 1982 Elections* 40 (October 9): 2481–2610.

*Congressional Quarterly Almanac.* 1990. Washington, DC: Congressional Quarterly.

Conover, Pamela Johnston, and Stanley Feldman. 1989. "Candidate Perception in an Ambiguous World: Campaigns, Cues, and Inference Processes." *American Journal of Political Science* 33:912–40.

Converse, Phillip E. 1964. "The Nature of Belief Systems in Mass Publics." In *Ideology and Discontent,* ed. David E. Apter. New York: Free Press.

Converse, Phillip E., and Gregory Markus. 1979. "'Plus ça Change . . . ': The New CPS Election Study Panel." *American Political Science Review* 73:2–49.

Cook, Elizabeth Adell, Ted G. Jelen, and Clyde Wilcox. 1994. "Issue Voting in Gubernatorial Elections: Abortion and Post-Webster Politics." *Journal of Politics* 56:187–99.

Craig, Barbara Hinkson and David M. O'Brien. 1993. *Abortion and American Politics.* Chatham, NJ: Chatham House.

Cronin, Thomas E. 1989. *Direct Democracy: The Politics of Initiative, Referendum, and Recall.* Cambridge, MA: Harvard University Press.

Dahl, Robert A. 1982. *Dilemmas of Pluralist Democracy: Autonomy vs. Control.* New Haven: Yale University Press.

———. 1989. *Democracy and Its Critics.* New Haven: Yale University Press.

Dalager, Jon K. 1996. "Voters, Issues, and Elections: Are the Candidates' Messages Getting Through?" *Journal of Politics* 58:486–515.

Damore, David F. 2004 "The Dynamics of Issue Ownership in Presidential Campaigns." *Political Research Quarterly* 57:391–97.

Decker, Cathleen, and Bill Stall. 1994. "Divisive State Campaign Lurches toward Finish." *Los Angeles Times,* November 6, A1.

Delli Carpini, Michael X., and Scott Keeter. 1996. *What Americans Know about Politics and Why It Matters.* New Haven: Yale University Press.

Donovan, Todd, and Shaun Bowler. 1998. "An Overview of Direct Democracy in the American States." In *Citizens as Legislators: Direct Democracy in the*

*United States*, ed. Shaun Bowler, Todd Donovan, and Caroline J. Tolbert. Columbus: Ohio State University Press.

Downs, Anthony. 1957. *An Economic Theory of Democracy*. New York: Harper and Row.

Druckman, James N. 2004. "Priming the Vote: Campaign Effects in a U.S. Senate Election." *Political Psychology* 25:577–94.

Druckman, James N., Lawrence R. Jacobs, and Eric Ostermeier. 2004. "Candidate Strategies to Prime Issues and Image." *Journal of Politics* 66:1205–27.

Dubois, Philip L., and Floyd Feeney. 1998. *Lawmaking by Initiative: Issues, Options, and Comparisons*. New York: Agathon Press.

Ellis, Richard J. 2002. *Democratic Delusions: The Initiative Process in America*. Lawrence: University Press of Kansas.

Erikson, Robert S., Gerald C. Wright, Jr., and John McIver. 1993. *Statehouse Democracy*. New York: Cambridge University Press.

Finkel, Steven E. 1993. "Re-examining the 'Minimal Effects' Model in Recent Presidential Campaigns." *Journal of Politics* 55:1–21.

Fiorina, Morris P. 1981. *Retrospective Voting in American National Elections*. New Haven: Yale University Press.

———. 1996. *Divided Government*. 2nd ed. Needham Heights, MA: Allyn and Bacon.

Fiske, Susan T., and Shelley E. Taylor. 1991. *Social Cognition*. New York: McGraw-Hill.

Franklin, Charles H. 1991. "Eschewing Obfuscation: Campaigns and the Perceptions of U.S. Senate Incumbents." *American Political Science Review* 85:1193–1214.

Garrett, Elizabeth. 1999. "Money, Agenda Setting and Direct Democracy." *Texas Law Review* 77:1845–90.

Gelman, Andrew, and Gary King. 1993. "Why Are American Presidential Election Campaign Polls So Variable When Voters Are So Predictable?" *British Journal of Political Science* 23:409–51.

Gerber, Elisabeth R. 1996. "Legislative Response to the Threat of Popular Initiatives." *American Journal of Political Science* 40:99–128.

———. 1999. *The Populist Paradox: Interest Group Influence and the Promise of Direct Legislation*. Princeton: Princeton University Press.

Gerber, Elisabeth R., and Arthur Lupia. 1995. "Campaign Competition and Policy Responsiveness in Direct Legislation Elections." *Political Behavior* 17:287–306.

———. 1999. "Voter Competence in Direct Legislation Elections." In *Citizen Competence*, ed. S. Elkin and K. Soltan, pp. 147–60. University Park: Pennsylvania State University Press.

Gilens, Martin, James Glaser, and Tali Mendelberg. 2001. "Having a Say: Political Efficacy in the Context of Direct Democracy." Paper presented at the Annual Meeting of the American Political Science Association, San Francisco, August 30–September 2.

Goldstein, Ken, and Paul Freedman. 2000. "New Evidence for New Arguments: Money and Advertising in the 1996 Senate Elections." *Journal of Politics* 62:1087–1108.

Gomez, Brad T., and J. Matthew Wilson. 2001. "Political Sophistication and Economic Voting in the American Electorate: A Theory of Heterogeneous Attribution." *American Journal of Political Science* 45:899–914.

Gordon, Stacy B., and Gary M. Segura. 1997. "Cross-National Variation in the Political Sophistication of Individuals: Capability or Choice?" *Journal of Politics* 59:126–47.

Greene, William H. 2000. *Econometric Analysis*. Upper Saddle River, NJ: Prentice Hall.

Gronke, Paul. 2000. *The Electorate, the Campaign, and the Office: A Unified Approach to Senate and House Elections*. Ann Arbor: University of Michigan Press.

Harden, Blaine. 1996. "Dole Tailors Immigration Remarks to Audiences in California." *Washington Post*, October 28, A8.

Herrnson, Paul S., and Kelly D. Patterson. 1998. "Agenda Setting in Congressional Campaigns." Paper presented at the 1998 Annual Meeting of the Western Political Science Association, Los Angeles, March 19–22.

Herrnson, Paul S., and Clyde Wilcox. 1997. "The 1996 Presidential Election: A Tale of a Campaign That Didn't Seem to Matter." In *Toward the Millenium: The Elections of 1996*, ed. Larry J. Sabato. Boston: Allyn and Bacon.

Hershey, Marjorie Randon. 1989. "The Campaign and the Media." In *The Election of 1988*, ed. Gerald M. Pomper. Chatham, NJ: Chatham House.

Hibbing, John R., and John R. Alford. 1982. "Economic Conditions and the Forgotten Side of Congress: A Foray into U.S. Elections." *British Journal of Political Science* 12:505–13.

Higgins, E. Tory. 1996. "Knowledge Activation: Accessibility, Applicability, and Salience." In *Social Psychology: Handbook of Basic Principles*, ed. E. Tory Higgins and Arie W. Kruglanski. New York: Guilford Press.

Higgins, E. Tory, and Gilliam King. 1981. "Accessibility of Social Constructs: Information Processing Consequences of Individual and Contextual Variability." In *Personality, Cognition, and Social Interaction*, ed. Nancy Cantor and John F Kihlstrom, Hillsdale, NJ: Lawrence Erlbaum Associates.

Hoetker, Glenn. 2002. "Confounded Coefficients: Accurately Comparing Logit and Probit Coefficients across Groups." Working paper. College of Business, University of Illinois at Urbana/Champaign.

Hogan, Michael J. 1994. *The Nuclear Freeze Campaign: Rhetoric and Foreign Policy in the Teleopolitical Age*. East Lansing: Michigan State University Press.

Holbrook, Thomas M. 1996. *Do Campaigns Matter?* Thousand Oaks, CA: Sage Publications.

Holbrook-Provow, Thomas M. 1987. "National Factors in Gubernatorial Elections." *American Politics Quarterly* 15:471–83.

Howell, Susan E., and James M. Vanderleeuw. 1990. "Economic Effects on State Governors." *American Politics Quarterly* 18:158–68.

Huckfeldt, Robert, and John Sprague. 1995. *Citizens, Politics, and Social Communication: Information and Influence in an Election Campaign*. New York: Cambridge University Press.

Hunt, Albert R. 1983. "National Politics and the 1982 Campaign." In *The American Elections of 1982*, ed. Thomas E. Mann and Norman J. Ornstein. Washington, DC: American Enterprise Institute.

Hutchings, Vincent L. 2003. *Public Opinion and Democratic Accountability: How Citizens Learn about Politics*. Princeton: Princeton University Press.

Initiative and Referendum Institute. 1998. *1998 Election Post Election Report*. Washington, DC: Citizen Lawmaker Press.

———. 2000. *2000 Election Post Election Report*. Washington, DC: Citizen Lawmaker Press.

Iyengar, Shanto, and Donald R. Kinder. 1987. *News That Matters: Television and American Opinion*. Chicago: University of Chicago Press.

Iyengar, Shanto, and Adam Simon. 1993. "News Coverage of the Gulf Crisis and Public Opinion: A Study of Agenda-Setting, Priming, and Framing." *Communication Research* 20:365–83.

Iyengar, Shanto, and Nicholas A. Valentino. 2000. "Who Says What? Source Credibility as a Mediator of Campaign Advertising." In *Elements of Reason: Cognition, Choice, and the Bounds of Rationality*, ed. Arthur Lupia, Mathew D. McCubbins, and Samuel L. Popkin. Cambridge: Cambridge University Press.

Jacobs, Lawrence R., and Robert Y. Shapiro. 1994. "Issues, Candidate Image, and Priming: The Use of Private Polls in Kennedy's 1960 Presidential Campaign." *American Political Science Review* 88:527–40.

Jacobson, Gary C. 1980. *Money in Congressional Elections*. New Haven: Yale University Press.

———. 2000. "Party Polarization in National Politics: The Electoral Connection." In *Polarized Politics: Congress and the President in a Partisan Era*, ed. Jon R. Bond and Richard Fleisher. Washington, DC: Congressional Quarterly Press.

———. 2001. *The Politics of Congressional Elections*. New York: Longman.

Jacobson, Gary C., and Samuel Kernell. 1983. *Strategy and Choice in Congressional Elections*. New Haven: Yale University Press.

Jacobson, Gary C., and Raymond E. Wolfinger. 1989. "Information and Voting in California Senate Elections." *Legislative Studies Quarterly* 14:509–29.

Jerit, Jennifer. 2004. "The Best Offense Is a Good Defense: Priming and Engagement in the Health Care Reform Debate, 1993–1994." Paper presented at the Annual Meeting of the Midwest Political Science Association, Chicago, April 15–18.

Jerit, Jennifer, and Jason Barabas. 2003. "Bankrupt Rhetoric: The Debate over Social Security Reform and Citizen Knowledge." Working paper. Department of Political Science, Southern Illinois University.

Johnston, Richard, Andre Blais, Henry E. Brady, and Jean Crete. 1992. *Letting the People Decide: Dynamics of a Canadian Election*. Stanford: Stanford University Press.

Jones, Bill. 1996. *Financing California's Statewide Ballot Measures: 1996 Primary and General Elections*. Sacramento: Political Reform Division, Secretary of State.

Jones, Bryan D. 1994. *Reconceiving Decision-Making in Democratic Politics: Attention, Choice, and Public Policy*. Chicago: University of Chicago Press.

Joslyn, Mark R., and Donald P. Haider-Markel. 2000. "Guns in the Ballot Box: Information, Groups, and Opinion in Ballot Initiative Campaigns." *American Politics Quarterly* 28:355–78.

Judd, Charles M., and Joel T. Johnson. 1981. "Attitudes, Polarization, and Diagnosticity: Exploring the Effect of Affect." *Journal of Personality and Social Psychology* 41:26–36.

Just, Marion R. 1997. "Candidate Strategies and the Media Campaign." In *The Election of 1996: Reports and Interpretations*, ed. Gerald M. Pomper. Chatham, NJ: Chatham House.

Kahn, Kim Fridkin, and Patrick J. Kenney. 1999. *The Spectacle of U.S. Senate Campaigns*. Princeton: Princeton University Press.

Karp, Jeffrey A. 1998. "The Influence of Elite Endorsements in Initiative Campaigns." In *Citizens as Legislators: Direct Democracy in the United States*, ed Shaun Bowler, Todd Donovan, and Caroline J. Tolbert. Columbus: Ohio State University Press.

Kenney, Patrick J. 1983. "The Effect of State Economic Conditions on the Vote for Governor." *Social Science Quarterly* 64:154–62.

Kernell, Samuel. 1977. "Presidential Popularity and Negative Voting: An Alternative Explanation of the Midterm Congressional Decline of the President's Party." *American Political Science Review* 71:44–66.

Key, V. O., Jr. 1966. *The Responsible Electorate*. New York: Vintage Books.

Kiewiet, Roderick D. 1983. *Macroeconomics and Micropolitics*. Chicago: University of Chicago Press.

Kinder, Donald R., and Lynn M. Sanders. 1996. *Divided by Color: Racial Politics and Democratic Ideals*. Chicago: University of Chicago Press.

King, Gary, Robert O. Keohane, and Sidney Verba. 1994. *Designing Social Inquiry: Scientific Inference in Qualitative Research*. Princeton: Princeton University Press.

King, Gary, Michael Tomz, and Jason Wittenberg. 2000. "Making the Most of Statistical Analyses: Improving Interpretation and Presentation." *American Journal of Political Science* 44:347–61.

Klingemann, Hans-Dieter, Richard I. Hofferbert, and Ian Budge. 1994. *Parties, Policies, and Democracy*. Boulder, CO: Westview.

Koch, Jeffrey W. 2001. "When Parties and Candidates Collide: Citizen Perception of House Candidates' Positions on Abortion." *Public Opinion Quarterly* 65:1–21.

Krasno, Jonathan S. 1994. *Challengers, Competition, and Reelection: Comparing Senate and House Elections*. New Haven: Yale University Press.

Krikorian, Greg, and Dave Lesher. 1994. "Huffington Declares Support for Prop. 187." *Los Angeles Times*, October 21, A1.

Krosnick, Jon A., and Laura A. Brannon. 1993. "The Impact of the Gulf War on the Ingredients of Presidential Evaluations." *American Political Science Review* 87:963–75.

Krosnick, Jon A., and Donald R. Kinder. 1990. "Altering the Foundations of Support for the President through Priming." *American Political Science Review* 84:497–512.

Kuklinski, James H., and Gary M. Segura. 1995. "Endogeneity, Exogeneity, Time, and Space in Political Representation." *Legislative Studies Quarterly* 20:3–22.

Kuklinski, James, H., Paul J. Quirk, Jennifer Jerit, and Robert F. Rich. 2001. "The Political Environment and Citizen Competence." *American Journal of Political Science* 45:410–24.

Kuklinski, James H., Paul M. Sniderman, Kathleen Knight, Thomas Piazza, Philip E. Tetlock, Gordon R. Lawrence, and Barbara Mellers. 1997. "Racial Prejudice and Attitudes toward Affirmative Action." *American Journal of Political Science* 41:402–19.

Kunda, Ziva. 1999. *Social Cognition: Making Sense of People*. Cambridge, MA: MIT Press.

Lee, Frances E., and Bruce I. Oppenheimer. 1999. *Sizing Up the Senate: The Unequal Consequences of Equal Representation*. Chicago: University of Chicago Press.

Lee, Ryan. 2004. "Gay Marriage Ban Proposed for Georgia." February 23, http://www.southernvoice.com/2004/1-23/news/localnews/gaymarr.cfm.

Lesher, David. 1996. "Affirmative Action Fades as GOP Issue in California." *Los Angeles Times*, June 13, A1.

Lesher, David, and Larry B. Stammer. 1996. "Battle over Prop. 209 Heating Up." *Los Angeles Times*, September 4, A1.

Leyden, Kevin M., and Stephen A. Borrelli. 1995. "The Effect of State Economic Conditions on Gubernatorial Elections: Does Unified Government Make a Difference?" *Political Research Quarterly* 48:275–90.

Lippmann, Walter. 1922. *Public Opinion*. New York: Free Press.

Lodge, Milton G., and Ruth Hamill. 1986. "A Partisan Schema for Political Information Processing." *American Political Science Review* 82:737–61.

Lodge, Milton, Kathleen McGraw, and Patrick Stroh. 1989. "An Impression-Driven Model of Candidate Evaluation." *American Political Science Review* 83:399–419.

Lodge, Milton, Marco R. Steenbergen, and Shawn Brau. 1995. "The Responsive Voter: Campaign Information and the Dynamics of Candidate Evaluation." *American Political Science Review* 89:309–26.

Lombardi, Wendy J., E. Tory Higgins, and John A. Bargh. 1987. "The Role of Consciousness in Priming Effects on Categorization." *Personality and Social Psychology Bulletin* 13:411–29.

Lubenow, Gerald C., ed. 1991. *The 1990 Governor's Race: An Inside Look at the Candidates and Their Campaigns by the People Who Managed Them*. Berkeley, CA: Institute of Governmental Studies Press.

———. 1995. *The 1994 Governor's Race: An Inside Look at the Candidates and Their Campaigns by the People Who Managed Them*. Berkeley, CA: Institute of Governmental Studies Press.

Lupia, Arthur. 1994. "Shortcuts versus Encyclopedias: Information and Voting Behavior in California Insurance Reform Elections." *American Political Science Review* 88:63–76.

Luskin, Robert C. 1990. "Explaining Political Sophistication." *Political Behavior* 12: 331–66.

MacKuen, Michael. 1984. "Exposure to Information, Belief Integration, and Individual Responsiveness to Agenda Change." *American Political Science Review* 78:372–91.

Magleby, David B. 1984. *Direct Legislation: Voting on Ballot Propositions in the United States*. Baltimore: Johns Hopkins University Press.

———. 1994. "Campaign Spending and Referendum Voting." Paper presented at the Annual Meeting of the Western Political Science Association, Albuquerque, New Mexico, March 10–12.

———. 1995. "Direct Legislation in the American States." In *Referendums around the World*, ed. Austin Ranney and David Butler. Washington, DC: American Enterprise Institute.

———. 2002. *The Other Campaign: Soft Money and Issue Advocacy in the 2000 Congressional Elections*. Lanham, MD: Rowman and Littlefield.

Mann, Thomas E., and Norman J. Ornstein. 1983. "Sending a Message: Voters and Congress in 1982." In *The American Elections of 1982*, ed. Thomas E. Mann and Norman J. Ornstein. Washington, DC: American Enterprise Institute.

Mann, Thomas E., and Raymond E. Wolfinger. 1980. "Candidates and Parties in Congressional Elections." *American Political Science Review* 74:617–32.

Marelius, John. 1996a. "Dole Quiet on Affirmative Action." *San Diego Union Tribune*, August 7, A1.

———. 1996b. "Wilson Bemoans Dole Effort Here: Governor to Devote Energies to GOP Races for Legislature." *San Diego Union Tribune*, October 12, A1.

Markus, Gregory B., and Philip E. Converse. 1979. "A Dynamic Simultaneous Equation Model of Electoral Choice." *American Political Science Review* 73:1055–70.

Martin, Leonard L. 1986. "Set/Reset: Use and Disuse of Concepts in Impression Formation." *Journal of Personality and Social Psychology* 51:493–504.

Martin, Leonard L., and John W. Achee. 1992. "Beyond Accessibility: The Role of Processing Objectives in Judgment." In *The Construction of Social Judgments*, ed. Leonard L. Martin and Abraham Tesser. Hillsdale, NJ: Lawrence Erlbaum Associates.

Mayhew, David R. 1974. *Congress: The Electoral Connection*. New Haven: Yale University Press.

McCombs, Maxwell, and Donald L. Shaw. 1972. "The Agenda-Setting Function of the Mass Media." *Public Opinion Quarterly* 36:176–87.

McCrea, Frances B., and Gerald E. Markle. 1989. *Minutes to Midnight: Nuclear Weapons Protest in America*. Newbury Park, CA: Sage Publications.

McCuan, David, Shaun Bowler, Todd Donovan, and Ken Fernandez. 1998. "California's Political Warriors: Campaign Professionals and the Initiative Process." In *Citizens as Legislators: Direct Democracy in the United States*, ed. Shaun Bowler, Todd Donovan, and Caroline J. Tolbert. Columbus: Ohio State University Press.

McDonnell, Patrick J., and Dave Lesher. 1994. "Clinton, Feinstein Declare Opposition to Prop. 187; Immigration: President Calls Measure Unconstitutional. Senator Admits Her Stance Could Cost Her the Election." *Los Angeles Times*, October 22, A1.

McGuigan, Patrick. 1985. *The Politics of Direct Democracy in the 1980s*. Washington, DC: Free Congress Foundation.

Mendel, Ed. 1995. "GOP-Backed Drive to End Affirmative Action Slows." *San Diego Union Tribune*, November 3, A1.

———. 1996a. "Prop. 209 Race Gets Tighter as Election Nears." *San Diego Union Tribune*, October 30, A1.

———. 1996b. "Prop. 209 Regains Big Lead." *San Diego Union Tribune*, November 4, A1.

Mendelberg, Tali. 1997. "Executing Hortons: Racial Crime in the 1988 Presidential Campaign." *Public Opinion Quarterly* 61:134–57.

———. 2001. *The Race Card: Campaign Strategy, Implicit Messages, and the Norm of Equality*. Princeton: Princeton University Press.

Mendelsohn, Matthew. 1996. "The Media and Interpersonal Communications: The Priming of Issues, Leaders, and Party Identification." *Journal of Politics* 58:112–25.

Mendelsohn, Matthew, and Fred Cutler. 2000. "The Effect of Referendums on Democratic Citizens: Information, Politicization, Efficacy and Tolerance." *British Journal of Political Science* 30: 685–701.

Meyer, David S. 1990. *A Winter of Discontent: The Nuclear Freeze and American Politics*. New York: Praeger.

Miller, Joanne M., and Jon A. Krosnick. 1996. "News Media Impact on the Ingredients of Presidential Evaluations: A Program of Research on the Priming Hypothesis." In *Political Persuasion and Attitude Change*, ed. Diana C. Mutz, Paul M. Sniderman, and Richard A. Brody. Ann Arbor: University of Michigan Press.

———. 2000. "News Media Impact on the Ingredients of Presidential Evaluations: Politically Knowledgeable Citizens Are Guided by a Trusted Source." *American Journal of Political Science* 44:295–309.

Miller, Judith. 1982. "Nuclear Freeze Debate Important in Few Races." *New York Times*, October 19, A18.

Miller, Warren E. 1955–56. "Presidential Coattails: A Study in Political Myth and Methodology. *Public Opinion Quarterly* 19:353–68.

Mondak, Jeffery J. 1990. "Determinants of Coattail Voting." *Political Behavior* 12:265–88.

———. 1995. *Nothing to Read: Newspapers and Elections in a Social Experiment*. Ann Arbor: University of Michigan Press.

Moskowitz, Gordon B., and Robert J. Roman. 1992. "Spontaneous Trait Inferences as Self-Generated Primes: Implications for Conscious Social Judgment." *Journal of Personality and Social Psychology* 62:728–38.

Nagler, Jonathan. 1991. "The Effect of Registration Laws and Education on U.S. Voter Turnout." *American Political Science Review* 85:1393–1405.

Nakato, Annie. 1996. "Prop. 209 Backers Unveil Provocative Ad." *San Francisco Examiner*, October 9, A8.

Nicholson, Stephen P. 2003. "The Political Environment and Ballot Proposition Awareness." *American Journal of Political Science* 47:403–10.

Nicholson, Stephen P. 2005. "The Jeffords Switch and Public Support for Divided Government." *British Journal of Political Science*, forthcoming.

Nie, Norman H., and Kristi Anderson. 1974. "Mass Belief Systems Revisited: Political Change and Attitude Structure." *Journal of Politics* 36: 541–91.

Nie, Norman H., Sidney Verba, and John R. Petrocik. 1976. *The Changing American Voter*. Cambridge, MA: Harvard University Press.

Norpoth, Helmut, and Bruce Buchanan. 1992. "Wanted: The Education President: Issue Trespassing by Political Candidates." *Public Opinion Quarterly* 56:87– 99.

Novak, Robert D. 1996. "A GOP Retreat from Colorblindness." *San Diego Union Tribune*, July 16, B6.

Oppenheimer, Bruce I. 1996. "The Representational Experience: The Effect of State Population on Senator-Constituency Linkages." *American Journal of Political Science* 40:1280–99.

Orlov, Rick. 1996. *Los Angeles Daily News*, September 7, p. 1.

Osborne, David. 1990. *Laboratories of Democracy*. Boston: Harvard Business School.

Page, Benjamin I., and Calvin Jones. 1979. "Reciprocal Effects of Policy Preferences, Party Loyalties, and the Vote." *American Political Science Review* 73:1071–89.

Page, Benjamin, and Robert Shapiro. 1992. *The Rational Public*. Chicago: University of Chicago Press.

Pantoja, Adrian D., and Gary M. Segura. 2003. "Fear and Loathing in California: Contextual Threat and Political Sophistication among Latino Voters." *Political Behavior* 25:265–86.

Pantoja, Adrian D., Ricardo Ramirez, and Gary M. Segura. 2001. "Citizens by Choice, Voters by Necessity: Patterns in Political Mobilization by Naturalized Latinos." *Political Research Quarterly* 54:729–50.

Partin, Randall W. 1995. "Economic Conditions and Gubernatorial Elections: Is the State Executive Held Accountable?" *American Politics Quarterly* 23: 81–95.

Patterson, Thomas E. 1989. "The Press and Its Missed Assignment." In *The Election of 1988*, ed. Michael Nelson. Washington, DC: Congressional Quarterly Press.

Peltzman, Sam. 1987. "Economic Conditions and Gubernatorial Elections." *American Economic Review* 77:293–97.

Peterson, Kavan. 2004. "Battle over Gay Marriage Goes to Voters," May 4. http:// www.stateline.org/stateline/?pa=story&sa=showStoryInfo&print=1&id= 366573.

Petrocik, John R. 1991. "Divided Government: Is It All in the Campaign?" In *The Politics of Divided Government*, ed. Gary W. Cox and Samuel Kernell. Boulder, CO: Westview.

———. 1996. "Issue Ownership in Presidential Elections, with a 1980 Case Study." *American Journal of Political Science* 40:825–50.

Petrocik, John R., and Frederick T. Steeper. 1986. "The Midterm Referendum: The Importance of Attributions of Responsibility." *Political Behavior* 8:206– 29.

Pomper, Gerald M. 1972. "From Confusion to Clarity: Issues and American Voters, 1956–1968." *American Political Science Review* 66:415–28.

Popkin, Samuel L. 1991. *The Reasoning Voter: Communication and Persuasion in Presidential Campaigns*. Chicago: University of Chicago Press.

Price, Vincent, and John Zaller. 1993. "Who Gets the News? Measuring Individual Differences in the Likelihood of News Reception." *Public Opinion Quarterly* 57:133–64.

Quirk, Paul J. 1989. "The Election." In *The Election of 1988*, ed. Michael Nelson. Washington, D.C.: Congressional Quarterly Press.

Quirk, Paul J., and Jon K. Dalager. 1993. "The Election: A 'New' Democrat and a New Kind of Presidential Campaign." In *The Election of 1992*, ed. Michael Nelson. Washington, DC: Congressional Quarterly Press.

Rahn, Wendy M. 1993. "The Role of Partisan Stereotypes in Information Processing about Political Candidates." *American Journal of Political Science* 37:472–496.

Ramirez, Ricardo. 2002. "Race, Social Context and Referendum Voting." Working paper. Department of Political Science, University of Southern California.

Redlawsk, David P. 2001. "You Must Remember This: A Test of the On-Line Model of Voting." *Journal of Politics* 63:29–58.

RePass, David E. 1971. "Issue Salience and Party Choice." *American Political Science Review* 65:389–400.

Riggle, Ellen D., Victor C. Ottati, Robert S. Wyer, James Kuklinski, and Norbert Schwarz. 1992. "Bases of Political Judgments: The Role of Stereotypic and Nonstereotypic Information." *Political Behavior* 14:67–87.

Riker, William H. 1982. *Liberalism against Populism: A Confrontation between the Theory of Democracy and the Theory of Social Choice*. Prospect Heights, IL: Waveland Press.

———. 1986. *The Art of Political Manipulation*. New Haven: Yale University Press.

———. 1993. "Rhetorical Interaction in the Ratification Campaigns." In *Agenda Formation*, ed. William R. Riker. Ann Arbor: University of Michigan Press.

Romer, Thomas, and Howard Rosenthal. 1978. "Political Resource Allocation, Controlled Agendas, and the Status Quo." *Public Choice* 33:27–43.

Rourke, John T., Richard P. Hiskes, and Cyrus Ernesto Zirakzadeh. 1992. *Direct Democracy and International Politics: Deciding International Issues through Referendums*. Boulder, CO: Lynne Rienner Publishers.

Rudolph, Thomas J. 2003. "Institutional Context and the Assignment of Political Responsibility." *Journal of Politics* 65:190–215.

San Diego Union Tribune. 1996. "Dirty Tricks with 209: Opponents Resort to Dishonest Tactics." *San Diego Union Tribune*, October 31, B10.

Schaffner, Brian F., and Matthew J. Streb. 2002. "The Partisan Heuristic in Low-Information Elections." *Public Opinion Quarterly* 66:559–81.

Schattschneider, E. E. 1960. *The Semi-Sovereign People*. New York: Holt, Rinehart and Winston.

Schleuder, Joan, Maxwell McCombs, and Wayne Wanta. 1991. "Inside the Agenda-Setting Process: How Political Advertising and TV News Prime Viewers to Think about Issues and Candidates." In *Television and Political Advertising Volume 1: Psychological Processes*, ed. Frank Biocca. Hillsdale, NJ.: Lawrence Erlbaum Associates.

Schmidt, David D. 1989. *Citizen Lawmakers: The Ballot Initiative Revolution.* Philadelphia: Temple University Press.

Schneider, Sandra K., and William G. Jacoby. 2003. "Public Attitudes toward the Policy Responsibilities of the National and State Governments: Evidence from South Carolina." *State Politics and Policy Quarterly* 3:246–69.

Schrag, Peter. 1998. *Paradise Lost: California's Experience, America's Future.* New York: New Press.

Schultz, Jim. 1996. *The Initiative Cookbook: Recipes and Stories from California's Ballot Wars.* San Francisco: Democracy Center.

Schumpeter, Joseph A. 1976. *Capitalism, Socialism and Democracy.* New York: Harper and Row.

Sears, David O. 1988. "Symbolic Racism." In *Eliminating Racism*, ed. Phyllis A. Katz and Dalmas A. Taylor. New York: Plenum Press.

Sears, David O., Leonie Huddy, and L. G. Schaffer. 1986. "A Schematic Variant of Symbolic Politics Theory, as Applied to Racial and Gender Equality." In *Political Cognition*, ed. Richard R. Lau and David O. Sears. Hillsdale, NJ: Lawrence Erlbaum Associates.

Sears, David O., Richard R. Lau, T. Tyler, and H. M. Allen. 1980. "Self-Interest vs. Symbolic Politics in Policy Attitudes and Presidential Voting." *American Political Science Review* 74:670–84.

Sears, David O., Colette Van Laar, Mary Carillo, and Rick Kosterman. 1997. "Is It Really Racism?" *Public Opinion Quarterly* 61:16–53.

Shepsle, Kenneth. 1989. "Studying Institutions: Some Lessons from the Rational Choice Approach." *Journal of Theoretical Politics* 1:131–47.

Sherman, Steven J., Diane M. Mackie, and Denise M. Driscoll. 1990. "Priming and the Differential Use of Dimensions in Evaluation." *Personality and Psychology Bulletin* 16:405–18.

Sigelman, Lee. 1984. "Doing Discriminant Analysis: Some Problems and Solutions." *Political Methodology* 10:67–80.

Simon, Adam F. 2002. *The Winning Message: Candidate Behavior, Campaign Discourse, and Democracy.* New York: Cambridge University Press.

Simon, Dennis M. 1989. "Presidents, Governors, and Electoral Accountability." *Journal of Politics* 51:286–304.

Simon, Dennis M., Charles W. Ostrom, Jr., and Robin F. Marra. 1991. "The President, Referendum Voting, and Subnational Elections in the United States." *American Political Science Review* 85:1177–92.

Simon, Herbert. 1957. *Models of Man: Social and Rational.* New York: Wiley.

Smith, Daniel A. 1998. *Tax Crusaders and the Politics of Direct Democracy.* New York: Routledge.

Smith, Daniel A., and Caroline J. Tolbert. 2001. "The Initiative to Party: Partisanship and Ballot Initiatives in California." *Party Politics* 7:739–57.

———. 2004. *Educated by Initiative: The Effects of Direct Democracy on Citizens and Political Organizations in the American States.* Ann Arbor: University of Michigan Press.

Smith, Eric R.A.N. 1989. *The Unchanging American Voter.* Berkeley: University of California Press.

Smith, Mark A. 2001. "The Contingent Effects of Ballot Initiatives and Candidate Races on Turnout." *American Journal of Political Science* 45:700–706.

———. 2002. "Ballot Initiatives and the Democratic Citizen." *Journal of Politics* 64:892–903.

Spiliotes, Constantine, and Lynn Vavreck. 2002. "Campaign Advertising: Partisan Convergence or Divergence?" *Journal of Politics* 64:249–61.

Stall, Bill. 1996. "Voters Back Prop. 209, but Margin Declining." *Los Angeles Times*, July 21, A6.

Stapel, Diederik, Willem Koomen, and Marcel Zeelenberg. 1998. "The Impact of Accuracy Motivations on Interpretation, Comparison, and Correction Processes: Accuracy x Knowledge Accessibility Effects." *Journal of Personality and Social Psychology* 74:878–93.

Stein, Robert M. 1990. "Economic Voting for Governor and U.S. Senator: The Electoral Consequences of Federalism." *Journal of Politics* 52:29–53.

Stein, Robert, and Kenneth N. Bickers. 1994. "Congressional Elections and the Pork Barrel." *Journal of Politics* 56:377–99.

Stokes, Donald E., and Warren E. Miller. 1962. "Party Government and the Saliency of Congress." *Public Opinion Quarterly* 26:531–46.

Strack, Fritz, Norbert Schwarz, Herbert Bless, Almut Kuebler, and M. Wanke. 1993. "Awareness of the Influence as a Determinant of Assimilation versus Contrast." *European Journal of Social Psychology* 23:53–62.

Sullivan, John L., James E. Piereson, and George E. Marcus. 1978. "Ideological Constraint in the Mass Public: A Methodological Critique and Some New Findings." *American Journal of Political Science* 22:223–49.

Taylor, Shelley E., and Susan T. Fiske. 1978. "Salience, Attention, and Attribution: Top of the Head Phenomena." In *Advances in Social Psychology*, ed. Leonard Berkowitz. New York: Academic Press.

Terkildsen, Nayda. 1993. "When White Voters Evaluate Black Candidates: The Processing Implications of Candidate Skin Color, Prejudice, and Self-Monitoring." *American Journal of Political Science* 37:1032–53.

Thomas, Tom E. 1990. "Has Business 'Captured' the California Initiative Agenda?" *California Management Review* 33:131–47.

Tidmarch, Charles M., Lisa J. Hyman, and Jill E. Sorkin. 1984. "Press Issue Agendas in the 1982 Congressional and Gubernatorial Election Campaigns." *Journal of Politics* 46:1226–42.

Tolbert, Caroline J., and John A. Grummel. 2003. "Revisiting the Racial Threat Hypothesis: White Voter Support for California's Proposition 209." *State Politics and Policy Quarterly* 3:183–202.

Tolbert, Caroline J., and Rodney E. Hero. 1996. "Race/Ethnicity and Direct Democracy: An Analysis of California's Illegal Immigration Initiative." *Journal of Politics* 58:806–818.

Tolbert, Caroline J., John A. Grummel, and Daniel A. Smith. 2001. "The Effects of Ballot Initiatives on Voter Turnout in the American States." *American Politics Research* 29:625–48.

Tolbert, Caroline J., Daniel H. Lowenstein, and Todd Donovan. 1998. "Election Law and Rules for Using Initiatives." In *Citizens as Legislators: Direct Democ-*

*racy in the United States*, ed. Shaun Bowler, Todd Donovan, and Caroline J. Tolbert. Columbus: Ohio State University Press.

Tolbert, Caroline J., Romana S. McNeal, and Daniel A. Smith. 2003. "Enhancing Civic Engagement: The Effect of Direct Democracy on Political Participation and Knowledge." *State Politics and Policy Quarterly* 3:23–41.

Tomz, Michael, Jason Wittenberg, and Gary King. 2003. CLARIFY: Software for Interpreting and Presenting Statistical Results. Version 2.1. Stanford University, University of Wisconsin, and Harvard University. January 5. Available at http://gking.harvard.edu.

Tufte, Edward R. 1975. "Determinants of the Outcomes of Midterm Congressional Elections." *American Political Science Review* 69:812–26.

Valentino, Nicholas A. 1999. "Crime News and the Priming of Racial Attitudes during Evaluations of the President." *Public Opinion Quarterly* 63:293–320.

Valentino, Nicholas A., Vincent L. Hutchings, and Ismail K. White. 2002. "Cues That Matter: How Political Ads Prime Racial Attitudes during Campaigns." *American Political Science Review* 96:75–90.

Walker, Jack L. 1991. *Mobilizing Interest Groups in America: Patrons, Professions, and Social Movements*. Ann Arbor: University of Michigan Press.

Walters, Dan. 1996. "Politicos Take 209 Command." *Sacramento Bee*, October 25, A3.

Waters, M. Dane. 2003. *Initiative and Referendum Almanac*. Durham, NC: Carolina Academic Press.

Weaver, David H., Doris A. Graber, Maxwell McCombs, and Chaim H. Eyal. 1981. *Media Agenda-Setting in a Presidential Election*. New York: Praeger.

West, Darrell M. 1997. *Air Wars: Television Advertising in Election Campaigns, 1952–1996*. 2nd ed. Washington, D.C.: Congressional Quarterly Press.

Westlye, Mark C. 1991. *Senate Elections and Campaign Intensity*. Baltimore: Johns Hopkins University Press.

Wolak, Jennifer. 2004. The Context of Political Learning. Ph.D. diss., University of North Carolina at Chapel Hill.

Wright, Gerald C. 1990. "Misreports of Vote Choice in the 1988 NES Senate Election Study." *Legislative Studies Quarterly* 15:543–64.

Wright, Gerald C., and Michael B. Berkman. 1986. "Candidates and Policy in United States Senate Elections." *American Political Science Review* 80:567–88.

Wyer, Robert, and Thomas K. Srull. 1989. *Memory and Cognition in Its Social Context*. Hillsdale, NJ: Lawrence Erlbaum Associates.

Zaller, John R. 1992. *The Nature and Origins of Mass Opinion*. Cambridge: Cambridge University Press.

Zaller, John R., and Stanley Feldman. 1992. "A Simple Theory of the Survey Response: Answering Questions versus Revealing Preferences." *American Journal of Political Science* 36:579–616.

Zisk, Betty H. 1984. *Money, Media, and the Grass Roots: State Ballot Issues and the Electoral Process*. Newbury Park, CA: Sage Publications.

# INDEX

*Page numbers in italics refer to tables or figures.*

Abbe, Owen G., 22, 24

*ABC News/Washington Post* exit polls, 64, *66*

abortion issues, 34, 45–48; in congressional elections, 50–56, *58*; educational levels and, 54; information environments and, 15; methodology for study of, 53–56, 59; partisan stereotyping and, 24; priming effects and, 135; in senatorial elections, 55–58

advertising, campaign, 2, 17–18, 93, 115, 118

affirmative action issues, 34, 112–29; campaign spending on, 114–16; in down-ballot races, 121–27; methodology for study of, 119, 131; in presidential elections, 116–21, 123; priming effects and, 135; as wedge issue, 14, 93, 94–95

agendas: conditional effects of, 26–30; definition of, 2–3; democracy and, 132–37; explanation of, 25–26; issue voting and, 10–13, 20, 132; mass media and, 17–19; national, 25–26, 138; setting of, 13, 16–19, 24, 32–41, 44, 49–50, 64, 67–70, 91–93, 133–37; visibility of, 26–29, 31, 34–35, 67–68, *68*, 74, 78, 80, 109, 122

Allision, Paul D., 73

Alvarez, R. Michael, 95

Ansolabehere, Stephen, 17, 22

Arizona, elections in, *46*, *62–63*, *69*

Arkansas, elections in, *46*

Arterton, F. Christopher, 44

Atkeson, Lonna Rae, 7, 30, 143n.11

attention. *See* voters, attention to politics of

attitude strength, 48

ballot measures: agenda-setting and, 25–26, 32–41, 44, 49–50, 67–70, 91–93, 134–37; campaign-specific issues contrasted with, 30; campaign spending on, 35, 40–41, 43–44, *62–63*, 114–16; democracy and, 135–37; effects of, on political life, 32–33, 136; increasing use of, 2, 32–33; interest groups and, 40, 91, 134–

35; methodology for study of, 13, 36–41, 64; number of, 2, 32–33, 44; partisan stereotypes and, 24–25, 63–64, 95; signature gathering and, 40–41; top down flow and, 40, 65, 133–34; visibility of, 34–35, 67–68, 74, 78, 80, 122, 138; as wedge issues, 93–96, 136. *See also* initiatives; referenda

Barber, Benjamin, 10, 133, 137

Behr, Roy, 17

Beilenson, Anthony, 110

Berelson, Bernard R., 11

Beyle, Thad L., 78

Bickers, Kenneth N., 6

Bowler, Shaun, 40

Brace, Paul, 36

Bradley, Tom, 35

Brandeis, Louis, 36

Brannon, Laura A., 18

Branton, Regina P., 25

Briggs, John, 35

Brown, Jerry, 35

Brown, Kathleen, 1, 98

Bush, George H. W., 18, 43–44, 94

Butterfield, Tara L., 95

California, elections in: ballot measure requirements in, 40; nuclear weapons freeze issues and, *62–63*, *69*–-70, 75, 78; partisan stereotypes and, 25; spillover effects in, 22; tax issues in, *46*. *See also specific propositions (e.g., Proposition 5)*

California Civil Rights Initiative (CCRI). *See* Proposition 209

campaign-specific issues: advertising of, 2, 17–18, 93; contrasted with initiatives, 30; as evaluative criteria, 5; in gubernatorial elections, 77–78; matching of candidates to, 9, 11; methodological choice of, 8–10; spending on, 12, 35, 43–44

Campbell, Angus, 11, 36

candidate-centered campaigns, 141n.8

candidates: ballot measure sponsorship by, 35, 91–93; campaign-specific issues and, 5, 8–10, 77–78; characteristics of, 11;